Activation

Activation

The Core
Competency

EDMUND J.
FREEDBERG, PH.D.

HarperBusiness
HarperCollins*PublishersLtd*

http://www.harpercollins.com/canada

First edition

Canadian Cataloguing in Publication Data

Freedberg, Edmund J. (Edmund Jerome), 1939-
Activation : the core competency : converting individual & corporate
potential into optimal performance

"A HarperBusiness book".
Includes index.
ISBN 0-00-255748-7

1. Success in business.   2. Self-management (Psychology).   I. Title.

HF5836.F733 1997   650.1   C96-931890-1

97 98 99 ❖ HC 10 9 8 7 6 5 4 3 2 1

Printed and bound in the United States

To my parents,
who taught me the value of learning

My children,
the value of life

My wife,
the value of living

CONTENTS

BOOK ONE

ACTIVATING THE ORGANIZATION

INTRODUCTION

There is virtually no aspect of any organization's performance-management system that does not have, as its ultimate focus, the managing of immediate performance. This is a book about the most important manager in any organization — the manager of that immediate performance.

Immediate performance is the doing. If the doing is effective, so is the organization; if not . . . Because immediate performance is the organization's critical asset, the manager of immediate performance is its critical manager. The only person who can directly support and directly determine, the only person who has sole authority over the immediate performance of an individual, is the individual himself. In an organization ten thousand strong, there are ten thousand managers of immediate performance, managing or perhaps mismanaging their critical and exclusive area of management responsibility. The manager of immediate performance is the self manager.

It is more than simply a matter of interest to note that there are few, if any, organizations whose performance-management system even recognizes, let alone deals with, its most important and largest management force — its self managers. Mind you, self managers need not wait for recognition to exist. They are not granted the authority to manage their own immediate performance by the organization. They have that responsibility because it is theirs and can be no one else's. However, an organization does have the choice of recognizing and including the self manager in, or excluding the self manager from, its stated performance-management system. Regardless, that manager is there and working.

The consequences of inclusion, of recognizing and then dealing with the existence and function of the self manager, can be to create a structure and processes that support the carrying out of that most critical of management responsibilities — the managing of immediate performance. The consequences of exclusion, the consequences of ignoring this most significant reality — the reality of the self manager —is to leave his level of functioning largely unsupported.

An organization can include or exclude the self manager from its training thrust and again, since this critical management force remains largely unrecognized, exclusion is, for all intents and purposes, the universal order of the day. The cost of exclusion is likely very high. It means that all self managers have an undetermined and unsystematically attained set of skills with which to carry out their responsibilities. Their degree of management effectiveness is a matter of chance, and the promotion of any systematic growth in the functioning of the self managers is left unattended.

Although organizations might set objectives, provide resources, select and train the necessary job specific skills, it is the self manager, recognized or not, trained or not, who must manage these skills and resources. It is the self manager who must manage the immediate performance needed to reach those objectives. Can we afford to continue not recognizing and not dealing with our most important management resource?

This book is not only about the most important manager in organizations, however. It deals with the self manager as activator of ability, regardless of whether the focus is on occupational or on personal life. We are all self managers. We all manage our immediate performance. We all activate our abilities in every aspect of life.

The functioning of the self manager is as important to our nonwork lives as it is to our occupational existence, and in our personal lives we are "it." We are the ones who have to determine our own objectives, recognize and seek out the skills needed, make the time and expend the energy required to meet those objectives. There is no formal management structure in place outside of ourselves to lend support.

We are all self managers. Of that there is no question. The question that does exist is, "Do we self-manage well?" Perhaps the even more critical question — "Could we self-manage better?"

The fact is, that although we have this most critical management function with regard to all aspects of our lives, although we are responsible for managing our own immediate performance, for activating our abilities, our potential, minute by minute, hour by hour, we have received virtually no systematic training directed at doing this self-management job.

The second part of this book offers a systematic process designed to address this serious deficit. It focuses on ways to manage the three critical areas of activation — self-confidence, self direction and self commitment. It provides a number of practices that, in turn, build, protect, maintain and strengthen the practices of self management so that we can more effectively convert our potential into the performance that serves both our occupational and personal existence.

chapter 1

THE MANAGEMENT VACUUM

THE PERPETUALLY CHANGING KALEIDOSCOPE

One of the major newspapers of our city celebrated its hundredth anniversary recently by reprinting old articles throughout the year, starting with 1892 and gradually moving to the near present. In a sense, readers were given a time machine that allowed us to travel from the end of the nineteenth century all the way to the last decade of the twentieth.

There was a very good chance that on any specific morning we would be exposed to a fascinating world, very different from the one that we had read about, the morning before. Although we may have traveled only a few years in time, we were likely to find differences that impacted significantly on the everyday lives of the average resident of the period being observed.

Had there been daily newspapers during the Middle Ages, and had we been offered the same kind of time travel, the voyage would have probably been a very different one. The trip through a century may have had little to offer in the way of novelty. The language, the vocabulary, the mode of expression, but more importantly, the value system, the attitudes, the concerns, the costumes, the toys, the worldview and especially the everyday experiences of the average member of medieval society, may all be virtually the same through the ten decades. We might not even notice that we're reading an article four generations rather than four hours old. We may even be able to travel two or even three centuries back in our time machine without noting very many significant differences in everyday life as we go.

Time-traveling through our century would bring with it very different experiences. One decade would not that closely resemble another, and looking at the last quarter century, in some instances, dramatic differences between twelve-month periods would be perceived. Photographs and advertisements would illustrate dramatic change in tastes. The objectives of the day would be very different indeed. There might even be some slight shift in language, and new words would likely appear. Many concepts and larger concerns being discussed might not have been in evidence a year earlier. A change in value system, in the worldview and in the technology already being taken for granted, may well be evident. In fact, with regard to change, yesterday's century may seem worth about today's month and a half.

We certainly recognize the existence and rapidity of change as being a significant and somewhat unique aspect of the world we now live in, as reflected in the number of seminars being offered, designed to teach us how to manage change. That is not to say that our century has cornered the market; that change didn't begin until 1900. We recognize, however, that while the pace of change has been increasing rapidly over the last few hundred years, a marked acceleration distinguishes the present.

The signposts of Kitty Hawk and the first walk on the moon are often used as dramatic illustrations of the incredible changes that have occurred in the short span of the current century. The process has become what feels like a positively accelerating curve. Living in our world is much like traveling in a time machine, moving forward at constantly increasing speeds. From the first moon landing to the present, there have been, and continue to be, remarkable changes in the everyday lives of people in the industrialized world. Living a day in 1965, in 1975, in 1985 and in 1995 were very different experiences. Roles, functions, tools and overall frame of reference show dramatic shifts, not as we move through various ages, different centuries, but as we move through decades — even individual years.

When I was a young child, one of my favorite toys was a kaleidoscope, a circular tube with pieces of dazzling colored glass and mirrors, constructed so that when I held it to the light, I would see a beautiful, symmetrical, complex, multicolored pattern. I turned the kaleidoscope, the glass moved and the pattern changed. When an especially beautiful pattern came into existence, if I held my hand very still, I could admire that picture for a long time. But once I moved, it was gone; the world inside that kaleidoscope altered forevermore.

What has been happening in our world over the past hundreds of years is that the kaleidoscopic patterns have been changing more and more rapidly. On our time travel through the Middle Ages via our medieval newspaper, often the kaleidoscope would not appear to have moved from one stop to another, the pattern remaining virtually the same. In the last number of centuries it could be said that there has been a significant increase in the number of pattern changes. In the twentieth century, the interval between pattern shifts has continuously become shorter and shorter.

Today we are living in still another reality, a reality in which the kaleidoscope seems never to stop. It feels as if there are no longer any intervals, that the patterns keep altering continuously and relentlessly. It is said that we have now moved from the industrial to the information age. Perhaps the major factor that differentiates our time from yesterday is not so much the increase in amount of information, as it is the related shift in the rate of change that this increase has created. Continuous adaptation to an ever-turning kaleidoscope has become a fundamental demand of our time.

THE CHANGING ROLE OF MANAGEMENT

What has been the effect of this significantly increasing rate of change on the occupational world generally, and more specifically, on the role of management?

But a few years ago, most managers within the occupational world had a pretty clear idea of what was required of them in the sense that for some extended period, the jobs for which they were responsible were well defined and remained relatively static. A manager knew what he was being paid to manage.

A particular management function could be represented by a learning curve that a manager would start climbing at his appointment. When he reached the top, he'd stay there for a good while and soon become well seasoned in his specific management responsibilities. When it was time to take on a new position or perhaps respond to a move of the kaleidoscope, either the learning curve would alter somewhat and require a bit more climbing, or in some instances, a new learning curve would have to be scaled. There would, however, be long periods of time when our manager could look in the mirror and see a seasoned veteran staring back.

Today, because of the reality of ongoing change, as soon as a manager catches a glimpse of the peak of a learning curve being scaled, a new one appears. (This experience is generally mirrored by his managees.) The manager then finds himself once again at the bottom, as objectives, methods of management, even roles and functions seem to be altering at an ever-increasing pace. Instead of seeing the mirror image of a veteran, a rookie keeps staring from behind the glass. *The management job grows larger.*

The Moving Job Description

There is a particular kind of change, having to do with the *now* that deserves a focus of its own — virtually constant and rapid informational/technological growth. Continuing with the analogy of the kaleidoscope, it is not just that the pattern continues to change, but the size and number of pieces of colored glass, as well as the complexity of the patterns themselves, continue to grow, again, at a positively accelerating rate.

Because of this informational deluge, this continuing technological advancement, the occupational community is becoming one that is made up only of experts, each unique from the other in his area of expertise.

A job description, in the very recent past, could be viewed as something relatively static, something that included specific responsibilities related to specific skills and objectives. Because of the continuous technological, informational advances, as well as the proactivity being demanded with ever-increasing vigor, an individual's job description is constantly changing, with new skill sets and responsibilities appearing on an ongoing basis. Often, it is only the individual himself that is in a position to write this constantly changing job description representing what he is doing today — but only today.

It was not very long ago that the manager was the person who knew better than any other member of a department what it was that staff members should be doing and how they should be doing it. Now, the manager must have a fairly clear sense of what each managee needs to get done over the long haul; what must be done to get there and how to get there generally relates to the knowledge and skills of the managee, not the manager. The "Renaissance Manager" is a thing of the past. Managers now face the challenge of managing people whose jobs, skill sets and necessary activities are, to some degree, a mystery to them. *The management job grows larger.*

The Contest

That our planet has become one very large and highly competitive bazaar is becoming a more focused and increasingly insistent reality. A highly competitive world marketplace is not a brand new phenomenon, but we in the Western world have been paying more and more attention to it of late, largely because, as contestants, we have not been experiencing the same degree of success that we were a few decades ago and earlier. Our diminished victories have heightened our perception of this worldwide economic community as a serious challenge rather than as a gift.

Competition is greater within our own industrial community and very much greater outside of it. In an alarming number of instances, we are losing the competitive battle for our own marketplace as well as for other world markets. Our relative competitiveness has taken an unexpected beating, the result being, not that a world contest has just arisen, (it's been around for a very long time), but that victory can no longer be taken for granted.

Because of this growing competition, we must constantly change and do things differently, and at the same time, better and better. In order to do this, we must manage our material and people resources with increasing effectiveness. *The management job grows larger.*

THE MANAGEMENT VACUUM

To be successful, a corporation must be able to compete effectively. This effectiveness must carry with it as low a price tag as is possible. The focus on costs has necessarily increased. Corporations have recognized that being too "fat" could result, eventually, in not being at all.

Complacency, too often a dangerous side effect of long-term success, is, in large part, responsible for the weight problem suffered by our occupational community. The effectiveness of other societies has rudely shaken us out of our self-satisfied state, forcing us to look in the mirror and so come to grips with the necessity of an often rather dramatic weight-reduction program.

The delayering of organizations, with whole levels of management being removed, has been and continues to be one of the significant cost-reduction processes common to many organizations. Even within remaining organizational levels, the numbers of people have also been reduced. This has created a very real challenge. The constant altering of how we do business, what business we are in, shifts in internal organization, the rapidly altering needs of the marketplace, the changing definition of who we are as organizations and as individuals within those organizations, makes the job of managing more complex, more difficult and at the same time, more critical. The information and skill distance between manager and managee also creates new and larger demands upon managers. The need for, and difficulty in, maintaining a competitive edge, taxes management effectiveness still further.

Yet as the management job grows larger and larger, the number of people in place to do that job, to carry out that responsibility, continues to decrease. The result of each of these processes, individually and together, the growth of the responsibility, at times paired with the shrinking of the numbers of people to carry it out, is the creation of a management vacuum, a vacuum that in our present, highly competitive, ever-changing world, we can ill afford.

chapter 2 | EMPOWERMENT — THE DESPERATE BLESSING

Whether formally identified or not, the management vacuum has been recognized to exist. This recognition, in turn, has given rise to what could be called "The Empowerment Movement." As management forces decrease in number, the management job continues to grow larger and larger. The corporate world cannot afford to reverse the trend, however, simply by hiring more managers to fill the vacuum.

Even if it could, would the increase in payroll fit the bill? Most likely not. Overall change, in combination with constantly increasing specialization, suggests that a significant increase in management numbers by itself, affordable or not, would not bring about the necessary solution — would not really fill the management vacuum.

Question: "What will?"

The Popular Answer: "Empowerment!"

The Blessing

There appears to be a dialogue going on within many executive offices of corporate North America that goes something like this.

Executive #1: "What are we going to do? We're not doing an effective job of managing all these people, but they've got to be managed effectively."

Executive #2: "Perhaps we have to hire a slew of new managers."

Executive #1: "We can't afford to do that."

Executive #3: "And anyway, just a few months ago, we had a lot more managers than we do now and had that been the answer, they'd still be here."

Executive #1: "Well, maybe our managers are just going to have to work harder."

Executive #3: "There are only so many hours in a week and those hours have already been used up."

Executive #1: "Yes, but somebody has to do the job."

Executive #4: "I've got an idea. Why don't we give our people some of the management responsibility for themselves? Let them take up the slack. Psychologists tell us that if you give people more responsibility, more power for decision making, you increase their commitment and their productivity. Anyway, somebody's got to do it and our people are the only somebodies around."

CEO: "So, we must empower our people to manage themselves. We must ask them to fill this management vacuum — to take greater responsibility for making the right things happen. They've got to become more proactive, more creative. They've got to make more of the decisions that relate to their own personal productivity. Is that what we are talking about?"

Executive committee: (in unison) "Yes! That's exactly what we're talking about."

CEO: "I want you to assemble all the people working in this organization . . . and get me my robes!"

The masses are gathered together and the corporation's leader, robes flowing, raises both arms, symbolically covering the heads of his flock, and in a loud and booming voice utters the blessing, "Be thou empowered!" There's a burst of lightning and a clap of thunder, accompanied by the desperate hope that the management vacuum has now been filled. (If the CEO doesn't have the time to utter the Empowerment Blessing in person, it can always be delivered via E-mail.)

The organization's masses have now been commanded "to go forth and manage yourself." This command was not meant to give each individual total management responsibility for himself, but rather to ask each person to share in that management responsibility — to take up the slack — to fill the vacuum.

DISEMPOWERMENT AND THE TRADITIONAL MANAGEMENT MODEL

Within the context of our present organizational structures, what is likely to be the effect of this empowerment blessing? Will it, in fact, create the opportunity for empowerment to occur? Will the management vacuum be filled?

In all likelihood, all that will be created is frustration and disappointment, the disappointment of promises not kept.

Intrinsic to the Traditional Management Model, the management model within which we have operated for decades, perhaps centuries, are a number of disempowering mechanisms. While some of them arise directly from the structure of the model, others relate more to the perceptions that are generated by it.

Disempowerment Direct

There is a perception of power in a vertical hierarchy that is intrinsic to it. The power resides, always, in the level above.

One of the most important characteristics, long built into the organizational structure of our occupational community, has been its ability to disempower. Many structures and mechanisms, both formal and informal, have been constructed and continuously reinforced, in an ongoing attempt to support the disempowering capabilities of our organizations.

The Traditional Management Model is often visually represented as a triangle whose very shape is supportive of the function to disempower — a triangle with the power at the very top, with many levels to its base, in which each level disempowers the level immediately below. The exception to this is, of course, the bottom level, only because it is the bottom and has no level below it.

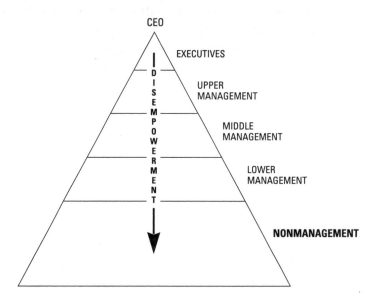

There's nothing inherently incorrect, nothing morally wrong or necessarily destructive of productivity, in the building of a disempowering organization. Once the assumption is made that there is, and should be, a person or a small group of people, responsible for making virtually all the organization's significant decisions, then this disempowering triangle serves to empower the appropriate decision maker to effectively shape the organization.

Theoretically, at least, disempowerment helps ensure that the decision of a CEO will be carried out by removing the power to change the direction of the organization's leader from the level below, then the level below that and so on. The structure of the organization supports the ability of each level to push the decisions coming from the level above through to the level below so that the staff, who are in a position to carry out the decision from above, are mandated by it. Again, once one accepts the assumption that decision making must be concentrated at the top, then this disempowerment is not only acceptable, it is desirable.

But is this assumption, in fact, a useful one? One could argue that, in the not too distant past, people who moved to the top of the corporate ladder in organizations were, generally, through a process of "natural selection," the people best suited to make the critical organizational decisions. Therefore, an organizational structure built to ensure the carrying out of those decisions was an appropriate one. And anyway, a look at the success of the industrialized world over the past century, and longer, highly recommends the Traditional Management Model in that it seems to have worked very well, or at least well enough.

The relevant question with regard to today, however, is, does it remain an appropriate, even acceptable model? Let's look once more at the rapidly moving kaleidoscopic world of today.

The Fallible Leader

The accelerating deluge of information and technology, and the increased complexity and specialization of the world that we have created, strongly attack the assumption that in today's universe all critical decisions can, and more importantly, should be made by one person or a very small group of people. This assumption is a shaky one because it is based on a further assumption that individuals are equipped with the information needed to determine, not only the long-term, but the day-to-day significant directions of an organization. Our world has become a sufficiently complex and fluid one to make the picture of an all-knowing individual at the helm of an organization an unrealistic one. The picture creates expectations virtually unreachable.

There is no doubt that some kinds of critical decisions can, should and often must be made at the top. However, there are other significant decisions that, both because of immediate knowledge and of long-term expertise, can be made only by specialists at various levels within the hierarchy. It is, in part, the recognition of this specialization, running throughout an organization, that has helped fire the empowerment movement.

The Leading Edge of Lip Service

We must empower people within our organizations to make and carry out the decisions that only they are qualified to make, or the organizations will malfunction under the direction of inappropriate decisions. Sharing decision making becomes essential for the survival and growth of an organization and, so, the Empowerment Blessing.

However, the blessing by itself, while correct in its intent, is not enough. It expresses the need to appropriately redistribute decision making, *but it neither creates the opportunity nor the structure within which that redistribution can effectively occur.*

The Empowerment Blessing, offered within the confines of the Traditional Management Model, gets chewed up by the disempowering structure and mechanisms within that model. An organizational structure that, by its very essence, is designed and built to disempower, will continue to do so regardless of any empowerment objectives it may hold. Culture change is not brought about simply by asking a culture to be something very different than it is.

Performance — A Singular and Indivisible Entity

Performance management, within the context of the Traditional Management Model, includes a fundamental perception that must ultimately block any move to truly empower those people functioning within its confines.

Any performance-management system is concerned with two fundamental and separate elements: the management of performance and the doing of that performance. Within the Traditional Management Model, it is the manager who manages and it is the managee who performs. Performance is treated as a singular and indivisible entity, requiring two separate functions, carried out by two separate forces. Managing this singular entity, called performance, is the responsibility given to the manager, while the actual performing itself is the responsibility of the managee. Simple. Manager manages. Managee does.

Any derivative performance-management system, therefore, concentrates primarily on the functioning of the *manager* and is designed to build skills, structures and processes that will aid that manager in managing the performance of his managees. Its primary concern is the supporting of the management function, again, a function carried out by the manager.

Enter the recognition of the need to empower and its ensuing Empowerment Blessing.

Let's look at a possible conversation between a CEO and the just-blessed employee immediately after the clap of thunder.

The Impossible Expectation

Employee:	"First, I would very much like to thank you for having empowered me a few minutes ago. It's something that I think I've wanted for a very long time. However, I do have a few questions, if you don't mind."
CEO:	"Mind? Hardly. Ask anything. After all, you are empowered now."
Employee:	"Yes, I know. . . . But . . . what does being empowered mean? Exactly what's different now that the blessing has been given?"
CEO:	(Incredulously) "What's different? Well . . . before the blessing, you weren't empowered. Now you are."
Employee:	"Empowered to do what?"
CEO:	"Empowered to be your own person. To make your own decisions. To manage yourself."
Employee:	"Ohhhh . . . to manage myself."
CEO:	"Exactly."
Employee:	"That's great. Now that I manage myself, what does my manager do?"
CEO:	"Your manager? Well, your manager manages you."
Employee:	"Oh, I thought you said I managed me."
CEO:	"Well, you do. You manage you and your manager manages you."
Employee:	"Oh . . . I see. Uh, just one other question."

CEO: "Yes?"

Employee: "What do I manage and what does my manager manage?"

CEO: "Look. I'm certain that you and your manager can work that out. But, as I'm sure you realize, that's not the important thing. The important thing is that I've given you this tremendous opportunity to make a difference. Don't let's get details in the way. You are now empowered. Go out and make that difference. I'm confident that you will live up to the challenge!"

An expectation virtually impossible to fulfill has been created. Within the Traditional Management Model the granting of empowerment becomes a desperate restatement of need in the guise of an action. It cannot be the satisfier of that need. With performance being treated as a singular, indivisible entity, the sharing of management responsibility by manager and managee can only be pretended. It is impossible to share in a responsibility when the shares have not been clearly defined and can't be separated. What do I manage and what does my manager manage? is an absolutely fundamental question that requires a very clear and workable answer, without which empowerment cannot occur. The question goes to the very core of what we perceive as the management responsibility within corporations and the ownership of that responsibility.

Without a workable and meaningful answer to the question, the granting of empowerment can be, in itself, disempowering, if only because it becomes a promise unkept. I, as managee, have just been given a responsibility that hasn't been defined. I may get the sense that I have been granted more power over determining my fate, but I neither know how much power nor the aspect of that fate. However, from the moment I walk back into my immediate work environment, while I see no concrete changes, I immediately feel the effects of those formal and informal mechanisms busily and effectively functioning to negate that power.

If I am a manager within the corporation, the apparent creation of an empowering organization may impede my effectiveness. I may feel disenfranchised in that I know my justification for existence is the managing of other peoples' performance. Although letting people manage themselves may seem like a good idea, practically speaking, this singular responsibility of performance management is something one either keeps or gives away. The problem is, if I give it away, what will I have left? My options don't appear to be many.

Empowerment Under Sufferance

There is, perhaps, one option that I have as an empowering manager, even within the Traditional Management Model. I can't give my responsibility away and for that matter, even if I wanted to, it wouldn't be allowed. But perhaps I could *loan* pieces of it to my managees. I could let people make some of their own decisions but with the proviso that the moment I note what I consider to be a problem decision being made, I'll simply take my responsibility back. This could be termed "Empowerment under Sufferance" — nicely descriptive but a contradiction in terms.

Even if a manager intended to empower his people, not as a whim, but as a nonnegotiable aspect of his performance-management practice, the intention may be a very difficult one to convert into reality. If the performance-management system of the organization continues to be based upon the typical version of the Traditional Management Model, expectations will be placed upon our empowering manager's shoulders that will be very difficult to live up to.

The empowering manager will be expected to exert a greater degree of control over the everyday performing of his managees than is reflected in the intent to empower. Disempowering orders may be issued by our empowering manager's "superior," the expectation being that those orders be moved at least one step further down the organizational hierarchy.

When our empowering manager is asked by his manager, "How is employee X doing with regard to Project A and how, specifically, is Problem Y being handled?" the answer, "Things appear to be going well, but I don't really know exactly how Problem Y is being handled" may be greeted with less than a great burst of enthusiasm. Instead, the observation may be forthcoming, "But you should know! You should know exactly! It's your job to know!"

Although our empowering manager may see himself as living up to his management responsibility, in concert with the objectives of the empowerment blessing, our "traditionalist" may perceive, in contrast, a relinquishing of management responsibility.

It is not enough that, in an organization, I, as manager, perceive what share my managees have in the management of their own performance. That perception must be an organizational one for it to be optimally supportive.

The Illusion of Control

The underlying meaning of the term "manager," and the rights and responsibilities attached to the title, support the process of disempowerment. A manager is a kind of boss. If one gets past the formal "book-learning" definitions of management by unexpectedly asking people the question, "What does a manager do?" and insisting that they answer immediately, they are likely to reply, "Well, a manager is a boss. He tells people what to do."

The response carries with it an important implication. Not only does the manager, the boss, tell the managee what to do, but the managee does it. That is, there is an assumption within the Traditional Management Model that a managee is a resource, controlled by the manager. The reality reflected by the Traditional Management Model is, I am the manager. I am the boss. I tell you what to do and you do it. It is not, I tell you what to do and you do it — if that's what you decide to do. The performance decisions belong to the manager. The manager owns the performance potential of the managee. Management has been defined as the process of getting work done through others. The managee may do it, but the manager gets it done.

Often this illusion can be destructive of not only the managee's but the manager's productivity as well. When a manager, "in the face" of his managee, orders that a result be brought about in the manager's way and then leaves with no way of ensuring or even knowing what will occur, his future influence is likely to be severely damaged. It's difficult to respect the emperor with no clothes.

The Traditional Management Model is not primarily a model concerned with communication flow. It is a model describing the movement of power. It is primarily designed to reflect, perhaps reinforce, perhaps even *create* the direction of authority. It is not concerned with reflecting reality. Regardless of what reality might be, the Traditional Management Model assumes, even promotes, this concept of control. Therefore the perceptions, the structures and the practices emanating from the model reflect this assumed reality.

The Illusion of Empowerment

Some general practices that move through many different management processes appear, on the surface, to significantly increase the "empowering quotient" of an organization. Intense scrutiny, however, promotes a different or, certainly, a more conservative conclusion.

The Power of Dialogue

Perhaps the most common component of leading-edge management practices is that of mutual dialogue — two-way communication, giving the opportunity for both manager and managee to input whatever decision-making process is being targeted. One is given the impression of a kind of partnership within which decisions are arrived at through a process of negotiation, compromise and mutual agreement.

However, the opportunity to give input and the power to decide are neither mutually exclusive nor are they synonymous. While opportunity to give input, standing on its own, can carry with it great value and can influence decision making, it is important to recognize those situations for which the opportunity does not carry with it any control over the decision-making process. Within the confines of the Traditional Management Model, even if the intent is to share, not only observations and opinions, but decision-making power as well, the intent is seldom actualized. Ultimately, the final decision is made by the manager, the person seen as responsible for the managing of performance.

The Power to Set Objectives

Let's look at activity management and setting objectives. Here the manager has the last word. The manager decides what the managee should be doing and how he should be doing it. Management-training courses recommend that the manager take into account the skills and experience of the managee, and even consult him in determining the job to be assigned and the management support necessary to get it done.

The managee may act as advisor. The advice may be followed. But, still, it is the manager who decides. The empowering manager may let his managee "alone" for months at a time, recognizing that no external direction is needed. Nevertheless, the manager has the power to change his mind, to intervene and redirect activities at any point during that period. Again, empowerment under sufferance.

It is often recommended that the setting of longer-term objectives for an employee be represented by a process, actively entered into by both employee and manager. In most organizations that recommend this practice, it is carried out in varying degrees by its different managers. The variance itself reflects the optional nature of the practice. Even with the managers that vigorously involve their managees in the process, judgment ultimately rests with the manager. A highly empowering manager may be perceived as one who consistently agrees with the objectives generated by his managees, but even here we are looking at empowerment under sufferance. (The manager may, in fact, be dysfunctional rather than empowering.)

The Coaching-Skills Luxury

We give coaching skills to our managers at an ever-increasing rate. In large measure, these skills are designed to increase the manager's effectiveness as influencer rather than as dictator. They are aimed at the process of selling ideas, directions, objectives, skills and attitudes, rather than ordering. It could be argued that coaching skills and the approach they support function to empower.

However, these coaching skills are presented within the framework of how to become a *better* manager, how to manage *more* effectively, not how to become a manager, and how to manage effectively. The adoption of coaching skills are, again, optional. Many are the human resources people who bemoan the vigorousness with which coaching skills are often left on the shelf by the people managers in their organization.

For those managers who choose the option of practicing these coaching skills, of influencing rather than dictating, there is frequently an application up to the point where it becomes clear that influence isn't working; where the managee isn't "cooperating." It is here that, more often than not, the attempt at influencing is abandoned and authority takes over. Again, empowerment under sufferance.

The Performance Appraisal Option

Performance appraisal is perceived, in intent if not in practice, as being an ongoing process rather than an event, and one involving both manager and managee. In interacting with many corporations in different industries, I have often heard the statement delivered by managers that they truly buy into the performance-appraisal process recommended by their organization and would have very much liked to carry it out, if only there had been time.

In theory, performance appraisal is considered a process, but in practice, it can so easily become the same kind of singular event it has been for decades — forty-five minutes spent in reviewing the last year and planning the next. In theory, it is mutually involving but in practice, a judgment by one, the manager, and a brief opportunity to comment by the other, the managee.

The Manager as Motivator

Commitment — commitment to the organization overall, commitment to the objectives of the organization, an individual department or a work team — is critical to an organization's success. Under the Traditional Management Model, we automatically, however, slip into viewing commitment as something that resides in the managee but is, in large part, generated by the manager. Motivation is perceived as being a precious commodity in the care of management, whose responsibility it is to somehow distribute it to those who wait below.

The Insufficiency of Cosmetic Change

There is no intention here to devalue those current management practices that involve the managed more intensively than has often been the case in the past. The application of coaching skills, involvement in the decision-making process — even if only in an advisory capacity — frequent evaluation of, and dialogue about, ongoing performance, attention to the individual's skills, experience and needs — all of these things help increase the effectiveness of performance management within the Traditional Management Model. Yet if the empowerment movement has stemmed from the need not simply to give people greater opportunity for input, but to give them greater decision-making *authority* in their areas of expertise and their specific responsibilities, and if that need is a valid and critical one, then we are far from the mark. The practices may be very constructive. They are not, however, sufficient.

The problem is that on the surface, many of our current management practices give the illusion of empowerment. Management feels that they are empowering, and often the managed feel that they have been empowered. After all, having your input taken seriously and being given decision-making authority even if only when you make the "right" decisions or when only related to relatively unimportant things, is, nevertheless, positive and useful.

The Need for a New Management Model

Even though it may create "happy campers" of both manager and man-agee, it is important to recognize that the management vacuum discussed earlier is not being filled by these new performance-management thrusts. We may be doing better at what we were already doing before, but that's not good enough. We have to be doing something else. We cannot afford to experience a false sense of security arising from the illusion that we have fulfilled a critical need. That fulfillment must be a reality and that reality, requires a different management model.

Management is often heard to say, and with sincerity, "My most important resource is my people." This very statement vividly reflects the implications of the Traditional Management Model. "My people" are a resource controlled by me, their manager.

Without a significant culture change, without a change in management model and therefore in the perceptions, structures and performance-management practices and systems ensuing from that model, the Empowerment Blessing cannot be anything but an expression of the importance of presenting and fulfilling the opportunity for empower-ment. It is, however, in itself, neither that opportunity nor its fulfillment.

An Altered Frame of Reference

The awareness that we must make real changes within our organizations is growing. We have a clear idea of what many of those changes must be.

- We must allow people to make the decisions that will free them to do their jobs more effectively.
- We must open communications.
- We must listen more effectively.
- We must reduce the distance between various levels of responsibility within the organization.
- We must work more closely as groups so that we can benefit from the synergy that arises from team effort and identification.
- We must increase the adaptability quotient of our organization.
- We must, in turn, increase the flexibility of the individuals in the organization.
- We must increase the proactivity of each individual.
- We must create the opportunity for that proactivity to bear fruit.
- We must become constantly better at helping our people grow, giving them new skills, new knowledge, new information, new attitudes.
- We must give each individual greater input into the overall activities and objectives of the corporation.
- We must increase individual identification with, and loyalty for, the organization.
- We must ensure an accountability system that is both real and relevant.
- We must release more of the performance potential within the organization.
- We must empower.

. . . and the list goes on.

We do know the changes we want to make, and see many of them as being necessary for our survival and growth as individual organizations and as an occupational community. There is a problem, however, in that, as was illustrated with the Empowerment Blessing itself, often we slip into the error of behaving as if, once a need is identified, effectively verbalized and collectively understood, it has somehow been satisfied.

However, knowing the desired changes and even going after those changes head on, is often not enough. They cannot even be approximated, in the absence of a new management frame of reference. We must change the model. We must mean something different when we talk about performance management, when we look at who is responsible for managing, when we look at what a manager does. We recognize the necessity of redistributing management responsibility within our organizations, but that redistribution cannot occur within the confines of the Traditional Management Model, at least as it is presently perceived.

chapter **3** | # THE SHARED-MANAGEMENT MODEL

THE REQUIREMENTS OF A NEW MANAGEMENT MODEL

Empowering the Managee and Manager

In empowering the managee, the new management model must not, at the same time, disempower the manager. Moving the "crown" from one head to another is not the answer. It won't serve the purpose and it will be resisted, understandably. Just as we cannot afford to waste the potential of the managee, nor can we afford to waste the potential of the manager. So the new model must bring about the redistribution, not simply the reassignment, of management responsibility.

As long as performance is regarded as a singular, indivisible entity, redistribution becomes impossible. It must be seen as being divisible so that the responsibility for performance management can be shared. At the same time, the sharing of responsibility must support the kinds of changes that organizations must make to survive and grow.

We must ensure that new responsibilities are accompanied by the authority required to carry them out. At the same time, it is important that we establish accountability for those responsibilities, so that they do not rapidly convert to the old structures.

The Requirements for Effecting Change

To bring about these significant changes, must we as individuals and organizations change significantly? How much do we have to alter before the desired differences can come about?

The answer to that question had better not be "a remarkable amount." Human beings and organizations of human beings seldom make change via gigantic leaps. We don't respond well to turning ourselves inside out. We create significant change not by changing significantly, but through a process of many small changes that cumulatively bring about the desired result. And so this new model, while its difference has to be significant from the model that we have used well, and for a very long time, must not require that we, as organizations or individuals, become "a new species."

Before continuing, let's look at a summary of what would likely be some of the requirements of this new management model.

- To avoid the malfunctioning of our organizations under the yoke of inappropriate decisions, we must empower people within our organizations to make and carry out the decisions that only they are qualified to make. We must give people greater decision-making authority in their areas of expertise and their specific responsibilities.
- Performance management must be understood as a shared responsibility, shared by manager and managee.
- The redistributed management responsibilities must be accompanied by the authority required to carry them out.
- Accountability must be established around those responsibilities.
- The share of management responsibility an individual is given, if it is to have organizational impact, must not simply arise from the perception of individual managers, but must be an inherent part of the organization's performance-management system.
- It must be understood that control of an individual's activity rests not with his external manager, but with that individual.
- The new, or altered, management model must empower both managee and manager.

THE PERFORMANCE CYCLE

The Shared-Management Model satisfies the requirements of an empowering model discussed above. It accomplishes this by identifying an important member of an organization's management team, heretofore ignored — *the self manager*. This model establishes the significant role of the self manager in the management of performance. It frees the external manager to focus on the growth of his people. By viewing performance, not as a single indivisible entity but as a three-phased cycle, the "Performance Cycle," it facilitates the sharing of management responsibilities.

PHASE 1 — THE PREPARATION PHASE
The Performance Cycle

Phase 1

P R E P A R A T I O N		

Defining the Job

The first phase of the Performance Cycle could be categorized as the *before-the-job* phase, the phase that paves the way for immediate performance to occur. It is here that a managee's long-term objectives are determined. This phase is concerned with what *should* be done.

Determining the Necessary Resources

With having decided what the job is, the skills and the material and human resources needed can be determined. In other words, the question, What will an individual need to make the job happen? can be answered. Identifying the necessary abilities and resources not already in place is the business of the Preparation Phase of the Performance Cycle.

While certain aspects of the Preparation Phase may be carried out at the beginning of an extended time period, for example, the start of an operating year, this initial phase of the Performance Cycle is also ongoing in that new or altered objectives arise, and previously unidentified skill needs may very well become evident. Static objectives, chiseled in stone, are becoming a less common feature of our constantly moving occupational landscape.

Selecting and Training for the Job

Let's zero in on the issue of the skills needed to carry out the objectives. This is, of course, an extremely important and fundamental performance-management issue. A high correlation must exist between the work to be done and the abilities of the people chosen to do it. This correspondence may be brought about through a selection process — selecting the right person to do the job. Often it happens through a combination of appropriate selection and new training. There may be new information, new skills required, if the objectives are to be reached. The training needed is identified and the method of fulfilling the need established.

This new learning represents the most important growth function of the Preparation Phase of the cycle. Earlier, we looked at the reality of our changing world and the demands that those changes put upon an organization and the people within it. We must continue to grow, continue to adapt to the constantly forming, novel, kaleidoscopic patterns. The new learning supporting this growth, whether it be formal or informal, at the job site, in front of a computer terminal or in the seminar room, occurs here in Phase 1 of the Performance Cycle, and is an important element sustaining individual and organizational adaptability.

That ongoing training is critical to the continuing viability of an organization is a "parenthood" statement, difficult to dispute. Nonetheless, when a corporation's performance takes a dive, frequently because it stood still with regard to the skills and stance of its people, often the budget allotted to new learning is the first to go. It is seen as supporting a luxury, now unaffordable.

To neglect the growth aspects of Phase 1 in our constantly changing and highly competitive reality, whether in the face of great success or its relative absence, can very quickly become expensive folly.

Establishing the Accountability Process

In preparing people to do a job effectively, it is important that they know what they can expect if they reach their objectives, if those objectives are exceeded or if they are missed. Not only must standards of performance be established and communicated here in the Preparation Phase, but the accountability process should be defined and installed.

Phase 1 Mismanagement

When the Preparation Phase is not being managed properly, a number of negative things can occur. If, in setting objectives, the individual's potential has been underestimated — even when those objectives are carefully specified, standards defined and consequences described — the performance and growth of that individual will not come close to reflecting his potential. On the other hand, overestimation of potential can result in the creation of unattainable objectives — a set up for failure.

If the objectives do, in fact, fit the individual managee's potential, but the resources needed to reach those objectives are not provided, then again, performance potential and growth will not be realized.

If an effective accountability system is in place but not shared with the managee during the Preparation Phase, then even if performance is high, the delivery of positive consequences becomes a deserved surprise, after the fact, rather than an incentive and ongoing performance support, while the job is being done.

If an effective accountability system is neither described nor applied, then the relationship between performance and consequences resembles more closely the workings of a gambling casino than of an optimally constituted workplace.

The people growth and organizational productivity arising from a Preparation Phase, well managed, can be dramatically significant. The loss of individual and organizational potential represented by a Preparation Phase, poorly managed, can be equally dramatic.

The Preparation Phase, then, is concerned, longer term, with what job should be done. The focus is also on how the job is to get done. As well, it is here that an individual's accountabilities are laid out. The standards of performance are defined here, methods of evaluation are described, the monitoring system is installed and the system supporting the defined accountabilities is presented. The way has been paved for effective, immediate performance.

PREPARATION: AN EXTERNAL MANAGER'S PRIMARY RESPONSIBILITY
The Performance Cycle

Phase 1
PREPARATION

E X T E R N A L M G R		

The managing of Phase 1 of the Performance Cycle, the Preparation Phase, belongs primarily to external management, represented here by the external manager. It is the external manager's function to:

- establish the long-term objectives of the managee;
- ensure that those objectives are clearly communicated;
- select the right person for the job;
- ensure that the necessary material and people support are in place to carry out those objectives;
- identify and satisfy the necessary training needs without which a high degree of success vis-à-vis those established objectives cannot occur;
- spell out the accountability system related to the managee's performance objectives.

Communication skills, and increasingly, coaching skills — skills that permit the external manager to more effectively influence the performance of his managees — are becoming more prominent aspects of the training of external managers. This training represents an acknowledgement that preparation isn't a once-a-season, or perhaps even a once-a-year function, but an ongoing, critical responsibility, belonging to the external manager.

All of the above responsibilities are either directly or indirectly related to people's growth and, in fact, the responsibilities listed tell us nothing new about the assumed job of external management. How well these responsibilities have been carried out is, however, another question and one to be looked at later in this chapter.

PHASE 2 — THE ACTIVATION PHASE
The Performance Cycle

Phase 2

	A C T I V A T I O N	

✻   ✻   ✻

This second phase of the Performance Cycle concerns itself with, not the work to be done, but the work getting done. It is the *on-the-job* phase of the cycle, and immediate performance happens here. Phase 2 represents the "performance moment of truth." It is eleven o'clock on Thursday morning, that specific point in time when the job will either get done adequately, well, poorly or not at all. Here, in the second phase, the Activation Phase of the Performance Cycle, exists the potential to apply abilities, to utilize resources, to perform in service of the objectives set out in Phase 1. If Phase 1 is concerned with what should be done, then Phase 2 is concerned with what *will* be done. The job, for better or worse, happens here.

Phase 2 Mismanagement

Mismanagement of the Activation Phase of the Performance Cycle brings about a reduction or absence of results. It represents a waste of potential, not only of the person supposed to be doing the job, but of the resources put in place in Phase 1 to support performance. Significant potential of people whose performance is dependent upon the results of someone else's mismanaged Activation Phase will also not be realized.

Activation: An External Manager's *Pretended* Responsibility

It makes little sense to assume that something as critical as immediate performance does not require managing. Since the external manager has been traditionally seen as the only real manager that exists, then by default if nothing else, the responsibility of managing immediate performance has been perceived as falling to the external manager.

This perception brings with it some interesting challenges. For starters, how does one directly manage on-the-spot performance without being on the spot? Most of the time, when a managee is doing his job, the external manager is nowhere to be seen. He is not around. The external manager is with another managee or at his desk or at a meeting or. . . . The only person who, most of the time, can possibly manage immediate performance is the only person present — the managee.

In addition, while the external manager may be in the position to appropriately determine what should be done in the long term, the performance needs of the moment generally require the services of the self manager. Even if the external manager were physically present, the technical, knowledge-based expertise of the managee with regard to his specific job and the appreciation of the immediate factors affecting performance make the self manager the only appropriate manager of immediate performance.

The misassignment of management responsibility springs from the Traditional Management Model mistakenly ascribing ownership of someone else's immediate performance to the external manager who then takes responsibility for managing the doing. He sometimes even takes responsibility for the doing itself. One of the most common, pained complaints of managees is that their managers won't allow them to do the job but all too frequently attempt to take over. When said disdainfully, this is often what's meant by the term "hands-on manager." The manager drops in on his managee for a few moments, watches, disapproves, says, "I not only want you to do the job, you're to do it this way," and then walks, assuming that his word is his managee's command. (As a test of the assumption, I've often asked managers to look back into their past to a time when they weren't in management and examine how irresistible many management commands really are. Rather sheepish smiles appear on their faces as they remember the times that they decided not to follow orders.)

And so, frequently, we have a significant portion of external-management energy being expended in an attempt to directly manage other people's immediate performance — even, at times, to take over and carry out other people's performance responsibilities. This may account, in part, for many of the ills of our occupational community, ills that indirectly prevent the optimizing of immediate performance. The attitude reflected in the statement, "I just work here" and all that it implies, is hard to set right when your external manager pretends an expertise and control over you that is, in fact, not his but yours. It may be that much of the energy wasted on playing destructive power games, of resisting contribution rather than contributing, would not be nearly as popular a corporate pastime if people were recognized as being in the best position to manage their own on-the-job performance, and allowed to go about *their* business.

I do not suggest that within the Traditional Management Model the managing of immediate performance is, in fact, carried out by the external manager. It isn't, because it can't be. However, that reality has not stopped us from pretending the illusion. The point being made here, however, is that in the absence of identifying who really has the control, whatever the reasons for that absence, there is no doubt that somebody must be made responsible for managing, for owning immediate performance. We have given the assignment to the external manager in an attempt to fill a role that must be filled, and we seem to have gotten away with living the illusion, for a very long time, that we can own someone else's performance. However, our recent recognition of the need to empower suggests the realization that the costs of the illusion can no longer be afforded.

The Misperception of External Manager as Primary Motivator

Managing someone else's immediate activity is not the only inappropriate responsibility given to external managers, although it probably takes up the lion's share of the time. Another, often perceived as critical, primary and belonging to external management is the responsibility to motivate.

Here we have an interesting contradiction — two belief systems functioning simultaneously.

If you were to ask a group of people, virtually any group of people "Who is the only one in a position to motivate an individual?", in all likelihood, the majority would answer, "That individual himself. Motivation must come from within. We are the only ones who can motivate ourselves." Had you asked that same group another question instead, "What are the primary responsibilities of a people manager?", in all likelihood, one of the responses would be, "To motivate his people."

The first statement, in large measure, reflects a belief, given lip service, but one that remains a belief only, rather than one translated into action. The second response, even though perhaps not believed with the same intensity as the first, is, nevertheless, the belief translated, albeit most often ineffectively, into action. We really do, more often than not, perceive the external manager as being the prime motivator of his people.

At eleven o'clock on Thursday morning, can someone else motivate me to carry out a specific direction? They may have influence, certainly, but whether the decision is made to carry out that direction or not, is determined by no one else but myself. At eleven o'clock on Thursday morning, I'm alone. There is no one else to light the fires of commitment within me, but myself. Nor is there anyone else who can put those fires out if they are already burning, but myself. Even if someone else were standing beside me attempting to lead, attempting to motivate, whether I accept, whether I allow myself to be influenced, is determined, again, by me. The activation of immediate performance is the self manager's responsibility.

It is true that providing motivation is an important function of the external manager, but not in Phase 2 of the Performance Cycle. Providing the motivation to carry out a specific direction right now must be the job of the self manager. No one else can do it. The external manager can certainly act as an important secondary source of motivation, and can, through influence, increase the probability of effective performance. However, this motivational support is generated primarily in Phases 1 and 3. Whether or not something gets done remains to be determined by the self manager.

In the Preparation Phase, the external manager may explain the importance of the job to be done, highlight the importance of the potential contribution of his employees, may exert personal influence and may set out the consequences, positive and negative, that will be triggered by the level of future performance — all of this, potentially motivating. In the third phase of the Performance Cycle, yet to be discussed, again the external manager's motivational function is further supported.

But the primary determination in carrying out of a specific direction rests with the self manager. It is easy to assume a direct line from, for example, coercive authority in the hands of the external manager and the performance of the managee. However, it must be remembered that whether or not the managee is willing to pay the price of nonperformance is the decision of the managee. That history is replete with self-elected martyrs to a multitude of causes illustrates the role of the individual as his own primary motivator.

Effective accountability systems are extremely important (although somewhat rare in our occupational community). However, the descriptive equation, PERFORMANCE = ABILITY x PROMISED CONSEQUENCES, represents only a very small, albeit influential, part of the performance equation.

The Misperception of External Manager as Primary Support

One important function of the external manager is a very general one — creating an atmosphere conducive to optimal performance. This might include anything from physical environment, to quality of social interaction promoted by the manager, to trust shown in the potential of staff.

There is no doubt that a manager can, for example, play a positive role in the building of confidence or its opposite, confidence destruction, with regard to his managees. However, as with motivation, the person in the confidence driver's seat is the individual himself. The most important environment for the support of performance is not one's external but one's internal environment. How confident I am in my ability to perform is critical in determining how well I will perform, and how confident or unconfident I am is determined primarily by me.

A good confidence builder can effectively utilize confidence-building support from others and will neutralize or reduce the damaging effects of destructive external criticism. A poor confidence builder will quickly waste the support given by others but internalize their criticism and at great cost.

As with motivation, external managers have an important, albeit secondary, confidence-building role to play, but it can only be played out in the first and third phases of the Performance Cycle. Any attempt at giving the external manager the primary responsibility of confidence building in others will create unattainable expectations and leave the providing of an internal performance-supportive environment — that is, within individuals — largely up to chance, rather than up to the person really in charge — the self manager.

The Inefficiency of Managing Phase 2 Externally

The problem is clear. The assignment of Phase 2 management to the external manager is an unreasonable one — unreasonable and very costly. An incredible amount of time, energy and effort has been spent by managers attempting to manage the immediate performance of others. Precisely because of the perceived importance of the task — although an impossible one — often the lion's share of external management energy has gone into managing immediate performance and has been largely wasted. Because the management job is being attempted by the wrong person, even a minimal result has required an incredible amount of effort. In a sense, one could say that 90 percent of all energy often goes into creating, at best, a 10 percent return because the responsibility has been misassigned in the first place.

External Manager as Firefighter

External managers often complain that they spend an inordinate amount of time putting out fires, dealing with crises and performance deficits created by their managees. Management skills, organizational processes and structures are put in place in an attempt to lessen these deficits and so free the managers to do better things, but generally if the preventative measures are effective at all, they tend to only slightly reduce the firefighting demands.

What happens? Managers can seldom be physically with their managees to tell them what to do at each moment. As the span of control of managers increases — that is, as the number of people each manager manages increases — the amount of time that a manager can spend standing over any individual managee decreases. Consequently the external manager is assigned the responsibility of managing immediate performance, of directing immediate activity, but he is seldom there to do it.

The result? As long as things appear to be going well, as long as the managee seems to be doing what needs to be done, the manager is freed up to attend to other things. However, how can the manager really know if the managee is doing what needs to be done since he is seldom there to directly supervise the managee and, in fact, isn't really expected to be? Still, as long as things seem to be going well, the managee tends to be left alone.

The immediate-performance bulletin generally gets broadcast when things are not being done as they're "supposed" to be; that is, when a crisis occurs. And by the time it arrives on the manager's desk, it is almost always yesterday's news. Oftentimes, if the poor performance creates enough noise to get to the manager, it has been going on long enough not to simply create a minor results deficit, but through cumulative negative performance, a very real crisis. A puff of smoke in our very complex environment may not be enough to set off the alarm; it often requires a fairly respectable fire. Directing immediate activity, an absolute necessity and perhaps the most important management function of all, tends to occur in the absence of positive, or in the presence of negative, immediate performance.

We talk about managers having to prevent crises and to encourage growth in their people so that performance constantly improves, productivity increases and proactivity expands, but how realistic, really, is that when immediate performance must be managed and there is no one assigned to do it but the external manager? Even if an external manager is involved in fostering growth in a particular managee, there's a good chance that the alarm will sound signifying a fire somewhere else — started by an unattended managee — that must be put out. The manager is then taken away from the growth exercise.

It gets worse. Because the growth support could not be given to the managee just abandoned, he may be the next to start a conflagration to be put out by the external manager, and so it goes, until very quickly, there are just too many fires being lit to allow the manager to do anything but fight fires. The manager's managing of immediate performance becomes almost totally crisis intervention. People's growth, at least as reflected by most management-training curricula, appears to be the primary people-management function of external managers, but they have virtually no time to carry out this function. So much of the external manager's time is spent in his managees' Phase 2, not cultivating immediate performance, but often simply maintaining minimal acceptable productivity. In this situation, no one grows — manager or managee.

Immediate performance, the doing of the job, is the bottom line. It can't be ignored. It must be managed, and without the identification and formal installation of the self manager, somebody's got to do it and that somebody becomes the external manager. What we have, then, is a perceived critical responsibility, managing immediate activity, being carried out extremely inefficiently, ineffectively and at the same time taking most of the energy, time and expertise of the external manager. This valuable management potential is no longer available to support the growth of people in the organization, to help create the kind of adaptability and flexibility absolutely essential for organizational survival and success.

Will the Real Manager of Immediate Performance Please Stand Up

The external manager doesn't have control of the immediate performance of his managees. In fact, most of the time, in most organizations, the external manager isn't around when immediate performance is being demanded. Were the external manager present, there is a good chance that he wouldn't know what immediate performance is required. Furthermore, the external manager, as manager of immediate performance, is largely an illusion, albeit an expensive one. *The manager of immediate performance is, always has been and will always be, the self manager.*

The issue, then, is not whether the self manager is managing performance. He most definitely is. The critical question is, *how well is it being done?*

It is not until an organization recognizes that its primary managers of immediate performance are its self managers, that it is in a position to systematically support that most important of all management functions.

ACTIVATION: A SELF MANAGER'S PRIMARY RESPONSIBILITY
The Performance Cycle

Phase 2
ACTIVATION

	S E L F M A N A G E R	

*   *   *

It is now time not only to introduce the self manager into the Performance Cycle, but to take him seriously. Empowerment has confirmed the self manager's existence and often very dramatically (though, probably, not by name). The problem has been, however, that empowerment, stated but not supported, has created millions of self managers with nowhere to go.

Taking a closer look at the management requirements of Phase 2 clearly gives the self manager a destination and one that only he can reach.

The Phase 2 manager has to be in a position to control, to determine the immediate performance of the managee, minute by minute, hour by hour. The Phase 2 manager must have a strong grasp of the immediate situation, its requirements and its opportunities. He has to know what needs doing right now. The Phase 2 manager must be present at the time of that immediate performance management demand. *The self manager alone is in a position to satisfy these requirements.*

The managing of Phase 2, the Activation Phase of the Performance Cycle is, primarily, a self-management responsibility. It can belong to no one else.

It is the self manager's responsibility to:

- determine immediate objectives;
- build a performance-supportive attitude;
- manage on-the-job activity;
- provide on-the-job motivation;
- identify barriers standing in the way of getting the job done;
- remove those barriers wherever possible;
- ensure that the job gets done;
- recognize on-the-spot opportunities for performance enhancement.

It is the self manager, and the self manager alone, who has the authority, the opportunity and therefore the primary responsibility for the managing of immediate performance — the ultimate focus of all aspects of any and every performance-management system.

PHASE 3 — THE EVALUATION PHASE
The Performance Cycle

Phase 3

		E V A L U A T I O N

Phase 3 represents the *after-the-job* phase of the Performance Cycle and looks at performance, already happened. It focuses on the question, what *has* been done?

Monitoring

Monitoring is a critical aspect of Phase 3 and although the monitoring system may have been established and described in Phase 1, it is carried out here in Phase 3. Phase 3 is the data-gathering process that helps determine what occurred in Phase 2.

Evaluating

Evaluation happens here. The value of both the activity and results of the Activation Phase are determined in Phase 3. It is here in this third phase of the Performance Cycle that the accountability system is given life; here, depending upon the output of Phase 2, the delivery of consequences, positive or negative, occurs.

Training

Just as training is a very important part of the Preparation Phase, so it is an important part of the Evaluation Phase. However, the training that occurs in this latter phase tends to be of a more subtle nature and comes from review rather than preview. The fine tuning of abilities that can only occur in light of the observations of immediate activity and results happens here. Giving effective feedback and identifying strengths and weaknesses occur in this phase. The effective management of the Evaluation Phase helps determine the components of the next Phase 1.

Phase 3 Mismanagement

Too often accountability in an organization is given more lip service than real service. Without effective management of this third phase of the Performance Cycle, the kind of growth that organizations must have to survive and succeed cannot be expected to occur. The potential development, arising from the fine tuning of on-the-job performance, is not tapped.

If an accountability system is presented, but is not supported through time, then accountability as an overall performance support becomes, at best, an unfulfilled wish and both corporation and managee are placed in a position of sufferance with regard to what they can expect to receive from each other. When accountability is only a pretended part of the reality of an organization, the degree to which the potential success of that organization and its people is actualized, becomes seriously threatened.

If Phase 1 concerns itself with the work to be done and Phase 2 with the work being done, then Phase 3 (see page 45) has as its focus the work that has been done. This after-the-job performance phase completes the cycle.

EVALUATION: AN EXTERNAL MANAGER'S PRIMARY RESPONSIBILITY
The Performance Cycle

Phase 3
EVALUATION

		E X T E R N A L M G R

To the external manager also belongs the primary responsibility for managing Phase 3, the Evaluation Phase of the Performance Cycle. It is primarily the external manager's function to:

- ensure that activity and results are monitored;
- activate the accountability system so that rewards or their absence are consistent with performance;
- perform the fine tuning that observation of previous performance permits.

In fact, the quality of monitoring, of evaluating and of fine tuning, goes far in determining the degree to which the next Phase 1 actualizes the potential of the managee. If someone hasn't been assessed properly, if the opportunities for further growth have been misinterpreted or missed, then the question, What is this individual now capable of achieving? cannot be answered accurately.

Again, there is nothing new in the assignment of the primary responsibilities of Phase 3 to the external manager. After all, the growing focus on the import of performance appraisal includes and underlines the responsibilities mentioned above as belonging, primarily, to external management. And again, as was the case with the management functions belonging to Phase 1, they are primarily associated with the growth of people within an organization.

The question to be addressed, however, is not what the external manager's involvement in the management responsibilities of Phase 3 should be, but rather, in the real as opposed to the recommended world, what the external manager is doing vis-à-vis the carrying out of those responsibilities.

THE NEW MANAGEMENT TEAM

THE SHARED-MANAGEMENT MODEL
The Performance Cycle

Phase 1 PREPARATION	Phase 2 ACTIVATION	Phase 3 EVALUATION
E X T E R N A L M G R	S E L F M A N A G E R	E X T E R N A L M G R

＊　　　＊　　　＊

The redistribution of management responsibility, supported by the Shared-Management Model, removes responsibilities from the external manager that cannot, and that never could, be carried out effectively by that manager or by external management generally — the responsibilities of managing someone else's immediate activity. This elimination of an inappropriate, but heavy, workload frees him to carry out those critical, but often neglected, functions that have always been seen as a part of his domain, as reflected by the subject matter of management-training programs. It frees the external manager to take primary responsibility for Phases 1 and 3 of the Performance Cycle. It also demands that the self manager do the job that, although unrecognized, has always been his — the managing of immediate performance. Phase 2 is his responsibility.

Command and Control Redistributed

With the general acceptance that each individual has to take greater responsibility for his own productivity, with the perceived importance placed upon empowering, an unfortunate controversy arose. We tend to polarize, and so we decided that if empowerment was "in," then command and control must be "out," or vice versa. The "empowerers" understood that if we were to succeed, command and control must be banished. The traditionalists, even the more liberal ones, who felt the necessity for some command and control, had little choice but to turn their backs on the empowerment movement, in spite of the benefits that would be lost. (This controversy existed largely in the pages of human- and organizational-development literature. The real world can't afford to take these things too seriously.)

Of course, as with so many polarizations, neither position is sensible. Anarchy, even well intended, is probably not a formula for organizational success. There must be objectives, larger directions established, imposed and insisted upon, if organized effort is to occur. Perhaps today, more than ever, it is important that common and highly relevant collective objectives be formulated, clearly identified and energetically pursued. At the same time, even if one could give people no room to make their own decisions regarding the what and how of their performance, to do so would be highly destructive. The issue to be dealt with, then, is not who commands and controls, but who commands and controls *what*.

The Shared-Management Model illustrates clearly that command and control must be exercised and allows that to happen by appropriately redistributing management responsibilities. Phase 1 represents external management's "command" post. Not only *can* external management establish corporate direction and long term objectives, it *must*. Phase 3 represents the arena within which external management exercises its responsibility to control by ensuring that accountability is in place so that objectives are seen as more than the corporate "wish list."

Within the Activation Phase of the Performance Cycle, it is only the self manager that can and must carry out both the command and control functions of management. Self direction represents the command function related to immediate performance and self commitment, the function of control. Self-confidence could be said to support both in that the quality of self directions issued are, in part, determined by the level of self-confidence, and while self commitment increases the likelihood that the directions will be carried out, self-confidence increases the probability that they will be carried out more effectively.

The larger picture presented by the Shared-Management Model is one in which the functions of management must be actively applied to all phases of the Performance Cycle. This can only be accomplished when the management responsibility is appropriately shared by external and self managers within an organization.

chapter **4** | # THE SELF MANAGER'S JOB DESCRIPTION

In the last chapter we looked at some of the responsibilities that lie largely within the purvue of the self manager. In this chapter we are going to look at those responsibilities somewhat more closely, and also consider other aspects of the role of self manager.

THE MANAGING OF IMMEDIATE PERFORMANCE

Once one stops to examine seriously the statement that the manager of immediate performance is the self manager, the reality of that statement tends to come quickly into focus. When one looks at this statement, perhaps it is too easy to walk away and think, "Of course! Who else could it be, really? I've got that." However, the implications of that reality are of such importance that it should not be walked away from too quickly.

First, let's look at the degree of importance given to immediate performance by the occupational community, generally.

Performance-management systems tend to be rather complex and consist of numerous components, both formal and informal. For example, the selection procedures that are put in place are designed to increase the probability that immediate performance will be of the quality, quantity and kind that is needed by the corporation. The coaching and training that occurs has the same objective. Performance appraisal is designed to aid immediate performance by adding to an individual's potential through the fine tuning that is often an intrinsic part of the appraisal process. One hopes that it will also serve to provide a performance incentive.

Structural changes within an organization, such as changing the management structure, introducing or emphasizing the existence and importance of teams, identifying and adjusting processes, all are designed to have as their ultimate objective the strengthening of immediate performance.

There are many other things that happen in an organization that are not considered to be formally linked to its performance-management system but that, nevertheless, occur in the hope that immediate performance will be supported. This includes everything from purchasing equipment or technology necessary to do the job, to nonessential resources relating directly to doing the job, to redecorating the work space, to putting the corporate vision on the wall for all to see, nicely framed; all are expected to contribute positively to productivity. Organizations tend to choose to do nothing internally that is not expected ultimately to make a positive immediate-performance difference.

It is no wonder. The effectiveness of an organization's function at a specific moment in time is determined by the sum total of the immediate performance of each individual member occurring at that specific moment in time. It is immediate performance that creates the output that, in turn, determines organizational effectiveness. This is not, of course, an earth-shattering statement. We accomplish things by doing, and immediate performance is just that — the doing.

While we are actively attempting to influence immediate performance in any number of ways — many of them very indirect — through processes, procedures, purchases, pay, our performance-management systems ignore the one resource that doesn't simply influence, but determines immediate performance — the self manager. This self manager, because of the fundamental significance of his primary responsibility, is, in fact, the most important manager in our organizations — and is also the most numerous. To not pay serious attention to that management resource while investing tremendous energy and monies in less effective methods of immediate performance management, is expensive folly, especially in the face of the growing management vacuum. To recognize the need for empowerment without specific focus on the carrier of that empowerment, the self manager, makes even less sense.

People are hired and paid, not for what they are capable of doing, but for what they do — their output. That output is determined by their potential and the managing of that potential. It is the self manager that does the managing. Largely, we are employed and paid for the job of carrying out that function.

Managing Mind-Set

The term "mind-set" can mean many things. It might signify a value judgment, a belief system or a specific body of knowledge. The term is often synonymous with attitudinal stance or simply with the more general term, attitude. At times it may be seen as having emotion at its base, at other times, cognition, and sometimes, both, but regardless, it represents a filter of the mind through which we perceive ourselves and the world around us. Our mind-set not only refers to what we know or see or have experienced, but what we think or feel about what we know or see or have experienced. It has a major role in determining our immediate behavior. The decisions that we make, the issues upon which we focus our energies, the goals we set, the intensity and effectiveness with which we apply ourselves to those goals, are all affected, and often very significantly, by our attitude, by our mind-set.

Our attitudes are influenced by others. The advertising that continuously bombards us represents a persistent attempt to alter or to establish a positive attitude toward a particular product, service, political party or profession. Corporations do not only attempt to influence the mind-set of their potential customers, but of their employees as well. Some management practices are designed specifically to create a positive attitude toward the corporation, particular corporate objectives, the team to which one belongs and so on. A good people manager is seen as one who has significant influence over those he manages. Leadership, a highly valued management characteristic, refers, in part, to a person's ability to influence the attitude of others.

However, the greatest potential influencer of our mind-set is ourselves. At the same time that we are strongly influenced by our attitudes, we are in the position of being able to determine largely what those attitudes are. We can either be their victims or their creators. It is largely up to us. The problem is that while we do have a significant role to play, most of us seldom play it. We let our attitudes own us rather than the other way around. We acquire our mental set, in spite of ourselves. We don't take control. Often, we don't even try.

We all have many abilities. The effectiveness with which those abilities are applied depends on the strength and the kind of attitudinal foundation from which they are launched. It is the responsibility of the self manager to build and maintain that foundation.

Managing the Job

Each individual has the responsibility of not only carrying out his job description, but of managing that carrying out. Here we're talking about doing the job in its most concrete sense. What is too easily missed is that the doing needs managing and that managing can only be provided by the self manager. This management job includes a number of responsibilities that affect immediate performance, both quantity and kind.

Identifying the Blocks to Performance

There are often blocks that arise, standing in the way of our carrying out our Phase 2 objectives. These may have to do with our own lack of knowledge or specific skills needed to do the job. We may not have enough of the right resources, materials or technical support to succeed. There may be some problems within the corporation impeding task completion or some completely external condition blocking goal attainment.

An effective self manager is one who is the first and, often, the only one to identify barriers standing in the way of reaching objectives, and can frequently have much to say with regard to the solutions to those barriers. If there is something impeding performance, and resources outside the jurisdiction of the self manager are needed, be they material resources or skills, it is the self manager who will recognize and report the need. If the barrier cannot be overcome, but is nevertheless hampering getting the job done, that, too, is made clear as early as possible by the self manager.

All the above are manifestations of a self manager taking responsibility for doing *his* job.

However, a block to successful attainment of objectives can become very costly when the real Phase 2 manager, the self manager, is not recognized as such, and Phase 2 ownership is misguidedly assigned to another, usually an external manager. The self manager is in the best position to identify, spotlight and often do something to overcome the inevitable barriers that can block the attainment of objectives. If he remains passive, waiting for the sighting to be made by someone else — awaiting new immediate-activity directions, from someone else — that someone else, unfortunately, may not be in a position to recognize the problem in time to make the necessary adjustments; may not know what the necessary adjustments should be; may never even become aware of the barrier.

Ultimately, all that is recognized is a failed expectation, long after the optimal time for action is past. This deficit is then dealt with in that brief performance-appraisal meeting, occurring most likely many months after the barrier has done its damage. The lack of performance is noted. There is a rapid, after-the-fact search for the reasons underlying the failure and at best, some new learning takes place and the time for overcoming the barrier, in all likelihood, is long gone.

An organization that recognizes the self manager as the manager ultimately responsible for making the job happen assigns the responsibility of first-line identification of barriers to success where it belongs — on the shoulders of the self manager. (A good self manager accepts that responsibility, whether assigned or not, but when it is not recognized, he often has no one to talk to.)

There is a very dramatic difference between the statement, "I couldn't get the job done because . . ." and "I won't get the job done unless . . ." The latter represents the posture taken by the good self manager and insisted upon by the empowering organization.

Expanding the Envelope

In an organization, the broad parameters of a person's Phase 2 is established primarily by external management in that an individual's long-term objectives must, in some way, serve the objectives of that organization. However, that is not to say that the areas of responsibility assigned to an individual's Phase 2 must remain unaltered, awaiting the next formal long-term assignment. In fact, if anything, the opposite is becoming true.

More and more, we are asking people to be proactive, to initiate activity, to discover and solve problems, to ascertain needs related to their jobs, the corporation, the client, to satisfy those needs and to look for new, previously unidentified opportunities that, if responded to, might increase organizational success. What we are really asking people to do, more and more, is to continuously redefine their Phase 2 — to expand the envelope that represents the boundaries of their job descriptions.

Each time I reveal a need previously unidentified, each time I discover a new opportunity that without my involvement would not exist, I am adding responsibilities to my Phase 2. I am expanding my objectives. I now may require new skills, new or different resources, may have to alter the way I organize my time and focus my energy. While yesterday, it was I who determined what I would do, it was my organization that determined, with regard to my immediate performance, what I should do. Today, I determine not only what I will do, but, to a much greater degree, what I should do. Because, as self manager of my Phase 2, because of my unique area of expertise, my relationship with my own unique "theater of operations," I am in a position to see things that no one else can, and therefore can uncover needs and opportunities that would remain undiscovered without me.

For example, the salesperson or the individual providing service to a client corporation is frequently the expert regarding certain challenges, needs and opportunities. The manager of a group of people or the colleague of a particular staff member may have unique knowledge regarding untapped human potential in others, and the resources or support needed to help actualize that potential. Oftentimes, then, it is only the person on the spot who can creatively identify opportunities to reach new and more ambitious objectives. The request to be proactive, heard over and over again within our occupational community, is a request directed at its self managers, those responsible for managing the doing of the job.

Protecting the Investment in Material Resources

In order for an organization to survive, to grow, to be successful, it must have the material resources, the equipment, the technologies and the information systems necessary for reaching its objectives. This, generally, represents an extremely significant investment in both the present and the future.

All too often, the desperate cry heard from many a corporate headquarters is not, "We need more resources, more technology and more machinery if we are to be successful," but instead, "We've got all the necessary resources. All the required skills are in place and we're still not getting the results we need."

At first glance, it would appear that all the elements necessary for success have been attended to. The tools needed to do the job are in place. The people skilled in the use of those tools are assigned. It would seem to be simply a matter of putting the two together. However, it is that very meeting, the meeting between "man and machine," people and resources, that must be effectively managed if the potential of both are to be actualized. That meeting, while it can be planned for earlier, happens in Phase 2 of the Performance Cycle. It occurs within the context of immediate performance and is, therefore, largely an issue of self management.

To protect the critical and ongoing investment in material resources, not only must corporations have individuals capable of effectively utilizing those resources, but individuals who will consistently, energetically and creatively activate those capabilities. They must have individuals who are well self managed.

Managing the Primary Agent of Change

This book began by talking about the reality of change in our present occupational world and the impact that that has on us. Organizations are constantly beset by change and, in ever-growing degrees, their survival and their success rests upon the degree to which they are able to adapt to that change. However, organizations are people and in order for an organization to change, to adapt to ever-increasing new demands, the individuals within those organizations must adapt. If its people remain static, an organization cannot move.

From the pulpits of organizations we can regularly hear the sermon on change. Members of an organization are being told individually, in small groups, in larger groups, through speeches and through memos that they must be adaptable; that in order to respond to the change around them, they themselves must be willing to change. If this be true, and it appears inescapable, it may not be enough to simply say and then repeat how important it is for individuals to be constructively responsive to the demands of a changing world.

To simply tell people to change, and perhaps explain to them why it is necessary, implies that human beings are like chameleons — that all we need to do is understand the advisability of change and then we simply change. But is change the "natural," the simpler choice to make, or is it easier, generally, to maintain the internal status quo? Again, there exists an implicit assumption that wanting to change is itself a sufficient condition to bring about the desired change. In other words, explain carefully enough why change is necessary and it will happen.

In some instances that may be true. But there are many internal factors that make change an issue of somewhat greater challenge than is implied by simply making the request to change in the belief that the request alone will do. This is not the place to go into a lengthy discussion about the resistance to change as a tendency fairly common to most of us. Suffice it to say that it is a characteristic of which most of us are aware, certainly in others if not in ourselves. "You can't teach an old dog new tricks" is itself a very old expression, and one that is dealing with neither dogs nor the aged, but a recognition that relative rigidity as opposed to flexibility often better reflects the human condition.

In an organization, *the primary change agent is the individual*. It can be no other way. The important question then — who changes the change agent? Answer — *the self manager*.

Flexibility suggests many things: the tendency to be able to apply old abilities in new ways; to recognize novel situations; to evaluate when change is necessary and not rationalize the necessity away; to recognize the need for new skills and be willing and able to acquire and apply them; to take on new roles, new functions and at times, readily abandon old ones; to courageously recognize the need for change in the face of others whose resistance to change is high and vocal; and in contrast, to resist change only for the sake of change in the face of today's strongly supported "fad of the month."

For most of us, few of the above tendencies come easily. Do we have the capacity to acquire the characteristics of the incomplete inventory listed above? The pace of adaptation that is being manifested by us suggests the answer to be Yes. You can teach old dogs new tricks. *However, to change appropriately requires highly effective self management.*

Others can identify some of the changes that need to be made. Others can provide the skills, resources and information necessary to bring the change about. Only we as individual self managers can, however, make or block the change. Only we can promote within ourselves an internal environment that will support constructive flexibility. It's a self-management responsibility.

Protecting the Training Investment

In a world that is continuously demanding new and different things from its organizations, it is little wonder that those organizations are, in turn, demanding new and different things from their people. One of the most important ways to help people become effective agents of change is through training them for new skills and new conceptual frames of reference. The problem is that much of the vast sums of money spent on new learning annually is wasted. The opportunity for learning may be presented, but too often the learning or application of that learning does not come about. The serious byproduct of this lack is that the necessary adaptation to change and the creation of change do not happen.

Just as we often look to inappropriate sources for the management of immediate performance, so we tend to put the spotlight in the wrong place when searching for the primary activating factor in training. When a training initiative doesn't take (as is too often the case), we assume the deficit to be in the person facilitating the training, the content or the delivery system. The assumption then is if the participants didn't learn, the training is no good. That, of course, may be the case, but it is a dangerous assumption. The training may be very good. The problem may rest with the participants.

The primary responsibility for protecting the training investment belongs to the self manager. The most critical continuity factor in any training initiative is the receiver of that initiative. Whether the opportunity to increase potential through new learning is taken, whether the translation of that potential into performance occurs, is primarily determined by the self manager. Learning and its application reside squarely in Phase 2 of the Performance Cycle. It is about immediate performance.

This is a very serious issue in that we recognize the essential nature of continuous adjustment through learning, through training and their application. We must ensure that new offerings given present the necessary information and skills in a deliverable fashion, but that is only the beginning of any particular training journey. The moment the training is over, the real installation begins. Success now rests squarely on the shoulders of the self manager.

Precisely because the issue of new training is so critical, our performance-management systems must take into account the most critical player. Not only must the appropriate tools of change be identified and offered, responsibility for their utilization — both where the responsibility resides and whether it is honored — has to receive serious ongoing attention. *Again, protecting the training investment is primarily a self-management responsibility.*

Protecting the Effectiveness of External Management

We focus much time, energy, writing and doing on the role that external management has in the productivity and growth of the managee. We spend little, if any, time systematically looking at the reverse — the role the managee has in supporting the development and output of the external manager. And yet, this self-management role can be an extremely valuable one.

First, the obvious. No matter how thoroughly, no matter how appropriately the Preparation Phase of the Performance Cycle is carried out by external management, unless that potential is put to work by the managee in Phase 2, the potential represented by that preparation is wasted. When advice, training, critical and carefully thought out objectives and resources delivered by the external manager are ignored by the managee, from a developmental or outcome perspective, the delivery may as well not have occurred.

By the same token, the potential of an evaluation process, well thought out and energetically practiced, is to some degree largely wasted when, after the fact, the discovery of impoverished output is the outcome. (There is, of course, value in knowing that someone is unproductive.) The waste continues when the important learning that can come from effective evaluation, itself a kind of preparation for the future, is also ignored.

Other ways that the self manager can protect the effectiveness of external management, referred to in the discussion of the Shared-Management Model, are seldom given the attention they deserve. When a self manager is doing his job, is managing his immediate performance, the external manager is then freed to do the same. Management responsibilities that belong to the self manager do not have to take the time and energy of someone else.

A primary external-management responsibility is that of supporting the growth of the managee — increasing the managee's performance potential. This cannot be carried out effectively in the absence of well-self-managed employees. As was stated above, support, offered but not utilized, is of little value, regardless of its merit. An external manager, involved in putting out other peoples' fires, has little time to support the development of those people or of anyone else.

Perhaps the most important form of protection, offered by the self manager to his external manager, has to do with the quality and relevance of external support given. We tend to think of the managee as being the reactive member in the manager/managee relationship. We perceive the managee as being a resource for the manager. Both are true and often should be. However, at least as important are the reverse statements. The manager should often be reacting to the initiative of the managee. The manager should be perceived and should perform as a critical resource belonging to the managee. However, the last two "shoulds" can only occur when the managee is doing his self-management job well.

The reasons for this were set out earlier in this chapter. It is often an individual alone who is in a position to perceive a deficit in ability that may be interfering with his getting the job done. A self manager who truly takes responsibility for doing the job will seek the resources needed to overcome the deficit.

Developmental and resource needs often arise as a result of the well-self-managed, perceiving barriers, needs and opportunities evident only to the person on the spot who is actively looking. This, in turn, places the external manager in the position of being able to support energetically the growth in productivity of the well-self-managed in ways defined by their identification of new challenges.

chapter **5** | # THE TEAM AND THE SHARED-MANAGEMENT MODEL

THE TEAM AND WHAT IT ISN'T

Teams are in. Of that there can be little doubt. If labels are to be taken seriously, corporations that used to operate, in part, through work groups, committees and departments have, over the past decade and more, virtually abandoned those organizational structures. Work groups can no longer be found on the occupational landscape. Teams, however, are visible as far as the eye can see.

There are many reasons for this apparent proliferation: the success of teams in Japanese industry; the performance support ascribed to teams in athletics, along with the almost mythical properties sometimes given to that world by the world of business; the recognition that management, as we traditionally define it, often cannot know what needs to be done hour by hour, day by day and perhaps even more often, cannot know how to get it done; management's diminishing ability to "drive" the doing, especially as its ranks become thinner. These reasons offer strong justification for a greater and redirected emphasis on teams.

In addition, who better to know what activities and resources are needed to get the job done than the people doing it? Also, having a role in the decision-making process can bring about an increase in commitment to success — strong support, it would seem, for the self-directed team. No longer do we need a manager or a supervisor telling people what to do and making sure it gets done. The team will tell the people what to do and make sure it gets done. The team will become an answer, if not *the* answer to the management vacuum.

Before simply going with the tide, let's examine this a little more closely. Let's consider a self-directed team that meets every fourth Wednesday morning from ten-thirty until noon. It is now eleven o'clock on the first Thursday morning after the meeting. Where exactly is the team? Does it exist as a concrete entity? Does the team exert any *direct* control over the immediate activity of its members? Is it there to direct the here-and-now actions of the individuals belonging to it? Can the team tell its members what must be done *right now*? Can it make sure that what needs doing gets done *right now*?

The answer to each question is No. The team ceased functioning as an entity in real time the moment the team meeting ended, at twelve noon on Wednesday. Since that time and for the next month, it is nowhere to be found. It can't tell its members what to do at this moment because at this moment, the team doesn't exist. The decision as to what will be done right now by each individual member rests with each individual member. The team may have recommended what *should* be done, but that is not the same as directing immediate performance, as determining what *will*, in fact, be done. The team's existence as a reference group may increase its individual members' desire to perform, may influence overall commitment, may guide behavior but, again, that is a far cry from actually determining immediate performance. In the same way that the external manager does not, because he cannot, directly manage immediate performance, neither can the team. That responsibility does and must rest with the individual. It is the responsibility of the self manager.

Why the focus on building or restructuring team functioning within an organization? It happens, initially, in response to the perceived need to not only increase the opportunity for individuals to provide greater input into the decisions made by the organization, but to give them, when appropriate, the primary responsibility for doing so. The team creates an environment that allows individual expertise and initiative to have greater influence on organizational effectiveness. It also serves to provide an environment that can support and enhance the performance of its members. *The team is created, in large measure, to serve its individual members.*

However, once "on the road to team," it seems all too easy to lose sight of the destination, and the traveling itself is perceived as being the objective. We seem to work hard and with a high degree of success at walking away from the central importance of the individual and, generally, our treatment of the team is yet another illustration of this success. The focus tends to shift rapidly and in no time a memo is being issued to all members of all teams in the organization stating that team success is the raison d'être of each member's being; that the individual exists for the team. The team is perceived as being the fundamental element of the organization, this almost full-time abstraction that exists in the real world only rarely and for brief periods of time.

Virtually all aspects of a performance-management system, formal and informal, have as their objective, the support of immediate performance. The reason — output is created through doing. It is the individual that elicits immediate performance. It is the individual that determines immediate performance. The individual is the most important aspect of a performance-management system precisely because it is the individual that both does and manages the doing. The team can very effectively support the individual in carrying out those immediate-performance responsibilities. However, the clearer the perception of the appropriate team role, the more effectively that role will be exercised. Organization and individual members must not only appreciate what the team is, but *they must also understand what the team is not.*

It is *not* the manager of immediate performance. Although individuals working together in a team may, through some form of consensus, generate objectives and suggest directions for its members to take, those directions are then carried out (or not) by the individual members, who, in most instances, work independently during the time that their jobs are actually being performed. Ultimately, the outcome may be a team result in the sense that the objective is the cumulative output of the team members. That result, however, is produced through immediate performance, directed and carried out independently by individuals. The fundamental element in organizations, the individual, remains in control of immediate performance. To pretend otherwise cannot change that reality. It can, however, weaken that performance.

To see the team as the answer to the management vacuum, to see this useful, sometime abstraction as having primary responsibility for organizational success, to see it as center rather than support, is to expect from it the impossible and at the same time to ignore the expectation that can only be assigned to the individual. The importance of having an appropriate take on the role of the team is highlighted by the move in many organizations to have employees, computer programmers, service people, sales managers and salespeople work from their homes. It is interesting to watch some of these organizations hang onto the perception that it is the team that actually does the work when the members of the team, hopefully energetically productive, do not communicate, let alone find themselves under the same roof, for weeks at a time.

Is the performance-management role played by the team an important one? It certainly can be. The introduction and strengthening of teams in organizations can serve to dramatically strengthen Phase 1 and Phase 3 management in those organizations. Often members of a team, the people closest to the work, are in a better position to recognize opportunities for functional interdependence and to determine the intermediate directions to be taken by their members, than is a manager further removed from the doing of the job. There is a level of support and an accountability role that can often be carried out more effectively by a group of people "working together." In many instances, then, the team can add to the effectiveness of the external management by adding significantly to the quality of preparation and evaluation being offered its individual members.

But again, the danger lies in creating or strengthening the functioning of teams and then assuming for them a role that cannot be theirs. Recognizing the management responsibilities that do and must belong to the individual and then providing that individual with the environment and the skills to carry out those responsibilities more effectively is less likely to happen when a misassumption exists that those responsibilities can and are being carried out by something or someone else — in this instance, the team. By leaving the vacuum untouched, while assuming it is being filled, an even greater vulnerability is being created. The vacuum grows and nothing gets done that will bring about the primary organizational performance difference needed to fill it. *Although teams can add to the effectiveness of Phase 1 & Phase 3 management, they cannot manage immediate performance. That is and must be the job of the self manager.*

THE SELF MANAGER AS TEAM MEMBER

Just as a team can play an important role in determining the effectiveness of its individual members, so each member's self manager has an extremely significant role to play in determining the effectiveness of a team of which he is a member.

What any individual team member brings to the team is largely determined by his level of self management. A person, inappropriately unconfident in his knowledge of a problem facing the team, is unlikely to offer up a considered solution, even if that solution were, in fact, to be *the* solution. Negatively evaluating another team member's performance is a serious challenge for the unconfident. A team member with poor self direction inadvertently may have not done the "right" things before the meeting, in spite of his potential, and so brings less to it. An individual player with impoverished self commitment may have meant to prepare for the meeting, but somehow, something, or probably some things, got in the way. The result of this self-management deficit, operating both before and during the meeting, is that the team as a unit will not be nearly as effective as it could be in preparing its members for greater productivity.

In other words, a team meeting in which a number of its members are poor activators will be one in which those members will not bring their strengths to the table. Another way of expressing this is that the team will do a relatively poor job of preparing and evaluating its members. Weak membership equals a weak team.

Now, let's look at what the members can offer their team. Imagine a situation in which the team did an excellent job of preparing a team member to pursue an objective important to the team. Let's also assume that the individual sees the objective as important, that the team goals are important to him and that he has the ability necessary to succeed in reaching the objective. That is, he's got the ability, the desire and knows what the job is.

But there's one catch. This team member is a poor activator, a poor self manager. Whether his deficit lies in the area of confidence, of directing immediate activity, of self commitment or a combination of different areas, there is not a high probability that he will perform the tasks explained, supported and required by the team.

Once the team meeting is over, and the team has done its preparation for future performance or its evaluation of performance past, its job is done. Once the meeting is over, with regard to determining the immediate performance of this poorly self-managed team member, so is the team. Whether or not the job will get done is up to the doer. An apparently successful team meeting, one creating good directions and good support, will inadvertently waste much time and energy if, after the team breaks up, its players do a poor job of managing their own immediate performance.

Strong self managers, because of what they bring to the table, can create a vital team that can strongly support the performance of its members. Strong self managers can, in turn, make good use of that support. Regardless of the strength of the processes and structures surrounding team performance, without good management of immediate performance, the potential of the team and the individuals making up that team must remain relatively untapped.

If it is important that a team be flexible, adaptable and proactive, these characteristics can only be present in strength if the individuals belonging to that team are themselves flexible, adaptable and proactive. These characteristics are by-products of high levels of self-confidence, self direction and self commitment — of good self management.

chapter **6** | # ACTIVATION

THE PRIMARY CHALLENGE

We believe that our primary challenge, both as organizations and as individuals, is to continually increase our performance potential to satisfy constantly growing and altering demands. That is and will remain a constant challenge, but it is not our greatest one.

We know how to recognize new demands, and how to identify the skills and resources needed to satisfy them and devise the delivery systems to put the new potential in place. We have been doing exactly that at an ever-increasing rate over the last two decades. We've understood the need to change and how to bring those changes about. The problem has been that while massive increases in performance potential have occurred, brought about by retraining, retooling and restructuring, *there has seldom been anything close to a corresponding increase in the performance itself.* A flood in potential and only a trickle in performance.

The primary challenge facing us now and in the future is not the creation of potential but its conversion — turning the potential into performance.

THE INDIVIDUAL

The Fundamental Element

All information, all skills training, all organizational structures, all management strategies, all technical resources, all aspects of the physical environment — virtually everything that is input into an organization — has as its ultimate internal target, the individuals belonging to that organization. The quality, the kind and the amount of output of that organization, that is, the translation into performance of all that has been input, is carried out, again, ultimately by that fundamental element — the individual. The focus of the organization may be its customers, but the organizational or internal end user and end producer is the individual belonging to that organization. The success of an organization is ultimately dependent upon *the potential of its individuals and the degree to which that potential is translated into effective performance.*

Change and the Individual

In the first chapter of this book, "The Management Vacuum," we looked at the reality of change in our occupational world. The response to that change includes: constantly altering skill sets; growing knowledge and information; continuously expanding technology; changing attitudes; new management models, often with additional management functions; altered role definitions; the identification of processes; and the creation of processes that should be. While all these changes themselves continue to change, the one element that remains as a constant, the element that receives and must translate all these changes, is the individual, as is evidenced in the following diagram.

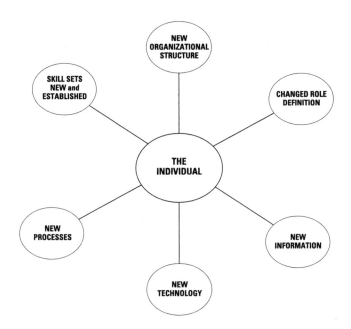

Again, the individual is the receptacle, processor and then translator of this ongoing, significant and expensive input. The occupational world continues to change. The individual remains the constant processor of that change.

And what do we do about this constant element? On the surface it would appear that we do much. After all, this changing input, be it skills or be it material, has, as its ultimate internal target, the individual. Are we not, then, constantly exerting significant energy aimed at increasing the potential of the individual? With each course given, for example, are we not augmenting the individual's flexibility? When we give a manager a new people-management course, have we not altered that manager's potential to manage his people? A course in customer service — does it not change the individuals receiving that course? The answer is Yes.

Then, apparently, we are taking care of the organizational constant — the individual — but in the way one changes one's computer by installing a new piece of software. A personal computer with no software does nothing. Install a software program and the PC has specific output potential. We do more. We change the quality of the software. We add programs having very different computing potential. The computer has now become more useful, more versatile.

There does come a point, however, when we recognize that our computer no longer has the memory or the speed to effectively process the potential represented by the new programming. We either revert to the older software or we acquire a more advanced central processing unit so that the potential represented by the new software can be actualized. (As a relative computer illiterate I have progressed through four generations of computers in the last decade.)

In a sense, the individual in organizations is analogous to the computer in that we are constantly loading new "software" into the individual. We continue to improve the way we do things organizationally, upgrade our performance-management systems and alter our corporate objectives to incorporate the potential represented by the new "software." However, we do little to change the individual. While the "software" and the systems may be upgraded and may make some positive performance difference, no alterations are brought about in the individual's ability to process the "software" to ensure that the potential of the upgraded programs and systems is optimally utilized. There are times when we are given the message that present capacity has been used up and still we attempt to load in the new "software" hoping that the message will just go away. We even find ourselves pouring expensive new "software" into unaltered individuals with the result that our "computers" freeze up and become unproductive rather than more productive. At that point we usually assume that either the "software" is no good or the "computers" just don't want to compute.

A Martian, visiting our planet and looking at the activities in most large corporations, would likely be impressed by the amount of effort given to delivering as much information, as much technology and as many skills to its individuals as it can. Were our visitor to hang around for a bit he would see that, if anything, the rate of delivery is continually on the rise. He could be excused if the conclusion he came to was that corporations have as one of their major objectives stuffing as much potential into their people as they can. He could not be blamed for missing the real objective — getting that potential out. Corporations are in the business of getting things done — not simply of making the doing possible. And yet all efforts focus on the latter. Virtually no systematic attention is given to the process of translating that potential into performance, the process responsible for creating the result.

The most significant and unattended opportunity to affect change in an organization is to change its individual employees — its primary agents of change. For organizations to become what they have to be to survive and succeed, change must start with the fundamental constant, its individuals. Again, we focus on management training, increasing competencies, new management structures, teams, but in any basic, systematic, intensive way, we keep clear of the individual, the place where change must occur, first and foremost.

This cannot be done simply by exclaiming the necessity of change, by the command "Make it so!" Individuals must be given the means to bring that change about. They must be provided with ways of systematically managing their attitudes rather than allowing their attitudes to manage them. They must have tools that will support making the right management decisions concerning their own immediate performance. They must be given the means to manage their own immediate motivation in the face of growing performance demands. They have to be in a position to manage building and strengthening their levels of proactivity and their degree of flexibility and adaptability. They must be given the capability to convert more effectively their increasing performance potential, whatever that potential happens to be, into the amount and kind of performance demanded of them—to process that new potential. They must be given the means to self-manage more effectively.

Empowerment and the Activated Individual

The belief that once an organization has created the empowerment opportunity, the individuals in that organization will, simply as a matter of course, now be empowered, is a common one. It can also be a very costly one.

If this belief is incorrect, the organization is in danger of needing empowered performance, requesting it, perhaps demanding it, possibly even providing the opportunity to allow it to happen, but from "disempowered" people who do not have the skills to respond to the demand.

Of course, the assumption that they do have those skills might be the correct one. The people given the empowering opportunity may be capable of taking advantage of it. But can we leave that up to chance? Can we afford to assign new, critical responsibilities to people and simply hope, rather than ensure, that the activation skills needed to carry them out are in place? Can keeping our fingers crossed be the appropriate action when rewards have come from following, not creating, orders — from behaving in an effectively disempowered rather than an effectively empowered fashion?

Can we, as individuals being given the opportunity to do more, to do better, to show greater initiative, to be more creative, to take more responsibility, to turn significantly more of our potential into performance, afford to simply assume that we are up to the challenge, that we are highly empowered people "just waiting to get out"? Can we assume that we have arrived as optimally effective self managers and all we need is the chance to prove it?

If empowerment is to be anything more than a wish, only sometimes fulfilled, the following requirement is essential.

Individuals must be given the skills *that will then allow them to take advantage of the empowerment opportunity.*

The Internal Conversion Rate

A bad day is a day when things go wrong even though we couldn't help it. A terrible day is a day when things go wrong even though we could. We could have reached our objectives. We just didn't.

How often do we, as individuals, have objectives that we truly wish to meet and realistically believe we can, but we failed to reach them? We wanted to get there. We had the ability to get there. But we didn't get there.

This is true, not only of goals related to work, but to objectives that relate to all of life — social, family, personal, leisure, health, financial as well as occupational. Most of us have numerous and significant demands placed upon us in varying aspects of our lives, demands arising from situations and people outside us as well as from within. In our rapidly changing world, if anything, the demands upon us continue to increase as do our intended achievements.

Most of us can't reach them all. Things get in the way. The outside world, in one way or another, may stop us from getting to where we wish to go. We may not have the ability to reach our objective, no matter what the conditions. *But then there are other objectives that are missed because of us but not because of lack of ability. We could have reached them. We just didn't and we pay the price.*

We are always having to pay a bill for reachable, but missed, objectives. The issue is not whether we receive such a bill. We all do. The issue is how high we allow it to become.

We may each define success differently, but regardless of our definition, we all want to reach success in all areas of life. We don't get up in the morning hoping that today will be the day that we fall flat on our face, that we fail dramatically. And yet often we don't reach our defined success, in spite of the fact that we had the desire, the ability and the opportunity to do so!

Part of being human is that few of us reach what we consider to be complete attainable success. The challenge is to get as close as possible and to continue moving in that direction. Helping satisfy that challenge is, in part, what this book is about.

We, as our own self managers, have the responsibility of translating our potential into performance. We are the activators of that potential. All of us could be said to have an internal environment or a set of built-in mechanisms that determine the amount of our potential that does actually get converted into performance. We have, as part of us, various releasers of potential, internal habits that activate, and various blockers, internal habits that de-activate. Together, the good and bad habits of self management determine our *internal conversion rate* — the degree to which we translate our potential into performance. Some releasers may be totally absent in us; others are very strong and easily triggered. Similarly, we may be lucky enough to not function under the burden of certain blockers but, at the same time, have an overload of others.

As individual self managers, our internal conversion rate has seldom come about through a planned and systematic process of installation. It tends to be left to chance and may be brought about by a combination of many things — who we are when we come into the world, the parenting we receive, the lessons given by teachers and peers, perhaps the movies we see, the television we watch and the continuing effects of our experiences. Whatever the sources, this critical performance determinant, our internal conversion rate, is, itself, largely determined by chance. As well, the habits that decide it tend to be so much a part of us that we are often not aware of what they are, when they are operating and how they are influencing our performance at any point in time.

A small example. Consider an individual who has a strongly developed tendency to look at the world pessimistically through very dark glasses. A situation arises containing numerous potential opportunities but also fraught with many possible pitfalls. In all likelihood, our pessimist will see this situation, categorically, as one to be avoided. Although the dangers will be perceived clearly, the opportunities may, for this individual, not even be seen to exist. The on-the-spot decision to "stay clear" will feel like an objective one brought about by the situation, when, in fact, it was brought about largely by a very limited appreciation of that situation — a conversion rate reduced by the habitual stance of pessimism.

THE PRIMARY PERFORMANCE DETERMINANTS

We human beings are always performing. As workers, as parents, as children of parents, as siblings, as spouses, as lovers, as friends, as golfers, gardeners, musicians, bakers and so on, we are always behaving, always acting, always doing, in the pursuit of something. We are always performing and how close we come to arriving at our pursuits determines the degree of our success. The better our performance, the more fulfilled we are.

The Performance Equation

In order to do a job, to reach an objective, to achieve the desired performance, whether it be crossing a busy intersection or performing heart surgery, two things have to be in place. We have to have the ability to do the job — the aptitude, the specific skills, the necessary information, the required experience, the essential tools, or a combination of some or all of these. If not, the job just won't get done. Without the ability to get something done, no matter how much we want it to happen, success will elude us.

However, while it's necessary to have the ability, that certainly isn't sufficient — we must put that ability to work. We must convert that potential. We must *activate* that ability in order for the desired performance to occur. Abilities left sitting on the shelf, no matter how great, do not result in performance. They either gather dust, deteriorate or both. For abilities to bring about performance they must first be activated.

Let's look at a simple, descriptive equation:

Performance = Ability x Activation®

Although both Ability and Activation are necessary for performance, which is more important? There is no doubt that if there's a job to be done and ten people are given the opportunity to do it, nine without required ability, there's only one who has a chance at success — the only one with the necessary ability. However, will the able person succeed? Only if the ability is effectively activated. Again, ability alone is not enough. He can do the job but will he?

Let's look at the same job with ten other applicants. However, in this instance, all have the necessary ability, but only one is an activator. Again, we have only one possible success — the activator. He can do the job and he probably will. Performance needs both ability and activation.

Now let's look at the issue a little differently. You've been given the responsibility for recruiting someone to fill an important position in an organization. In looking at the various applications, you come up with a candidate who seems likely to have stronger abilities pertaining to the job than virtually anyone else applying. This is the most able candidate.

Knowing nothing else, were you a betting person, would you bet a significant portion of your worldly belongings that this individual would be highly successful? After all, there's no doubt that the abilities needed are there. Chances are that most of us would be somewhat reluctant to bet a sizable amount on this person's being a dramatic success even though he certainly could be.

Now you look at another candidate. Judging from the application forms, you see that the abilities necessary to be successful are certainly there but not at the level shown by the previous candidate. However, looking at the information, you recognize that this person has shown a dramatically high level of activation in virtually all achievement areas over many years. Would you be willing to bet significantly more on that candidate's reaching a high degree of success? In all probability, most of us would be much more willing to take the chance.

The more critical question: of the two, which are you more likely to hire? I've asked the same question of many people over a number of years and almost invariably it is the second person that gets the job. Activation is perceived as being that important.

We've all seen it. The extremely bright student in school whose achievements don't come close to reflecting his potential versus the student who gets top grades but who is described as being a "plugger," someone who has to work for his marks. The natural athlete who comes a far second to the capable journeyman who puts in a consistent and total effort. The person with all the qualities to make a magnificent parent who doesn't give parenthood any focus versus the parent who doesn't come nearly as close to knowing all the right moves but is always conscious of doing the very best he or she can. The "natural" salesperson who sells little versus the somewhat "unnatural" salesperson who, through care and persistence, achieves a high level of success.

Perhaps of greater relevance is the reality that all of us, at least on some days, feel that we, unnecessarily, manage to waste our own performance potential. What we can accomplish is not the issue. It's what we *do* accomplish. And what we do accomplish is, in large measure, up to us.

It is *Activation* that tends to differentiate the successful from the less successful and the unsuccessful in virtually every area of life achievement. And yet, for which portion of the performance equation do we receive virtually all our systematic training? For the ability portion. There is virtually no systematic attempt to increase our proficiency in turning the constantly growing volumes of information, the ever-changing skills and attitudes that our continuously renewing world demands, into more effective performance.

From the time we first find ourselves in the grip of the educational system and even before, we are taught, we are practiced, we are tested, on the *ability* portion of the performance equation. We are taught how to read but seldom how to study. We are shown what to focus on but not taught how to focus. We are given an increasing number of skills but rarely, if ever, shown how to believe in them. We are told to be disciplined but are never shown the way. We are advised to be selective in our utilization of study time and energy but not told how.

During the last decade I have asked numerous groups to generate what they consider to be the important factors that determine performance. The list generated consists of many factors. Invariably at least 80 percent of those factors pertain to the *activation* portion of the Performance Equation. We know, without having to be told, how critical a performance factor, activation, is. Our appreciation of the significance of activation becomes apparent immediately upon asking the question. And yet, again, so little, if any, systematic teaching occurs with regard to this most critical of success factors.

Activating from the Outside

Would it be fair to say that we do nothing about activation other than recognize its importance when asked? In fact, we do quite a lot when it comes to trying to activate others. For example, that's what performance-management systems in organizations are all about. Formal and informal incentive programs are meant to be activators. Compensation systems are designed to activate, in that success is often rewarded by greater compensation or by promotion, and failure, by demotion or unemployment. Contests are events designed to activate, as is the promise of social recognition for a job well done. Many different practices plugged into the performance-management system of an organization are designed to help activate the people in that organization.

When we speak of leadership in organizations, we are not simply speaking of people with vision, although that is part of it. We are not simply speaking of people who are able to teach other people how to do more. We also are talking about people who have influence. Leaders are followed. Leaders "activate" their followers to go in a desired direction.

Our educational system attempts to build in sources of external activation, as well. Schools have exams, not only to keep up their own standards, but as a way of activating the student to learn and to illustrate his learning. The report card goes home, in part, with the hope that if the exams alone are not sufficient, then perhaps parental response to the marks will be. And generally, activation is something that parents spend a lot of time and energy doing to and for their children.

So, there is a recognition that performance is not brought about by ability alone. For performance to occur, the ability must be activated, and highly effective or not, highly systematic or not, we spend much time, money and energy attempting to provide the activation. This expenditure assumes the ability to perform (there's no point in activating what isn't there) but also assumes a possible inertia with regard to putting that ability to work. Titled or not, it is the activation factor that is designed to overcome that inertia. However, the primary activator for all of us cannot be others. It must be ourselves. Yet we do almost nothing to teach people how to activate themselves effectively — how to carry out this most critical self-management function.

Activating from the Inside

Although external sources contribute to the strength of a condition necessary for performance to occur, namely, the desire to do so, wanting and having the potential to succeed does not always bring about the activation of that potential. It may be a necessary condition, but it is often not a sufficient one. Few of us wish for failure and yet if success is defined as achieving what we can and want to, *there are many more capable people desirous of success than there are successful people.*

Without strong habits of activation, often we do not put our abilities to work in spite of ourselves. A weakness in our internal conversion rate, in our facility to convert potential into performance, can block performance even in the face of intense desire to succeed. Similarly, the weaker our conversion rate, the greater the level of external pressure that we need to get moving. Many of us say of ourselves that we work well under pressure. For some, that can be translated as, "I don't buckle when under the gun. I can still work effectively." For others, perhaps the majority, it really represents something else. It means, "I need a significant amount of external pressure to make me really productive. I don't look to myself for activation. I need something or someone external to me to get me moving. Not a weak shove but a strong push to overcome my inertia to activate."

Strong activation habits reduce that inertia so that significantly less motivation, internal or external, will be needed to convert potential into performance.

Replacing Desire with Habit

Complacency and Activation

Complacency can frequently function as an enemy of performance and somewhat paradoxically, success, often the result of strong activation, can act as a breeding ground for complacency. Complacency can be a kind of de-activator in that the drive to perform can be markedly reduced. Success can reduce the hunger to succeed.

An independent business person tends to fear the future less when immersed in a successful present. A managee's need to be appreciated by the boss tends to lessen immediately after a highly positive performance appraisal. A salesperson's rate of contacting new prospects often diminishes after a good quarter, in spite of the fact that the success was created largely through contacting new prospects.

The obvious answer to the problem seems to be to find a way of maintaining the same level of hunger, of need, regardless of the degree of satiation. However, it's often difficult to sustain a consistently high-drive level even when the immediate situation requires it, let alone when it does not.

An insistent drive to perform will often overcome the absence of strong activation habits. When the need is high, people will often perform, in spite of themselves. The lazy become motivated, even if only temporarily, the unconfident venture out, in spite of the lump in their throats, the indecisive pick a direction and move. With low drive, the lazy relax, the unconfident hide and the indecisive contemplate.

Reducing Motivation Dependence

Strong self-management habits significantly reduce the dependence on a high level of immediate motivation, whether generated by fear or want.

The activation trigger requires much less pressure to be fired. If one thinks of the activation factor in the Performance Equation, Performance = Ability x Activation$^{®}$, as determining the height of a wall, that wall representing inertia, the stronger the self-management habits, the lower the wall. Little energy is needed to step over a low barrier. Although self-management habits do not primarily create desire, they ensure that very much less desire is needed to activate ability. Complacency still must be guarded against, but its potentially damaging effects are dramatically reduced by the development of strong self management.

Refocusing the Role of External Motivator

In an earlier chapter we looked at the external manager as motivator. One of the reasons that external managers continue to try to motivate their people is that, at times, it works. It activates ability. However, even when it does, it does so temporarily. A momentary burst of desire is created and two things happen. First, a heightened level of performance may occur and second, a greater dependence on activation from outside is established. Conversely, the tendency to activate from within becomes threatened. A brief immediate benefit and a potentially high future cost. (I remember people in a sales organization wondering why sales activity finally reached an acceptable level only during the two major annual sales contests). With less self activation, more external motivation is required, and so the managee continues to feed at the trough of external motivation until the manager gets tired and the managee immune.

The picture changes markedly when strong self-management practices are in place. It takes much less motivation, less pressure, to activate, and so a relatively low level of motivation, whether generated internally or externally, is enough to convert potential to performance. Now, emphasizing the importance of objectives, generating mission statements and providing compensation for increased performance can be a constructive rather than destructive aspect of an individual's external environment, and can be utilized effectively as a secondary impetus to action.

THE ELEMENTS OF ACTIVATION

We have been talking about the important role that activation plays in determining performance and have identified the self manager as being primarily responsible for that activation. Now let's look at the main elements that determine the level of activation. There are three: one related to attitude, the second to immediate-activity decisions and the third to the area of motivation.

The first is **self-confidence**. A person may have the ability but he must be aware of that ability if it is to bring about anything close to optimal performance; if the ability is to be optimally activated.

The next is **self direction**. A person may have the ability and be confident in it, but he must direct that ability appropriately, must apply it effectively if it is to bring about anything close to optimal performance; if the ability is to be optimally activated.

The last is **self commitment**. A person may have the ability, be confident in it and determine how it is to be directed, but he must translate that direction into action if it is to bring about anything close to optimal performance; if it is to be optimally activated.

It is only when all three — self-confidence, self direction and self commitment — are effectively in place, that the performance potential of ability will be realized — that anything close to optimal activation will occur.

Activation has no ceiling. It is an area in which, with relatively little systematic effort, we can continue to grow. We can continue to improve the degree to which we are able to convert our potential into performance by continuing to increase our levels of self-confidence, self direction and self commitment.

Activation = Self-Confidence x Self Direction x Self Commitment

In a sense, everything until now serves as an introduction to the second book of this volume, titled "Activating the Individual." We are now coming to the core of the matter, the many things that we can do to *continuously* increase our level of activation. Book Two answers the question, How do I take systematic control over and continue to build my levels of self-confidence, self direction and self commitment so that I can more vigorously, more proactively and more flexibly activate my abilities — convert my potential into performance?

BOOK TWO

ACTIVATING THE INDIVIDUAL

INTRODUCTION

When we talk about the information age, the exploding technologies, the expanding communication channels opening throughout our world, the rapid pace with which all these harbingers of change continue to expand, the realization becomes more and more strongly underlined that we, as individuals, must continue to grow if we hope to keep up.

We spend a tremendous amount of time, energy and money, as a society and as individuals, attempting to increase our performance potential, whether that be performance in our jobs, our roles as parent or spouse or even in our leisure activities. We don't simply take up golf; we take golfing lessons or lessons in tennis, art, karate or whatever. Formal schooling begins at a very early age, and for many people, extends well into adulthood. We are constantly learning, ingesting new information, acquiring new skills, relating to new technologies.

This demand to increase our performance potential is, itself, rapidly increasing. Changes are occurring so quickly that we find ourselves having to acquire new knowledge, adopt new attitudes, learn new skills and often suspend the use of old ones at a rate that makes us feel that the status of "rookie" has become a lifetime condition. Understandably, then, as we approach the twenty-first century, we see, as perhaps the most critical challenge facing the individual, the need to continuously increase potential.

But is it? Perhaps there is another challenge as critical — the need to convert a greater portion of the potential we have into performance. Not only must we get more, but we must do more with what we've got. This, of course, is not a new song but a melody that has been playing since we began thinking about the nature of humankind. We perceive that as a species and as individual members of the species, what we accomplish does not come close to reflecting our capabilities. So much of our potential — our potential to do, to experience, to have, to grow — is not translated into performance. It exists largely as a resource, untapped.

There's more. Our constantly and swiftly altering landscape requires a greater ongoing flexibility and adaptability than ever. We have to translate our potential differently. Proactivity is becoming a more insistent demand as our kaleidoscopic world continues to turn faster. It seems that less and less is the path we take being defined for us by society, by the organizations for which we work, even by our past experiences. We are being asked to take responsibility for defining the immediate reality within which we perform. We are being asked to create the world within which we must then act. We must convert more of our potential, more creatively.

And to which of these demands do we respond? Increasing our potential or its conversion? As was said at the beginning of this introduction, from a very early age, we begin working on the systematic growth of our potential and that work goes on. Formal teaching in schools is replaced by the ongoing training that must be part of the occupational world if, as individuals or as organizations, large and small, we are to become or remain competitive. We are continuously increasing our performance potential, and with a vengeance.

What about our becoming more and more flexible so that we can effectively react to the changing situations that confront us, day to day? What are we doing to ensure that we are able to adapt to the larger changes that continue to occur? What measures are we taking to assure the application of greater proactivity in virtually all aspects of our occupational lives? Are we systematically working at a more vigorous conversion of the performance potential we have at any point in time?

Change management tends to focus largely on responses required by corporations and by people managers within those corporations. Little attention is given to the primary change agent, the individual, who has to both create and respond to the changes that are needed. The reality of change and the need to respond appropriately is stated frequently, as if repeated exposure will itself bring about the required accommodation.

Proactivity is dealt with in much the same way but perhaps in a still purer form. Organizations are telling their people over and over again that they must become more proactive, take more risks, identify and pursue new opportunities, new challenges, screaming repeatedly "Be proactive!" as if stating it loudly and often will make it so. While organizations present skills requiring proactivity, they do little to teach people how to be more proactive. Too often, organizations are made up of a lot of reactive people who have proactive skills but who show little increase in proactivity.

How about the larger issue — turning more of our potential into performance? In any direct, systematic sense, this primary human issue is given short shrift. We simply continue to mourn the great human potential that remains trapped within us, while noting that the demand for its release is constantly increasing.

This book is about the conversion of potential into performance and is written for the only person who is in a position to take primary responsibility for that conversion — the owner of the potential. This book is directed at self managers, the management force in the occupational and in the personal world that has the awesome responsibility of activating ability. It presents specific ways to strengthen the mechanisms of activation so that more and more of our potential today and tomorrow will be realized.

We each have two primary functions with regard to immediate performance. We each have the function of the performer, the person who does the job, and the function of self manager, the person who manages the doing. The performer represents our ability, our potential to perform. The self manager is the function that activates that potential. The activation habits represent a skill set, the self manager's skill set, that when applied, allows us to continually increase the effectiveness with which we are able to carry out the responsibility of managing our performer.

That's where the practice comes in. *By practicing, activation habits are built and strengthened; activation knowledge is translated into activating ability.* It's easy to do and takes minimal effort. Application happens in thought and doesn't interfere with doing other things simultaneously. Over time, application continuously strengthens activation, and minimal energy is required for maintenance and growth to occur. Perhaps their most important characteristic is that with relatively little effort, the activation practices become virtually automatic.

How well each of us is able to translate our potential, to turn our ability into performance, is the single most important determinant of the level of our fulfillment in virtually all critical areas of life. Don't leave it to chance. Take control.

PART I

MANAGING
SELF-CONFIDENCE

Knowing What Can Be Done

> *A person must have the ability, **must be aware of that ability**, must make the right immediate-activity decisions regarding the application of that ability and must translate those decisions into action, if the ability is to bring about anything close to optimal performance, if the ability is to be optimally activated.*

INTRODUCTION

Everyone knows about the importance of self-confidence. Ask anybody, "If you really have the ability to do something, but you have no faith in yourself, how are you likely to do?" and the answer will be, "Not very well." When we read the sports pages in newspapers or watch sporting events on television, how often are we told that a certain player isn't playing well because he's lost confidence or a team is on the rise because they're starting to believe in themselves? When people are about to face a challenge, are we not aware that giving them a vote of confidence may help them succeed in meeting that challenge? Sometimes we even go too far in assigning significance to this important activator. People will even be heard to say (and sometimes get paid to say it) that as long as you believe you can do something, you can do it. Personally, my height, age and shocking absence of athletic ability suggests that whether I believe it or not, I am not destined to ever be a center in the National Basketball Association. Self-confidence is not the answer to performance. The ability to do a job must also be in place if the job is to get done. It is, however, an extremely important performance determinant.

What Self-Confidence Is

Definitions of self-confidence differ, but generally, they all are similar enough to suggest that we share the same sense of what the concept means. Self-esteem, believing in yourself, having faith in your ability to do something, represent perhaps the most common definitions. A similar definition, but one that is more closely aligned with the Performance Equation, Performance = Ability x Activation®, is as follows:

> *Self-confidence is an optimistic, realistic and immediate awareness of one's abilities and capabilities.*

Optimistic because it involves focusing on one's strengths.

Realistic because believing that you can fly is unlikely to get you off the ground. Self-confidence does not permit us to do what we're not capable of doing. It frees us to do what we are able to do.

Immediate awareness because to activate, the awareness must be part of us — not an intellectual conclusion arrived at through lengthy analysis but a belief, immediately retrievable, almost without thinking.

It encompasses capabilities as well as abilities because it represents not only a belief in what we can do already, but in our potential to learn to do what we cannot, as yet.

The Variability of Self-Confidence

It's important to recognize that our immediate level of self-confidence, the amount of self-confidence we feel at any specific point in time, is not static but can be highly variable. When watching a tennis match, for example, you can almost see the confidence level of the players increasing and decreasing as the game progresses. You can describe a player: "That person is female, tall, has blue eyes and is confident." Eye color remains constant. Confidence does not. Although it's true that in a general sense we can categorize people as being more or less confident, within a short period of time, a day or even an hour, our immediate level of confidence can vary tremendously.

To illustrate, most of us know at least one person whom we would describe generally as being highly confident but who has experienced a significant setback — for example, the loss of a job—and is rendered temporarily unconfident.

Most of us have awakened, confident, on a specific day, but because of some unanticipated negative event, we are feeling useless by ten o'clock that morning. It may be because of something that has happened to us, something someone else has said, or it may even be the result of some of our own negative thinking about ourselves. The variability of self-confidence — that it is not a fixed characteristic — is really very good news. It puts us in a position to affect in a positive way our level of self-confidence on an ongoing basis.

Before we look at the kinds of things we do inadvertently that limit or decrease our level of self-confidence and then specific things that we can do to continuously protect and build the awareness we have of our potential, let's examine more closely the reasons that self-confidence is a critical ability activator. In other words, *we know that with self-confidence, there's a good chance that we will realize our potential. Without it, there is as good a chance that we won't.* Let's examine why.

The Costs of *Unconfidence*

Some of the reasons that self-confidence is important have to do with the fact that we tend to communicate to others our immediate level of confidence, the degree of confidence that we're feeling at a specific point in time. We do this in various ways, some of them so subtle that perhaps no one is aware of how confidence level is being communicated, but nevertheless the message is there. When we are unconfident, our posture changes, as does the way we move. Somehow our body language is saying, "I'm not really sure of this" or "I'm not really sure of myself." Eye movements may tell the tale. Some people, when feeling particularly unconfident, spend more time looking at their shoes. Voice tone can change. Some of us end our statements with a mild question mark. We may use a slightly different vocabulary when feeling confident than we do when we're not. In the latter case there may be more "I think," "I was wondering if perhaps," "I'm not sure if this makes sense but." Then there's a more extreme communication — silence. We are so unconfident that we manage to disappear while still in the room. "He didn't say anything" can easily be translated into, "He doesn't know anything."

Unconfidence is communicated and tends to communicate incompetence. We may have the necessary ability, experience and knowledge but our lack of confidence is communicating their absence. Many of our performance objectives, both in our personal and occupational lives, involve influencing others. It is extremely difficult to have a strong influence when one is communicating a lack of confidence. The unconfident manager who is asking his people to follow is likely to be leading a rather small parade. We have probably all witnessed some teachers being "eaten alive" by their adolescent students, not because the teachers lacked knowledge or the ability to convey it, but because they were clearly unsure of themselves. The unconfident salesperson may be using the words that convey, "I suggest that you take my advice," but may be communicating, "I don't believe in my expertise and I strongly recommend that you don't either." The unconfident member of a work team is less likely to be listened to regardless of the validity of his suggestions.

Often, then, the potential that we bring to a specific situation is decided, in part, by our ability to influence others. How influential we can be is partly determined by our level of confidence. Unconfidence can frequently lower influence.

Procrastination can be a serious de-activator. We put off things for many reasons, one of which can be a lack of confidence. We are more apt to postpone tackling challenges about which we don't feel confident. Sometimes we'll avoid the task or the situation by talking ourselves into believing that other things are more important. We convince ourselves that the worrisome top-priority activities don't really belong in that lofty category, and let the less consequential take on a somewhat overblown significance. We then label the comfortable a "must-do" and decide to do the former A-priority activity if and when there's time — carefully considered time mismanagement. We proceed to have a very busy day and end it feeling highly productive when, in fact, it was really spent doing some tasks so that we could avoid doing others.

A similar product of unconfidence is ability avoidance, which means that we don't avoid the task but we avoid activating some of our abilities appropriate to doing the task. This can be especially true when we have a choice of doing something the old way or doing it by a newly acquired method. Many cases of new skills, business processes and technologies not living up to their promise are the result of ability avoidance. The newly acquired potential just doesn't get out.

Resistance to change is often a child of unconfidence. The unconfident tend to hold onto yesterday for dear life, convincing themselves that yesterday's skills, roles and objectives are the right ones simply because they are yesterday's. Without confidence they desperately need yesterday's proof to know that they can do the job. We continue to tell people, often attempt to convince ourselves, that to be successful we must adapt to the new. However, in the absence of protected and continuously strengthened confidence, adaptability becomes a very tall order.

A cry of organizations to its people is "Be proactive!" This often means "Go and create a new world and then respond productively to it." Doing this requires courage. New situations frequently carry with them fewer guarantees of success, higher risk and the potential of difficulties yet to be identified. Courage, however, is, in part, a by-product of self-confidence. Self-confidence provides a reason to be courageous. Proactivity requires that it be effectively self-managed.

Entering situations uninvited can bring about an uncomfortable degree of rejection. (Mind you, for most of us, any rejection is uncomfortable.) For example, a person performing a sales function may receive a prospect's immediate, and sometimes strongly expressed, rejection. A manager, announcing a new and highly challenging objective, doesn't always get a heart-felt round of applause from his managees. Suggesting different and ambitious approaches to one's work team may not immediately result in the team's most-valuable-player award.

Precisely because we find rejection to be a rather painful experience, we tend to want to avoid it whenever we can. However, that avoidance can be costly. A high level of self-confidence can help. Self-confidence does not necessarily make rejection that much less painful, but it does make it less costly. Because rejection tends to reduce our immediate level of self-confidence, people who have little can ill afford the additional loss. Highly confident people are not as likely to be de-activated. They have a greater reserve to begin with, and good confidence builders are able to quickly replenish their confidence supply.

A related aspect of self-confidence is its function in the area of stress management. A lack of confidence is, understandably, accompanied by a fear of failure, with that failure being expected "any minute now." Getting up in the morning wondering, not whether you're going to fall flat on your face but how often, and when will the first time be, does not promote an internal sense of calm. The stress level of the unconfident can sometimes get a dramatic head start. High stress feeds on itself. We tend to make more mistakes when we are highly anxious. We also tend to exaggerate the negatives when we are feeling "uptight." Stress reduction is a rather difficult accomplishment for the unconfident. Stress magnification is easy.

The product of unconfidence, then, not only relates to decreased performance, but also to overall quality of life. Lessened fulfillment, as a result of deficient activation, the avoidance of potentially positive experiences, the presence of destructive levels of anxiety and unwarranted feelings of inadequacy, can, collectively, alter the joy experienced as one walks through life. Personal development in any number of such areas as playing a sport, traveling, learning a musical instrument or a new language or taking courses often represent challenges too great to be attempted in the eyes of the unconfident. Vacations might be spent in the backyard, the stated reason being, "I'm not interested in travel," when it may really be, "I'm not up to finding my way." For some, the couch-potato syndrome may not be the result of indolence or a love of television but an absence of the self-confidence to do much else. People's lives can be significantly impoverished as a result of a deficit in their level of self-confidence. *Effective self management of confidence not only helps us do better but perhaps, more importantly, it helps us enjoy the doing.*

Although it is not true that all we have to do to accomplish something is to believe we can, we do know that our expectations are related to our performance. If I have the ability to do something, am confident in that ability and expect success, the chances are good that my expectations will be realized. By the same token, however, if I have that same ability without the appropriate confidence level and therefore don't expect success, the chances are good that, again, my expectations will be realized. In other words, expectations are an important determinant of performance and, in turn, self-confidence is an important determinant of expectations.

When we think about expectations, we tend to be looking at things in the larger sense. "What do you expect to achieve over the next year?" "What are your life's goals?" The fact is, we generate expectations by the thousands as we go through life, everything from, "I expect when I turn the ignition key my engine will start," to expectations very much more ambitious. In the space of a day, we are confronted with many options. In a split second, we must decide whether to take a specific option or not. Expectation of success and we go down the road. Expectation of failure and we either look for another road or sit on the curb. Often success is determined by the immediate-activity decisions we make. Those decisions can be influenced by the instant expectations we generate — by the confidence or lack of confidence we have in our performance potential.

We all are aware that self-confidence is an extremely important performance determinant. There are many good reasons to support that awareness. Each of them provides an argument for not leaving our level of confidence to chance, but for taking control, managing it so that our level of activation can be continuously strengthened.

chapter 7

MANAGING SELF CRITICISM

THE EFFECTS OF DESTRUCTIVE CRITICISM

Most of us have a pretty good idea of what it feels like to be on the receiving end of destructive criticism — criticism for its own sake. The highly critical boss, parent, spouse, friend, sibling — someone we see frequently who is overly quick to inform us of our mistakes, of our weaknesses, with no honest attempt to give us counsel that would help us improve — is at best a pain in the neck and at worst, a threat to our self-confidence.

Let's look more closely at the boss whose criticism is destructive. What does the behavior look like and what is its impact? This person does not have very much that's good to say to you about you. He may or may not recognize the good. It's hard for you to know. But regardless, there is little communication about the positives. All the time is taken up talking about the "not positives." The mistakes, the weaknesses that get so much attention, don't have to be significant ones. Small mistakes that bring with them little, if any, cost seem to deserve just about the same degree of attention as do the big ones. Fortunately you make very few big mistakes, yet you find yourself on the receiving end of much destructive criticism. Blunders, weaknesses, omissions, big and small, all seem to get treated with close to equal "respect."

Mistakes can often be treated with such respect that even though they may have happened only once, they get talked about over and over. One mistake, taking but a few moments and having little impact on the world, can nevertheless become a topic of conversation that comes up again and again. So much mileage from so little fuel!

The most noteworthy characteristic of this campaign of destructive criticism is its extreme "purity." It is pure criticism. It is a description of what's wrong without any attempt to suggest what might be done to make the wrong, right. It is criticism for its own sake. It describes the perceived problem and doesn't even attempt to offer any possible solution — pure, 100 percent criticism.

What is its effect? What does it accomplish? It has only one primary effect — confidence destruction. No benefits here. Just cost.

If you were to ask this world-class criticizer the reasons for his behavior, the answer would likely come back, "It's my responsibility to get my people to grow; to increase their performance potential. To do this, I must point out their errant ways. How else can one expect positive change?"

There is a grain of truth in that. It may, in fact, reflect the intention of the boss or manager. If the person being criticized had not been aware that a mistake was made, the criticism might even help to positively alter performance in future.

There are some problems, however. There was no attempt to give positive suggestions. The benefits of correction were outbalanced by the associated confidence costs. The point was made upon first delivery of the criticism and the repetition served only to deflate. Because there was no attempt at constructive criticism, any possible small gain might be far outweighed by the damage.

It's important here to differentiate between constructive and destructive criticism. Although they both may have performance improvement as their aim, constructive criticism includes corrective input, but destructive criticism does not. It simply reveals, and frequently re-reveals, the problem.

Some of us have been on the receiving end of this exact experience and can probably recall the associated cost. It's hard to feel good about oneself, about one's potential, about one's abilities, in the face of this onslaught. The results of it can indeed be highly damaging to one's quality of life and certainly to one's performance. Even though our external manager spends only a limited amount of time "in our face," still the damage can be significant.

THE POWER OF DESTRUCTIVE *SELF* CRITICISM

While someone else, virtually anyone else, may be in our presence 1, 2, perhaps 5 percent of our waking hours, we are with ourselves 100 percent of the time. We can't escape ourselves even if we want to. If an external destructive criticizer, with us for a very small portion of our time, can do serious damage to our self-confidence, think of how much damage we can do if we're really good at destructive self criticism! After all, figuratively, we are always perched on our own shoulder, able to blast away at ourselves, virtually nonstop as we go through the paces of living. Unlike people outside of us, we don't even have to interrupt what we are doing in order to destructively criticize ourselves. It's something that happens inside our heads as we continue to be involved in doing other things.

What's the potential damage of this internal behavior? Severe damage to self-confidence. *We are, potentially, a greater danger to our own self-confidence than is anyone else.*

The Social Lesson

If there are no benefits to this destructive self criticism, or at least if the costs are much higher than the possible gains, why do many of us perform it with a vengeance and all of us perform it to some degree or other?

It begins with our tendency to focus on our weaknesses, on our mistakes, our omissions — on those pieces of performance in all areas of life that are not at the level we want them to be. It's understandable that we look at our mistakes. They are costly. After all, we function within the framework of objectives, whether they have been thought out, written down, communicated to others or not, and our blunders get in the way of our reaching those objectives. We focus upon those errors because they have impact. We focus upon them because we had better! Damage control and future improvement cannot happen if the mistakes are not noted.

When we were very young, most of us were taught a social lesson, that the world around us attends closely to our negatives. Unfortunately this lesson continues to the end of our days.

If a child were to bet a friend a quarter that he could get his parents' undivided attention within the next two minutes, what would the most likely avenue to greater riches be: good behavior or misbehavior?

As children growing up, even if our home were highly supportive, one of the things that most of us experienced was that negative behavior, misbehavior, was more likely to attract attention than positive. That is not to say, necessarily, that positive behavior was ignored but that negative had a greater likelihood of being noted and with some greater degree of accompanying drama. "Don't do that!" tends to get more play than does "Do that again!"

This social lesson that negative behavior — poor performance — tends to get the larger response, continues outside the home and into the school. Behaving in the classroom may get a rating of "Good" on the report card but is unlikely to get center stage while school's in session. Getting caught misbehaving, however, has a good chance of attracting the spotlight. Some kind of punishment is generally attached to being late, speaking out of turn, not doing one's homework, playing truant, to name a few, and may well be delivered with a liberal amount of fanfare. Not being late, not speaking out of turn, doing one's homework and coming to school rather than "playing hooky," have as their reward only the absence of punishment — a nondelivery and with no fanfare.

Academic performance, although perhaps to a lesser degree, tends to be treated in much the same way. Exceptionally positive performance is likely to get singled out by both home and school. An unexceptional positive performance does not usually attract a great deal of attention. But a twenty-four out of 100! That may deserve a call from the teacher, grounding for a month, the withdrawal of allowance, Lecture Number seventeen on the importance of education and any number of other creative reactions to the disappointing performance. The negative gets the noise.

The lesson continues into the workplace. Not always, and not everywhere, but as a general statement it is probably fair to say that if one hears, unexpectedly, upon entering work, the words, "The boss wants to see you," the response is not likely to be, "Me? The boss wants to see me? Wow! Is this my lucky day or what!" The first and perhaps second and third thoughts are more likely to be variations on the theme, "Oh no. What have I done now?"

The social lesson that generally accompanies us in varying degrees from cradle to grave is that we had better focus on our negatives if for no other reason than the rest of the world seems to.

The trouble, however, is not that we focus but that because of the imbalance inherent in the social lesson, many of us learn to overfocus on our negatives. In varying degrees, we mismanage and find ourselves on an ongoing Crusade of Self Criticism.

THE CRUSADE OF SELF CRITICISM

Dwelling on the Insignificant

One commonly found characteristic of this self mismanagement is that all our own mistakes, regardless of size, regardless of their importance or insignificance, become grist for this self-criticism mill. All omissions, all errors, no matter how small, are fair game and get our internal center stage. We've all experienced this. We've made a small mistake, perhaps a small social error. We examine and reexamine it. We may even add to the experience by then thinking about other mistakes we've made in the recent and not-so-recent past similar to this one. Before long, our self-confidence starts to wane.

The Relentless Review

A second characteristic of this crusade of self criticism has to do with the tendency to not just review the mistake once but to revisit it over and over and over again. We introduce someone at a party, or attempt to, but instead, forget the person's name and at three o'clock in the morning can be found staring up at the ceiling, vigorously replaying the video in our heads of the botched introduction.

From a confidence-cost point of view, this constant revisiting can be very expensive in that the effect on confidence of reviewing a mistake in one's head is very similar to the confidence effect of making the mistake in the first place. Very quickly a one-pound error takes on a one-hundred-pound weight.

Destructive Self Criticism

The third characteristic of this crusade of self criticism is the most damaging. So often the criticism we offer up is criticism for its own sake. We're not analyzing the situation. We're not intently looking for solutions or ways of avoiding the mistake in future. We are simply looking at our folly for the sake of looking at our folly. We are screaming internally, over and over again, "You idiot! How could you be so stupid?" just for the sake of the scream. No benefit — only cost. The cost of self-confidence.

I am not suggesting that we not examine our errors; that we not try to learn from our own mistakes; that we not constructively self-criticize. That kind of positive self coaching will be dealt with later in the book and represents an important self-management responsibility. What we are dealing with here is criticism that, often without even realizing it, is simply criticism for its own sake and carries with it only potential damage rather than potential benefit. Someone well practiced in destructive self criticism can inadvertently attack their own confidence from within, with the cumulative result over even a single day, let alone weeks, months and years, being a very high cost to confidence.

However, regardless of whether a person practices destructive self criticism vigorously or only sporadically, *the objective should be to reduce destructive criticism to as close to zero as possible.* Remember, destructive criticism carries with it no benefits. Only cost to confidence.

When we look at all life areas or the occupational world, specifically, we see a universe that is giving those of us who mismanage self criticism all kinds of practice. With the constant changes that are taking place, the new learning curves, the increased complexity of our jobs and the growing responsibilities being presented to us, we are being given what seems to be almost unlimited opportunity to make mistakes. This, in turn, allows the true practitioners of destructive self criticism numerous chances to apply their craft — to attack confidence from within, relentlessly.

THE ACTIVATION HABIT: SILENCE THE DESTRUCTION

However good we might be at destructive self criticism, it has taken us pretty well from birth to the present moment to get there. Fortunately we do not need anything close to that amount of time to significantly reduce this negative activation habit.

Precisely because destructive internal criticism can easily become a habit, can become virtually automatic, we are usually not even aware of when we are doing "it" to ourselves. We don't do anything about it because we don't realize it's there. "The Crusade of Self Criticism" seems to occur automatically and needs no help from us to keep going.

We've all experienced this. We are driving the car, for example, on our way to work and recall some mistake we made yesterday. We start reviewing it over and over again. Because we have been intensively involved in this destructive process throughout the trip, by the time we park the car we are, for reasons unidentified, feeling considerably less effective than we did when we started.

To reduce this negative habit, the first thing we must do is become aware the moment that the negative internal behavior starts happening. Again, we are unlikely to do anything about something if we don't realize it's occurring. The realization is an important first step. To promote it is simple.

When working on reducing destructive self criticism, begin the day by writing in your daily action plan the simple instruction, "Look out for destructive self criticism!"

Giving yourself this simple instruction will very quickly become sufficient to heighten your awareness of the negative internal habit. Writing rather than simply saying the instruction to yourself serves two purposes. First, the action of writing it increases the probability that you will remember. Second, the written word itself will serve as a reminder.

The next step is an easy one, taking an even smaller amount of energy than does the awareness training. It is a simple thought-stopping technique that markedly reduces the occurrence of destructive self criticism.

The moment that you become aware that destructive self criticism is happening, simply issue to yourself the order, "Stop it!"

The moment you become aware that it's happening again, even if that moment occurs on the heels of your last command, simply issue it again. It takes virtually no effort to give yourself the internal command, "Stop it!" It can be given five hundred times in a day without the loss of a single calorie. However, very quickly you will start noticing a significant decrease in both the frequency and duration of destructive self criticism. It will begin happening less and less often but when it does, "Stop it!" will result in its not being pursued with nearly the previous intensity. You will find that within only a few days there will be a marked decrease in destructive self criticism. With very little effort you will have given your immediate level of self-confidence significant protection.

Again, because destructive self criticism is just that — only destructive — the aim of a self manager should be to reduce it to its absolute minimum. Work on developing, maintaining and strengthening this counterproductive habit by coming back to the exercise over and over again to ensure that you continue to get better at reducing the negative crusade and that the destructive habit does not revitalize.

chapter 8

MANAGING SUCCESS

WITHHOLDING CREDIT

The Social Lesson

A kindergarten class is having a graduation party. Relatives have been invited, and during the party the guests are given the opportunity to see each of the students perform for the benefit of all lucky enough to be in the room. Some recite poetry, others dance, some sing and a few refuse to do anything at all. One child, a singer, clearly stands out as having a special talent and as she is giving forth, the pride her parents feel can be clearly seen by the expression on their faces.

The performance is over. Our star singer is overheard saying to her aunt, "Wasn't I terrific? Wasn't I just about the best in the class?"

Before she can continue the conversation she feels a hand on her shoulder moving her away from her aunt and to a more private spot in the room. It's her father (the same father that a few moments before was beaming with pride) who, looking rather

*sternly at his daughter, can be heard to say, "You're not sup-
posed to say things like that!"*

"Why not?" the child asks innocently. "It's true, isn't it?"

*The father then says, with the wisdom that often only par-
ents are able to muster, "That's got nothing to do with it.
You're not supposed to say good things about yourself to
other people!"*

When we find ourselves on the receiving end of a sincere compliment,
referring to something we've done or to something we are, most of us,
most of the time, feel pretty good about it. Even if we have difficulty
accepting compliments — feel somewhat embarrassed and uncomfortable, not knowing what to say, how to graciously accept the praise, even
then we still tend to review the compliment in our mind's eye, happy it
was delivered, despite our discomfort having suggested otherwise. And
it's no wonder. It is nice to be appreciated — to have our value recognized by someone else and through that, often gain an increased sense
of our own worth. Compliments build confidence and confidence feels
good. It's a good thing to have. One of the building materials of self-
confidence is the compliments of others.

Isn't it too bad, then, that most of the positive things we do go unnoticed. We don't live on center stage and so, while we may be accomplishing things, much of the time there is no one around to see us do it.
At other times, even if there are potential observers, our accomplishments may still go uncelebrated, unnoticed, unappreciated or simply
unacknowledged. So much confidence-building material wasted!

Were we able to somehow capture the confidence-building potential
of all our accomplishments, large and small, imagine what level of
awareness of our own ability and potential we would possess! There is
little doubt that level of self-confidence would be a consistent and significant contributor to our level of activation.

Although it is true that much of the time no one else is present or
paying attention to our accomplishments as they occur, hour by hour,
day by day, that is not to say that a witness is not present, and at all
times. We, ourselves are always there to see everything that we do,
including all our successes, large, medium and small. The problem is

that many of us, figuratively speaking, turn our backs on this most valuable of confidence-building materials — our own achievements.

The Lesson Revisited

Most of us have received intensive and systematic training in the art of ignoring our own accomplishments. The training starts early, the lead story at the beginning of this chapter providing us with an illustration of that training. The parent's response in this story may represent the first time that the child has been admonished specifically for telling the truth. What kind of truth is forbidden? A positive truth about oneself!

Interesting lesson. Of course, father is not saying, "Never think good things about yourself," or "Never say good things about yourself to anyone under any circumstances." There are a lot of qualifications to his instruction. It's just that there wasn't time to give them. And anyway, the most important thing to get across was that boasting is not an acceptable category of behavior and in that he seems to have succeeded.

The problem is that the message could easily be interpreted as suggesting that since we're not supposed to talk about our positives, perhaps they're not worthy of our attention. The way we are expected to talk to others about ourselves may very much influence the way we talk to ourselves about ourselves. The habit of withholding credit begins.

If we don't develop this strong habit to gloss over our achievements early in life, the world will likely continue delivering the lesson with the hope that one day it will stick.

> *An individual makes a presentation to colleagues at the annual meeting. After the presentation everyone meets for cocktails and the group is discussing how valuable and well delivered the information was. The speaker walks up to the collection of people and says, "Not bad, huh? I thought that came off really well. I mean, really well!" His colleagues answer with a rather quiet, "Ya. It was OK," and glance at each other as if to say "What a jerk!" and move off to leave presenter and his ego alone together for the rest of the evening.*

Interestingly enough, had the speaker apologized for a dreadful presentation, his colleagues would likely have responded with, *"Dreadful? We thought it was terrific!"* It's not acceptable to say good things about yourself but saying bad things is perfectly fine.

The Damaging Definition

There are a number of other lessons that many of us receive while growing up, often strongly reinforced in adulthood, that further support our skill at withholding credit for our positives, at not noting our own achievements. One has to do with what we see as an accomplishment that is worthy of any consideration.

When we think of an accomplishment, we are inclined to think in terms of a positive result and not the activities that were responsible for its happening. And not just any positive result. To get any attention at all it has to be one with dramatic significance —reaching a major objective. The problem is that we don't achieve many monumental results as we move from week to week, month to month, year to year. Reaching for the significant result tends to take a long time.

However, we don't "do" results. We do activities through which, we hope, the desired outcome will be brought about. We may be involved in a project requiring months of numerous accomplishments in an attempt to reach our goal. If we do attain our objective, we now perceive that we have one more accomplishment to our credit with which to build confidence. A small private bow and then on to the next project.

The interesting reality is, however, that there are very few positive results, large or small, that do not occur because of numerous small accomplishments, back to back. Realize it or not, we have many legitimate opportunities to take a bow.

Permit me a personal illustration. Many years ago I returned to university and began graduate school after having spent a few years in the real world. I felt as if I were beginning a long hard climb through what seemed an infinitely large mountain range. I had been well trained in the art of ignoring accomplishments and so, for me, receiving a doctorate was the one lone definition of achievement, sitting somewhere in time at the end of this long, arduous path — or not.

I vividly remember the moment of success. I completed my orals, having been interrogated by a number of professors, and was sent to a small adjoining room to await my fate. Only a few minutes passed and the door opened. I was asked to reenter the examination room at which point each professor shook my hand. "Congratulations, Dr. Freedberg" — words for which I had been working and waiting for what seemed a lifetime. Within moments of my long-sought-after success, all I could hear was Peggy Lee, somewhere at the back of my mind, singing, "Is that all there is?" The moment was gone as soon as it had arrived.

However, in a sense, receiving the degree wasn't really the accomplishment. It was the result of numerous accomplishments over many years that had brought it about. For example, staying up till three o'clock in the morning for days at a time, writing a major paper about a topic for which I could not have cared less and for a professor who I considered to be markedly less than brilliant — now that was an accomplishment!

I don't recall being highly confident during those years and it was not because I was achieving little. In fact, during my time at graduate school I was acquiring much new knowledge and many new skills, and even making some contribution to my discipline as I moved energetically from one learning curve to another. That the accomplishments did not increase my level of confidence to any great extent had to do, not with their absence, but with my not giving them their due. To get recognition, I had been taught that an achievement had to be pretty earth shaking — a final, not an intermediate, result and a big one.

It's not that we're not supposed to recognize and even celebrate our accomplishments. It's the weight they need to carry to be noticed. The significant promotion, graduating, the big raise — we're expected to view them as accomplishments. The problem is that in a lifetime there tend to be so few. Contrast that with the size a mistake needs to be to receive notice.

The Momentary Spotlight

That at least we are allowed to celebrate our larger accomplishments is good news of a sort, but another social lesson we are taught is that regardless of its significance, take the momentary applause and move on.

A child creates his very first piece of successful representa-
tional art, a tree that is recognizable. He runs to his parent
and presents his latest masterpiece. The parent, recognizing
the milestone, receives it with great enthusiasm, exclaiming
with much excitement, "It's a tree! It's a tree! And what a
magnificent tree! May I keep it?" The child answers, "Yes"
and immediately returns to his crayons and scrap paper to
create yet another magnificent tree. Directly after its comple-
tion he again runs to his parent to receive still more kudos. His
parent looks at the newest work and says, with a marked
decrease in excitement, "Oh, yes. Another tree . . . nice."

The young artist, feeling let down because of the lack of
conviction in his parent's voice, decides, understandably, that
perhaps his latest effort was not up to the quality of the first
and so he rapidly creates yet another, runs to his parent who,
with even less enthusiasm, responds to the showing with,
"Why don't you go away and draw a big forest and when it's
finished come and show it to me . . . if I'm not busy."

And this, only minutes after the child's first successful piece of repre-
sentational art! The learning — celebrate a milestone, once and quickly.
Then, for heaven's sake, move on!

The lessons are many and although perhaps not universal, nevertheless, they are all too common.

- Don't say good things about yourself.
- Only results are considered to be accomplishments.
- Only milestone accomplishments deserve recognition and
  celebration.
- An accomplishment deserves only one bow.

Is it any wonder that highly effective builders of self-confidence are not
very plentiful? The most important self-confidence-building material
tends to go unnoticed.

Focusing on Achievements

As we have seen, our large accomplishments come about through numerous small achievements. In a sense, we don't even do the big ones. They happen as a result of our doing the small ones, over and over again. It only makes sense, then, that our perception of personal success should at least include, if not be made up exclusively of, our accomplishments, our achievements, no matter how small. Since those achievements are the stuff of which success is made, they should also be the stuff of which self-confidence is built.

It is the self manager's responsibility to ensure that this most important confidence-building material — one's own achievements, large and small — is not ignored but is effectively utilized to support the strengthening of self-confidence.

Imagine what it would do to our self-confidence if we were to have someone beside us, at all times, whose only function were to recognize our accomplishments, all of them, large and small, and point them out to us, making sure that we noticed every one. We cannot possibly expect to have that someone else, but we ourselves are in a position to note all our achievements regardless of size — but do we?

The social lessons that most of us are exposed to tend to train us to be both poor observers and poor celebrants of our successes. The challenge for the self manager is to reverse that tendency, and once reversed, to continue to expand our observational powers with regard to our ongoing achievements. As we become better observers, as our ability to note and to appreciate our positive immediate performance increases, so will the level of our self-confidence.

*   *   *

Before we continue, let's examine what is meant by an achievement. *An achievement is a positive accomplishment, no matter its size.* When you begin working at becoming a better observer, if you're about to walk away from something you have just done, saying to yourself, "How can I consider something as small as that to be worth noticing?" ask yourself this question, "How would I feel about myself had I not done that?" If the answer comes back, "Not as good as I do now," your achievement deserves recognition.

It's interesting and rather sad to note that too often we recognize our accomplishments only in their absence. That is, when we haven't performed some positive act, we can easily become upset with ourselves. When we have, we can just as easily ignore the happening.

A personal example. I have a tendency to become very upset with myself when I am late for an appointment, be it a social or a business one. When I am on time, however, my tendency is to ignore the fact that I have just achieved something obviously important to me. Objectively, I am quite sure that if one reaction is valid, so must be the other. There is no doubt that no matter how often it happens and no matter how consistently, being on time remains one of my accomplishments.

A Plethora of Positives

There are so many everyday examples that should credit our self-confidence account but don't.

For most of us, the role of being a good friend is an important one. However, that status is not achieved only or mainly by our being there for someone else when they are in grave crisis. It's more the being there on an ongoing basis, providing undramatic but cumulatively valuable social support to others. It is similar with the role of good spouse, good parent and good relative. Achieving those objectives comes about through the small, everyday activities of life, not the significant events attached to the relationships. There are not simply a few opportunities to accomplish within the context of these important relationships. There are literally hundreds. They are important. Their presence defines success, their absence failure. Their occurrence, therefore, should justifiably serve to strengthen the confidence we have in ourselves, confidence that comes from real achievement.

When we look at our occupational lives, there is no doubt that there are some leaps, some defining moments that can make a real difference in the level of our success. However, in the main, for most of us, most of the time, the level of our success is defined primarily by the undramatic, recurring activities that form the foundation for occupational victory. Again, we create a tremendous amount of valid confidence-building material during our working hours, material that can only make a confidence difference when it is recognized — another example of the self manager's role in confidence building.

The self-management challenge, then, is how to get better and better at recognizing achievements as they occur.

THE ACTIVATION HABIT: RECOGNIZE SUCCESSES

We are on the scene in a position to witness every one of our successes no matter its size. The trick is to pay attention. Because most of us have not been strongly supported to become keen observers of our own accomplishments (if anything we've been supported to become keen ignorers), we have to retrain ourselves to pay heed to this most important confidence-building material.

The training program is a simple one. It is designed to do two things: first, to help us improve our ability to recognize our successes no matter how small, and second, to make the recognition virtually automatic. It requires some brief conversations with ourselves and little else.

On a week during which you are working specifically on strengthening this confidence-building habit, carry out the following. On days one and two, have a meeting with yourself every two hours to survey the last two hours and identify any accomplishments of any size that you achieved during that time period. As was mentioned earlier, if you are unsure that something is worthy of the label "accomplishment," examine how you would feel had you not achieved it. Although you are being asked to have as many as four meetings with yourself during each of those first two days, the task is really not an onerous one. It takes very little time and even less energy because we think very quickly. The meetings will only take a few moments.

It is important, especially when first beginning to develop this positive habit, to focus on relatively short time spans precisely because most of us do not start off being very good at identifying our immediate successes. This exercise done a number of times a day helps us in improving our powers of observation.

For the next three days you need call only three self-management meetings aimed at strengthening this habit. At lunchtime, review all accomplishments from awakening until noon. At dinnertime do the same with the time period between lunch and dinner. When you go to bed, review the remainder of the day, again looking for all successes of all sizes.

For the next two days of the week, you need only call one meeting just before you go to bed, for the express purpose of reviewing all the accomplishments, no matter how small, that you achieved during that day. One more step. Upon awakening the next morning, revisit the list of yesterday's accomplishments. It should spring to mind very quickly and provide a good, confident beginning for the day about to happen.

Why the review of accomplishments? A secondary reason is that an examination of one's most recent successes does have the effect of increasing one's immediate level of confidence. Try it and you will see that the glimpse feels good. However, *the main function of this success-review meeting is to build and continuously strengthen the habit of automatically recognizing accomplishments as they occur so that without effort, one goes through the day aware of one's successes as they happen. In that way, confidence is being realistically strengthened, continuously.* By getting into the habit of generating a list of one's daily accomplishments at day's end, one automatically becomes a collector of accomplishments as they occur, in readiness for the evening meeting.

This is a simple, but very important, habit to establish and continuously strengthen. If you are a parent of young children, consider giving them a head start by asking them at the end of their day to tell you what they accomplished and make sure that you point out to them, as best you can, the ones they might have forgotten. Within a short time their list will become comprehensive, and they will be well on their way as self-confidence builders. Nevertheless, continue having the meetings until they are older, at which time you can transfer the responsibility of initiating and holding that meeting to them.

Back to the activation habit. After the week focusing on building this habit, don't just walk away. Commit to having a success review at the end of every day and the beginning of the next. You might pair the meetings with brushing your teeth since you are pretty well stuck with nothing else to do. While practicing your dental hygiene, *review all your accomplishments for that day. Review that same list early the next morning.* By taking just a few moments to do this, you will be constantly strengthening the habit of immediate-accomplishment recognition and will, with very little cost, be building your confidence, realistically and ongoing.

chapter 9

MANAGING ERROR

You may have found yourself in a situation similar to the one that follows. You happen to bump into a friend and note that he is looking rather distraught. You ask, "Is something wrong?" and he answers,

> *"That's an understatement. I'll say something is wrong. I've got one big problem! I've been involved in a pretty ambitious and important project for a number of months now. Yesterday, out of the clear blue, I got some news that could blow this whole project out of the water. If that happens . . . don't ask! Of course, if the worst does occur, guess who will be to blame. That's right, you're looking at him. Even though, by the way, I've had nothing to do with creating the mess and don't have the authority to clean it up before it's too late. Look, I'd like to stand and chat but I got to get back to work and see if there is anything worth saving. See you."*

Understandably, during the next number of days you often find yourself thinking of your friend's plight. After ten days, you decide you just can't wait any longer. You've got to know what's happened. You pick up the phone, call your friend's number and as soon as he picks up the receiver, you ask,

> *"Well, how did it go?"*

> *"How did what go?"*

> *"How did what go! You know. The situation you told me about last week."*

> *"The situation. What situation? . . . . Oh ya, that. Ah, it was nothing. So how have you been?"*

Yesterday's disaster has barely survived as even a memory trace, today. It had certainly seemed to have the marks of a disaster to you, considering that your friend's behavior was consistent with being in the middle of a catastrophe. But then, how is a disaster or even the serious threat of one forgotten in so short a time? In fact, were you really dealing with disaster at all?

"CATASTROPHIZING"

The tendency to "catastrophize," to blow things out of proportion, is a very common one. Often, when it happens, it has not been preceded by a great investment in considered thought, but comes about as an immediate reaction, relatively devoid of careful analysis. It is so easy to immediately exaggerate the significance of a negative.

All of us probably do it to some degree. Some of us could be classified as "world-class catastrophizers." Perhaps you work with one. You may even see one staring at you in the mirror first thing in the morning. World-class catastrophizers have overreacting down to such a fine art that often they can get themselves and others almost in a panic before anyone has really identified what the problem might be. These are the general catastrophizers. Then there are the specific ones.

I, personally, fit nicely into the category of specific catastrophizer. It happens to me too often when I am behind the wheel of a car. If I were wired to the right kind of equipment, my guess is that blood pressure, heart rate, galvanic skin response, all reach magnificent proportions the moment I find myself driving behind someone who is going as much as five miles slower than the posted speed limit. Anyone looking at the readout of my life signs could immediately come up with the identification — catastrophe. The interesting thing is that this craziness can happen when I am one block from my office and at least a half hour early. Some catastrophe!

But it really is all too easy to overreact to negatives around us; to deal with them as if they are very much more serious than is, in fact, the case. However, the de-activator that we're focusing on right now is not concerned with the negatives around us but with those that we ourselves create. In a very real sense, we are the focus of our universe, not because of arrogance, but simply because we view the world from behind our own eyeballs. As the lead actor on stage, we tend to be very conscious of our own immediate performance. When we've "gone wrong," it is all too easy to automatically register the mistake and raise it to calamity status in a matter of moments. "I can't believe I did that" very quickly becomes "I can't believe I did *that*!" and often, the "that" keeps growing.

Whatever our tendency to catastrophize, it is frequently increased in the face of mistakes that we, ourselves, have made. We blow our errors out of proportion, turning a one-pound error into a perceived fifty-pound failure and by so doing, pay an unnecessarily heavy cost in self-confidence. Too many of us pay the price of having perpetrated one, or sometimes several, disasters upon our universe within the space of a single day. As in the illustration at the top of the chapter, these disasters will be forgotten within hours, likely to be replaced by other forgettable "catastrophes." By blowing our mistakes out of proportion, we can frequently feel like losers and suffer the de-activating effects of that perceived status.

This de-activation habit can have a serious impact upon performance, especially in situations in which less than perfect behavior is likely. We are constantly finding ourselves at, or near the bottom of, new learning curves that, by definition, create many opportunities for error. By an automatic inflation of the significance of the errors, our immediate level of confidence is under serious attack.

Risk, the risk of new learning and the risk of new doing, may be actively avoided, first because the self-created impact of error is so great and second, because the decrease in self-confidence increases aversion to risk. The very changes required in today's world continue to increase resistance to change when this de-activator, the catastrophizing of error, is prevalent.

THE ACTIVATION HABIT: "SO-ING"

The activation habit that blocks catastrophizing and so protects our immediate level of self-confidence is an easy one to understand and to apply. After a short time you will find that it is triggered automatically.

What tends to be occurring when we blow our mistakes out of proportion is this. We make the mistake. We notice it. We then immediately sound the internal alarm without really even checking to see what the implications of our error might be. In a sense, we assume the worst rather than investigate. There is nothing standing in the way of our self-confidence attack.

The solution, entitled "So-ing," simply puts something in the way. The exercise is as follows. The moment you notice that you have made a mistake or that your performance has been less than expected or hoped for, regardless of whether the internal alarms are ringing loudly or not, in the face of the error, ask yourself the question, "*So?*" Use the specific word "so" as the short form for the question, "What are the implications of your error?"

This is not a rhetorical question. It demands an answer. Check out the implications. We think very quickly, and in most instances since we do not create disasters on a regular basis, we quickly discover that our mistake has few, if any, serious implications. We realize we have created little, if any, damage and that realization, in turn, blocks the self-confidence attack. After all, it isn't easy to be down on yourself when you have done little or nothing to warrant the attack.

A word of caution. Do not make the mistake of thinking that "So?" is a short form for "So what?" "So what?" implies that mistakes don't matter and need not be looked at. That is not necessarily the case. The question *"So?"* is a real one and demands that the mistake be looked at in terms of its implications so that it can be kept in perspective.

Most often this results in a preservation of self-confidence because of the tendency to blow our mistakes out of proportion. Sometimes, of course, it has the opposite effect. By examining the implications, we may very quickly come to the conclusion that the mistake was, indeed, a serious one, perhaps even more serious than we initially realized. That conclusion may cost a greater amount of immediate self-confidence, but so be it. We can't afford to walk away from mistakes, to simply ignore our weaknesses or pretend they don't exist. That position, in itself, is a kind of de-activator. However, we also can't afford to have our mistakes cost more than is appropriate.

Making mistakes often is the very experience necessary to reach excellence so that in a way, many mistakes, while having to be recognized and corrected, should be welcomed. If instead, they create undue pain and destroy confidence, growth can be thwarted. "So-ing" allows us to adjust our performance while preserving the confidence necessary to adapt and to grow in our quest for fulfillment.

chapter **10** | # MANAGING CONFIDENCE THROUGH BEHAVIOR

THE POWER OF BEHAVING

Here is a common scenario that I live through more often than I would like.

> *I have just finished a long workday that felt even longer. I get into the car, tired, perhaps preoccupied and certainly not in the positive mood that I started the day with. And now comes the traffic! There are too many cars between my office and my house and all vehicles but mine, I convince myself, have idiots for drivers. By the time I get home, I am fit to be tied. At this point, patience is not my strongest suit and if anyone gives me reason to growl, part of me would probably welcome it.*
>
> *And now to our two cocker spaniels. They have no interest in what mood I bring with me when I return home in the evening. I doubt they even ask the question. All they seem to know is that they are very glad to see me back. So glad, in fact, that I am not allowed out of the foyer until I bend down and demonstrate something close to the level of affection that they have been showing me. After that's done, I'm permitted to continue.*

But something very interesting happens to me in those few moments. The negative effects of the trying and extended workday, the frustration that is created by my trip through traffic, dissipate — disappear into thin air. I no longer feel angry. I no longer feel frustrated. My mood is positive and I find myself looking forward to the remainder of the evening.

This illustration is not meant as an advertisement for household pets. The point here is the dramatic and often neglected effect that behavior can have on attitude. In the short time I spend relating to those spaniels, my behavior does not correspond to the negative attitude that I walked in with. In fact, it is much more consistent with feelings of affection than it is with feelings of hostility. Very quickly, my behavior begins influencing the way I feel so that by the time I straighten up, I find that I have also "straightened out." My mood now reflects my most recent behavior.

When we think about confidence, we generally consider the real effects that its presence or absence has upon the way we behave. We seldom consider the opposite, however, the effect that certain kinds of behavior can have upon our confidence. Yet, the way we behave can impact both, immediately and significantly.

Behaving Unconfidently

When we feel unconfident, we may inadvertently behave in ways that show our lack of confidence, behaviors we described earlier. But it doesn't stop there. The unconfident behaviors may lower our level of confidence still further. This, in turn, may alter our behavior yet again, further decreasing our confidence, and so the downward spiral continues. Refer to the diagram on the following page.

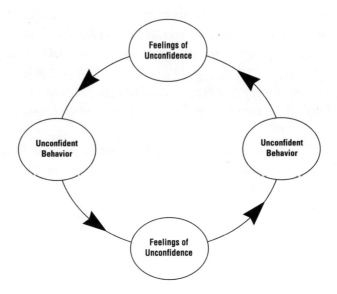

If you are having any difficulty "buying" the implications of the above diagram, or for that matter, if you are simply interested in experiencing the effects of unconfident behavior, try the following. First, assess your present level of confidence. Assign a representative number somewhere between one and ten, one being almost no confidence and ten being a tremendous amount. Then take a few minutes to "wimp around." Adopt an unconfident posture, an unconfident gait, use an unconfident voice tone in talking to others or if there's no one else around, try a wimp-like soliloquy.

I have seen some interesting illustrations of the impact of unconfident behavior over the years, through seminars I have given, or that client corporations have, themselves, facilitated. For example, people have been asked to "wimp around" for a ten-minute period and report on any impact on confidence. Invariably, a number of people report a marked decrease in their immediate level of self-confidence from what they know is simply a kind of self-imposed, role-play situation. A client facilitator told me that he gave some people an exercise in which he asked that they speak about their accomplishments and their strengths while consciously taking on an unconfident posture. People reported that while behaving unconfidently, it was difficult to think about, let alone communicate, their positives.

I worked with a National Hockey League team a number of years ago, which had an absolutely disastrous short- and long-term history when playing another specific team in the league. The day of the game you could almost touch the defeatist attitude that permeated the dressing room. This was clearly not a team filled with confidence. I then watched them skate during the warm-up. They seemed almost stooped, heads down, as they lethargically skated around the ice. They looked as if they were about to be led to slaughter and knew it. The next hour of play would prove them to be right. I believed that as unconfident as they felt before going on the ice, their behavior must have lowered their confidence still further.

The next time they met this same team, without even discussing their feelings, I asked them to straighten up and to skate energetically — to look as if they were going to have the other team for dinner. I can remember thinking that they looked like a different team on the ice and certainly their level of play and their victory suggested a high degree of confidence. In talking to them afterward, they reflected that they had felt more confident going into the game.

Not only does unconfident behavior have a potentially destructive effect on the level of self-confidence, but its opposite, confident behavior, can have an immediate and significant constructive effect. As was said earlier, we often focus upon the effect that attitude has on behavior but seldom on the effect that behavior can have on attitude. One of the positives with regard to behavior's effect on the confidence level is that it is generally easier to control one's immediate behavior than it is one's attitude. Therefore, using behavior as a confidence builder can be inexpensive, immediate and effective.

THE ACTIVATION HABIT: BEHAVE WITH CONFIDENCE

Just as we can generate various unconfident behaviors upon request, even when we're not experiencing an absence of confidence, by the same token, we can consciously decide to behave in a confident manner as reflected through our walking, our posture, our voice tone, facial expression and eye contact, whether or not we are feeling confident. That is, we can, to some degree, manage our immediate level of confidence through behaviors that are readily available to us.

Confident Behavior as a Corrective Tool

One of the things that we can do is employ confident behavior as a corrective measure. When recognizing a deficit in immediate self-confidence, we can voluntarily raise our level of confident behavior and by so doing, have a rapid, positive impact on our self-confidence. The changes may be subtle and not necessarily registered by others, but still may have a positive effect. A small, but conscious, change in posture, a slightly more determined walk, a more secure verbal delivery, all or any of these, can begin reversing the downward spiral. The behavior increases the level of confidence which makes confident behavior more easily elicited, which, in turn, raises the level of confidence still more, and so on.

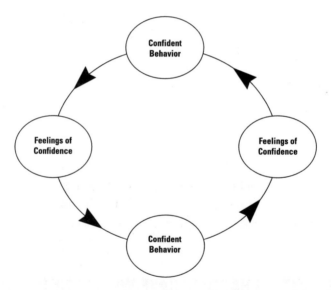

When we are alone, the behavioral fine tuning need not be as subtle. With no one to observe us, we can afford to behave in an overconfident, perhaps overbearing, manner. We can bang on the table, swagger and exaggerate the degree of certainty with which we express our opinions. Although this may not be recommended social behavior, it can, when social impact is not an issue, rapidly and more significantly take care of a confidence deficit that we may have seen within ourselves. It can act as a warming up exercise, preparing us to activate more effectively as we go into the world.

Confident Behavior as a Growth Tool

We have just been looking at how to use easily applied behavior to help fix a confidence deficit. We can also manage our behavior in another way that, long term, can have an even greater impact on self-confidence. This has to do with using confident behavior as an ongoing support, regardless of whether or not we are experiencing any immediate confidence problem. We can use behavior not only to correct a confidence deficit, but to support the maintenance and growth of our self-confidence on a continuing basis.

Make a habit of behaving confidently. Step back and look at your regular way of behaving to see if there are any aspects of it that might be labeled as unconfident, that might inadvertently be lowering your level of self-confidence or at least be doing nothing to maintain or foster it. The way you carry yourself may not be confidence supportive. Perhaps you have a tendency, in group discussions, to speak tentatively when offering your opinion. When disagreeing with someone, your expression may inadvertently be less definite than are your beliefs. There may be small and comfortable adjustments that you could easily make that would generally support a stronger overall level of self-confidence. Of course, often, our style of behavior comes so automatically that we are not really aware of it and so you might consider asking selected others if they see any behaviors in you that they might label as being less than confident.

There is no suggestion here that we must or should make ourselves over. However, you can identify ways that can help you easily and comfortably improve your confidence-supportive behavior. Consciously practice them so that they become second nature. When that has been achieved you will have provided a behavioral foundation to support your ongoing self-confidence without having to exert any energy thinking about it. The behavior will simply be there, supporting your self-confidence.

chapter 11

SELECTING OUT THE POSITIVES

MASKING THE POSITIVES

The de-activator discussed here is commonly practiced and highly threatening to one's level of self-confidence, but because of its subtlety, it can easily be hidden. Those of us who practice this destructive habit come by it honestly. It probably stems from the same experience that destructive self criticism does and is, in a sense, a variation on that theme, but a variation sufficiently unique and dangerous that it deserves its own spotlight.

Very briefly, as was discussed in "Managing Self Criticism," our negatives tend to receive the lion's share of the noise. The world around us actively recognizes our mistakes and our misbehavior more readily than it does our positives and so, understandably, we, too, can easily fall into the trap of giving our negatives more focus than is warranted. The de-activator in the following example is a symptom of this common tendency.

The hero of this story has just finished an important presentation to the management of his corporate division. The issue is an important one and so it was critical, he felt, that the case he presented be strong enough to influence his listeners in the direction that he knew to be the right one. His presentation took about thirty minutes, which for him seemed to be almost forever. From the voiced appreciation and then the ensuing discussion, it quickly became clear that his objective had been met. Because of his presentation, his division would be changing direction. With the meeting over, he walks back to his office and as he does, his silent conversation with himself goes like this.

"I can't believe I stumbled over those words right in the middle of my presentation. It was at such an important place in my argument and I so wanted it to impact. It impacted all right but the impact was me acting the fool. Not exactly what I had in mind. Did I look inadequate or what? It's not as if I hadn't practiced the presentation but it would seem that, for me, practice isn't enough. Mind you, at this point I would be hard pressed to figure out what would be enough. I can't believe I stumbled at that critical point in the presentation . . ." and on and on and on.

What has happened here? For one thing, he is practicing the crusade of self criticism and attacking his self-confidence virtually for the sake of the attack. But that's not the focus of the de-activator being looked at here. This silent monologue that he's having is not only overfocusing on a negative, *it is totally ignoring the existence of numerous and important positives.* There is a damaging selection process at work. In spite of the fact that twenty-nine minutes and forty-five seconds of his presentation were excellent, in spite of the fact that his primary objective was reached rapidly and conclusively, the only thing he is focusing on is the negative fifteen seconds.

This de-activator, however, is not about what he is doing. It's about what he isn't. Not only is he looking at the negative, he is ignoring all the positives surrounding it. From all that he has done, the only thing he's concentrating on is what went wrong — the negative is being allowed to virtually obliterate the reality of the many positives surrounding it. Had those uncomfortable fifteen seconds not happened, he would have been able to appreciate his positive performance and the victory that resulted and, by so doing, realistically build his level of self-confidence. Instead, the real accomplishments and the important victory were ignored. In the face of a negative and many positives, he selected out the negative, and as far as his self-confidence is concerned, the positives may as well not have happened. It's as if the presence of the negatives made the positives somehow nonexistent.

Many of us practice this de-activation habit, selecting out the negatives, vigorously. We may be able to recognize and appreciate our accomplishments unless an associated negative exists. At that point, we spotlight the negative and turn our backs on the very real positives that we achieved. Perhaps the negative should be taken into account, but that in no way must be allowed to obliterate the positives that did occur. By practicing this de-activator, we are able, often, to turn a silk purse into a sow's ear. What should have realistically and constructively built our self-confidence is allowed, through this self mismanagement, to instead, tear it down.

The Impact on Change of Masking the Positive

We have already looked at change and its impact a number of times. Because it is such a critical part of our reality, we must continue to do so. It has significant relevance to the habit of selecting out the negatives. Because we are continuously finding ourselves somewhere near the bottom of numerous new learning curves, we are also frequently performing at less than optimal levels. Simply put, to become good at something, we often have to first be not so good at it. At the same time that we are making our mistakes, we are also accomplishing a tremendous amount as we advance up these ever-appearing learning curves. If anything, most of us are accomplishing more and more as the weeks, months and years go by. The practice of selecting out the negatives virtually denies us this wealth of confidence-building material. So much important confidence-building material is lost and at a time when high levels of confidence are sorely needed. The level of activation is impeded and as a result, the readiness to climb the learning curves are in danger of being decreased as is the speed at which they are climbed.

Perfectionism

Before we go on to look at the activation habit that counteracts selecting out the negatives, let's first take a look at a quality that is often praised in our society — that of perfectionism. The perfectionist can be seen as someone who, within the limits of his capability, is likely to attain a very high degree of excellence in his pursuit of perfection. The good news is that the probability of having excellence as an objective is increased. The bad news is that the excellence is probably not appreciated.

The perfectionist tends to belong to that large group of us who suffer the burden of "selecting out the negatives," but the perfectionist suffers most. In the process of evaluating performance, the perfectionist uses a powerful magnifying glass to ensure that any flaws not visible to the naked eye will, nevertheless, be discovered. The moment the flaw is observed, all else disappears and our perfectionist is left with yet another failure . . . *and there is virtually always a flaw.* Selecting out the negatives, at its most powerful.

Of course, it is not true that perfectionists necessarily achieve optimal performance. At times, this dogged practice of selecting out the negatives can have a dramatic impact on their level of self-confidence and, therefore, their overall level of activation. Objectives may not even be attempted, with the perfectionist saying to himself, "Why bother? I know I won't get it right. My past performance has been so obviously impoverished." (Read, "imperfect.")

I remember, vividly, a comment by a seminar participant as we were discussing this aspect of self-managing confidence. He told the group that his passion was furniture building, an activity to which he devoted as much of his leisure time as he could. However, he got little satisfaction from his hobby because if he made the slightest error, one that would usually go unnoticed by anyone but himself, for him that piece of furniture was close to worthless. In fact, he had discarded pieces that everyone else thought were beautiful. He said that in thinking about his negative selection process, he realized that so much of what he had achieved he had not appreciated.

THE ACTIVATION HABIT: SELECT OUT THE POSITIVES

The activation habit to be installed or strengthened is a very simple one, but don't let its simplicity fool you. Although it may be simple to understand, even simple to do, that does not necessarily mean that the habit is established easily.

Many of us don't have to think about selecting out and then focusing on our mistakes. We just do it. It seems to come naturally. That is, immediately and automatically, the negative is selected out. The activation habit, selecting out the positives, is not automatic for most of us, and so its establishment takes conscious effort.

The moment that you find yourself focusing on a mistake that you have made, on what you did wrong, ask yourself the question, "*What did I do right?*" and *demand an answer.* Look at the larger picture, other aspects of your behavior related to the target situation or other activities associated with the task at hand and identify all your accomplishments, large and small. (Before tackling this activation habit, it would probably be a good idea to have a first run, at least, at "Managing Success," so that your ability to home in on accomplishments will have been strengthened.) Remember, we think very quickly, and so the survey of positives should not take but a few moments. Interestingly enough, at the beginning you may really have to work at responding to the self-imposed question, "What did I do right?" because the mistake will continue to demand attention. For many of us, selecting out the negatives is a well-practiced, well-established habit.

Nevertheless, insist on a response so that your accomplishments will be recognized and no longer denied, whether or not you feel like celebrating them. By forcing them to become part of your reality, your on-the-spot evaluation of your behavior will no longer be based on a narrow and unrealistically negative picture of your performance, and you will have cleared the way for appropriate confidence building to occur.

This activation habit does not include ignoring the mistake. In fact, it's not even about the mistake. It is about the insurance that when an error has occurred and been recognized, it does not serve to camouflage the "non-errors," the accomplishments that may be surrounding it. A realistic level of self-confidence cannot be achieved by ignoring either our successful or our unsuccessful activities.

A reminder. The challenge here is not the recognition that even in the face of negatives, the positives remain real. Nor is it the ability to realistically respond to the question, "What did I do right?" *The challenge is to make the asking of the question a habit, especially in the presence of an error, of a situation in which taking into account the positives becomes of even greater importance.*

chapter **12** | # REHEARSING SUCCESS

"THE BERMUDA TRIANGLE"

I am not a golfer. I don't know very much about the game, but as hobbies go, it sure seems to create a high degree of frustration for many of its devotees. Though I've never played golf, I have had the occasion to watch the game being played. I can't possibly know what's going on in a golfer's head, but watching people playing the game does suggest some interesting thought processes.

I remember once being at a mountain resort that had a golf course. From my balcony I had a good view of the course, this view including the water hazard. Here's what I saw many times over. A player would tee off and hit his drive straight down the fairway. His opponents would do the same. But then they approached the water hazard. I had already seen the golfers hit the ball farther than they needed to in order to clear the hazard but, again and again, I watched the golfers hit the ball near or into the pond as if the pond were the golfing version of the Bermuda Triangle. After witnessing the strange attraction that the water seemed to hold for golf balls, I felt, rightly or wrongly, that I could almost hear what was going on in the golfers' heads just before they took their swing. It must have gone something like this:

"Well, here I am again, facing the dreaded pond. Feels more like the Atlantic Ocean to me. And I know what's going to happen. I can just see it. I'll want to avoid the water hazard. I'll take my swing and then somehow — splash! In it goes! I know it. It's happened so many times before, why should this time be different?"

What was happening, I believed, was a perfect example of rehearsing failure. Immediately before the demand situation, that is, a situation demanding a specific performance, what occurred was a rehearsal, not of the performance, but of the nonperformance. The golfer, by perceiving himself the loser, experiences an immediate loss of self-confidence which, in turn, decreases the probability of success. His failure rehearsal becomes a self-fulfilling prophesy.

Soon after returning from the resort, I asked a number of golfers to tell me what happens to them, what they think about just before tackling a water hazard. Many of them reported a monologue that paralleled the one I imagined I was hearing a few weeks before. A number have since told me that they go one better. They use cheaper balls on the hole with the hazard. This is an example of a failure rehearsal even before the failure rehearsal!

REHEARSING FAILURE

The de-activator that we're looking at here, then, is, rehearsing failure, an immediate and effective way to lower self-confidence just before it is needed. The golfing illustration is a good one because the demand situation is clearly defined and occurs over and over. Most of life isn't quite that clear-cut or repetitious. However, it resembles the golf course in that it consists of numerous demand situations. The unfortunate thing is that just before entering any demand situation, failure rehearsal is a very easy thing to do, and to do virtually automatically.

Immediately preceding a demand situation, and that situation may have been identified only moments before, the chances are very good that we will not be focusing on yesterday's dinner. In all likelihood we will be seeing ourselves performing in the demand situation about to occur. That is, in our mind's eye we will be rehearsing our performance. The key confidence question is, *"Will we be rehearsing success or failure?"* If we just let this internal rehearsal happen on its own, there's a good chance that we will see ourselves failing and by so doing, lower our self-confidence just before we must activate.

This failure rehearsal can take many forms, any of them requiring only moments to complete. In fact, it takes so little time that we can probably get in a number of failure rehearsals before we actually have to do anything. There are many ways that we can trigger seeing ourselves go right for life's water hazards. We can just say a simple, "I hope I don't make a mess of this." We can be more specific. "I hope I don't ruin it by making this mistake." We might take an autobiographical tack. "I better not do the same stupid thing I did last week." All of these, of course, bring the image of our doing exactly what we don't want to see happen. It's much like the statement, "Whatever you do, don't visualize pink elephants." Nice elephant.

The point is that immediately before a demand situation, chances are we are going to do one of two things. We will either rehearse success or failure. It makes little sense to risk the latter.

THE ACTIVATION HABIT: REHEARSE SUCCESS

The solution is a simple one. *Rehearse success before every demand situation.* That is, make rehearsing success a habit. When success rehearsal becomes virtually automatic, we give a boost to our immediate level of self-confidence just before a performance requirement. That is not to suggest that through momentary success rehearsal our self-confidence goes through the roof. However, it's much better to give self-confidence a small boost than it is to lower it. If success rehearsal becomes a habit, over time, the consistent increases in self-confidence will have significant positive impact.

"Virtual" Visualization

There are a number of ways to rehearse success. Probably the most widely known, as a result of its use in the sports world, is rehearsal through visualization. A person tries, in his mind's eye, to see himself actually doing the job and doing it well. Detailed visualization, in which the situation and specific behaviors required are clearly perceived, mentally, is probably the most demanding of the techniques of success rehearsal in that it requires a high degree of concentration, an ability to visualize, previous knowledge of what's ahead, what will be needed and the time to do the rehearsal. By the same token, however, it can be very effective.

Most of us deal with many different kinds of demand situations in a day, requiring the application of different abilities and different applications of the same abilities. Often, these situations arise as part of the day's challenge, unexpectedly, and have to be dealt with now. Because they can't be anticipated until they arise, imaging a full rehearsal before actually answering the demand is not always an available option.

Fortunately, there are other ways to rehearse success that are more easily applied and more generally applicable than focused visualization. Although they may not be as powerful, because they are very easy to apply and can be practiced only moments before the demand to perform, they are often the self-management tools of choice.

Rapid Visualization

Another form of visualization, while perhaps not as powerful, is very much less time consuming and more readily applicable. Here, one sees oneself or perhaps feels oneself performing well and confidently, more as a general and instant impression than as a real script to be carried out in the mind's eye. We generally know, for example, what it feels like to be in top form. Generating that feeling immediately before a performance demand can make a positive-confidence difference.

Often we enter situations similar to previous experiences, situations in which we performed well. A way of rehearsing success is to identify one or two of these. Because we think very quickly, the mental review need take but a few moments. Then all that is needed is a reminder that "the person having done that good job is me." Yesterday's success is brought forward and the appropriate confidence building that comes from success is then carried into the present demand situation.

Review Relevant Performance Potential

Develop the habit of taking a rapid mental inventory of your strengths — the knowledge, the experience, the talents, the skills, that you bring to bear on the demand situation you are about to face. The review of strengths will serve as a kind of success rehearsal and will become a rapid and relevant confidence builder.

Employ one or a number of success-rehearsal techniques before responding to a demand situation. Because success rehearsal takes only a few moments, applying more than one technique for the same performance demand can easily be accomplished. Know how to rehearse success and be aware that it can make a positive difference, but more important, build it as an internal habit so that success rehearsal becomes an automatic mainstay of your activation practices. Not only will it serve to increase the level of self-confidence at very little cost and through numerous performance moments of truth; it will also block the rehearsal of failure and the confidence reduction that accompanies it.

chapter 13

MANAGING EXTERNAL CRITICISM

THE COST TO CONFIDENCE

For many of us, one way of ensuring that a day will stay in our memory for years to come is to have it include a criticism of us by someone else. It doesn't have to relate to anything especially significant. It often doesn't have to be from anybody especially significant. It just has to be a negative about us. The rest of the day will likely be forgotten within a few weeks. The criticism and probably the person who delivered it may remain an easily retrievable memory even till the end of our days.

Of course, criticism isn't always directly verbalized. It can come from a facial expression, a raised eyebrow, an obvious look of disdain. A great thing about these more subtle, nonverbal forms of criticism is that the criticizer can't easily be held accountable. We're not quick to ask people why their body language is communicating nonacceptance or to tell them that we would appreciate it if they would please lower their left eyebrow. We "hear" the criticism, but we can't even discuss it with the criticizer, and so it just sits there, raw and inviolate.

Many of us tend to be highly sensitive, perhaps highly oversensitive to criticism from others. It's not difficult to understand, considering we are social animals and gain much of our sense of worth from the people around us. Also, for reasons discussed in Chapter 8, "Managing Success," those people gain in importance because, generally, we have not been well taught to recognize our own worth. Compliments from others are usually highly valued and even if receiving them causes us embarrassment (another social lesson), we, nevertheless, often celebrate their existence, albeit quietly. Understandably, then, criticism can often be a powerful negative.

For the overly sensitive, a direct criticism can be extremely painful and as we relive the event in memory, it can become more painful with time. It can serve as a dramatic confidence destroyer whose ill effects can frequently be felt long after the person doing the criticizing has forgotten the event. It can function as a strong de-activator, much stronger than would appear to be appropriate. The slightest criticism can easily throw some people off balance for hours, days or even longer.

This oversensitivity can have other negative consequences. For example, teachers, managers, coworkers and often friends and relatives of oversensitive people are reluctant to criticize them, even when that criticism is truly constructive, because of their fear that the costs of the criticism are likely to be greater than its benefits. For those of us who are highly sensitive to criticism, we are between a rock and a hard place. If people become reluctant to criticize because we've communicated the devastating effect it has on us, we lose the lessons that might be gained from their criticism. On the other hand, if those people don't mind sending us reeling or we're good at hiding the seriousness of our wounds, we find ourselves frequently suffering a costly self-confidence drain.

All that being said, though most of us don't visibly curl up in a ball upon the delivery of a criticism, oversensitivity to criticism is probably a problem of the majority rather than the minority. For all sufferers, there isn't a lot of good news. Criticism from others is usually not all that hard to come by.

Let's take the workplace, for example. There is much lip service given to "management by positives." Positive management does not imply the exclusion of any negative observations. It does imply that there should be at least the same inclusiveness of positive ones. Reality suggests, however, that in most environments there seems to be little time for the acknowledgment of the positives. On the other hand, there has to be time to note the negatives, one reason being the need for damage control.

Because criticism, verbal and nonverbal, tends to be fairly prevalent, unless we learn to manage it, the result can be an ongoing and significant lowering of self-confidence. We may become very good at self-confidence building just to have the results torn down by some external criticism.

THE ACTIVATION HABIT: OBJECTIFY THE CRITICISM

The challenge for the self manager is to manage external criticism so that if it carries with it a lesson of some value, that lesson isn't lost, while at the same time, self-confidence is protected. Although there is likely to be some loss of immediate self-confidence upon receiving a valid criticism, that decrease should be appropriate to the criticism. An insignificant criticism should, at best, carry with it a very small confidence cost. The cost should be related to the worth of the criticism, not simply to its existence. The problem is, however, that many of us don't exercise judgment in the face of an external criticism. We automatically react to it strongly, but the reaction relates to *that* it is rather than to *what* it is.

Even those of us who are overly sensitive to external criticism seldom receive an opinion from someone without evaluating its worth. We apply our own perception of reality before we accept it as truth, modify it or reject it, but with one exception — if the opinion is negative and happens to be about us. Then our judgment grid is abandoned and the opinion moves from eardrum to ego in an instant.

It is the responsibility of the self manager to step in between criticism and reaction so that the criticism can be constructively dealt with; so that if there is something to be learned, the lesson is captured but without undue loss of self-confidence. However, because the pained and often costly response that many of us have to negative external criticism is automatic, we must make the managing of external criticism a habit. That is, the effective self-managing response must, too, become automatic. We must build in the habit of examining the criticism as objectively as we can, of treating it as an opinion to be judged rather than as a painful truth, simply to be accepted.

Here are four questions, the very asking of which can serve to reduce or avoid self mismanagement in the face of external criticism.

1. Do I respect the criticizer?

A very important question. I have the acquaintance of some people, just a few, whose movie, book or theater recommendations I accept gratefully because I then know what I wish *to avoid* at all cost. I place no value on their opinions but I must be careful because there is that one exception — if the opinion is negative and about me. Then, I automatically start writhing in pain as if they have been blessed with the wisdom of Solomon.

The first question, then, to be asked is concerned with taking into account the source of the criticism. A criticism by someone whose judgment you respect at least deserves serious consideration. The value given to a criticism by someone whose judgment you know nothing about should at least be tempered by the fact that you don't have enough information to evaluate his quality of judgment. A criticism by someone whose judgment you generally hold in disrespect perhaps should not totally be ignored but should surely take into account the perceived worth of the judge.

2. Do I care?

We all have too much on our plates to deal with everything. We make choices. We try to focus our energies first on those areas that matter, either because of their intrinsic value to us or because of the consequences attached to them. We make choices. We have to.

There are some areas of our lives that we consciously decide to ignore, or at least to neglect. However, unless we're careful, that decision can be forgotten in an instant — that instant when the area of neglect is under attack by an external criticizer. We can find ourselves writhing in pain about a deficit that we were not only aware of but decided to preserve.

A personal example — I do not keep a very neat desk. I tend to be dealing with a lot of things on a daily basis and organization is so much a weakness that I could easily spend a quarter of my day intelligently tidying my working surface. So, I made the decision a long time ago that, within reason, I would have to live with desk-top clutter. It works for me or at least until somebody says, "What a mess!" Unless I'm careful, it is so easy to completely forget that not only does the state of my desk not matter to me, I have decided that I can't afford to have it matter. I start behaving internally as if having a neat desk is perhaps my most important objective in life, or certainly should be.

In the face of an external criticism, the question, "Do I care?" ensures that criticism about things that aren't important to us will be reacted to, taking their value into account. By the same token, of course, criticisms about areas of import had best be examined carefully.

3. What do others think?

It becomes all too easy for many of us to isolate a criticism, to take it out of its context. If, for example, a number of people compliment us on something we've done and one person criticizes us about that same thing, the compliments can disappear and all that's left is the criticism. Again, a kind of selecting out the negatives.

It is not that the criticism should be ignored, but it makes at least as little sense to ignore the compliments. The question What do others think? is designed to ensure that both are taken into account. The positive opinions are considered along with the negative so that we deal with the response of others about us rather than with our own internal insecurity.

If the answer to the question What do others think? is that a lot of other people have expressed the same criticism, perhaps the criticism should be considered seriously. If, however, the answer is that most people have shown positive appreciation, then the criticism should perhaps be given a diminished weighting.

4. What do I think?

This, too, is a very important question to ask in the face of an external criticism. Most of us do not suspend judgment when evaluating the opinion of someone else except when that opinion is negative and concerns us.

With regard to our own behavior, our own being, we cannot always be totally objective, but when dealing with the assessment of our own performance, we cannot afford to, nor should we, suspend personal judgment. Ours should not necessarily be the only opinion looked at, but it most certainly should be one of them. The problem is that when criticized we can too easily forget to consider it. What do I think? brings our self manager, the person responsible for managing our immediate performance, back into the equation.

These four questions take a very short time to ask and respond to, internally. The answers, however, can be important in protecting the learning from an external criticism, while at the same time protecting confidence from undue attack. It allows us to utilize the criticism instead of simply dealing with the fact that we've been criticized.

Perhaps even more important than the opportunity to take into account the answers to the four questions is the fact that asking those questions gets in the way of the knee-jerk reaction that so many of us have to negative criticism. It helps put us back to where we belong — in an active decision-making stance rather than one of passive acceptance. Whatever the decision around the value of the activity or characteristic being criticized, the decision is ultimately made by us rather than by someone else.

Work on this area so that asking the questions in the face of an external criticism becomes automatic.

The Other Side of the Coin

Just as external negative criticism can reduce the immediate level of self-confidence, compliments can increase it. When someone values something we are, or have done, and tells us, this often results in an increase of our own sense of worth. Few of us are immune to compliments, sincerely offered. Many of us do have difficulty gracefully accepting them, however.

Perhaps it has to do with the value we place on humility; that we feel accepting someone's compliment is like agreeing with it, but whatever the reason, many people respond to a compliment by inadvertently insulting the giver, by rejecting the compliment out of hand. We may come back with, "It was nothing" or "You must not have been paying attention" or "Thank you, but you're wrong. I was absolutely awful." We may say nothing at all, just look uncomfortably at the ground, clearly wanting to escape the situation or make our admirer disappear. That is, we suggest that the person giving the compliment is stupid, tasteless or sadistic. That does not mean we didn't appreciate the compliment; just that we don't let the appreciation be known.

The trouble is, that without meaning to, we shut off the source of this confidence building. There is little joy in giving someone a compliment who appears either to disagree with it or not appreciate receiving it, and so future opportunities that present themselves to the giver may be ignored.

Graciously accepting a compliment is not difficult. A simple "thank you" for the gift of confidence will do. Practice it every chance you get. It will not only be appreciated by the person giving the compliment; it will add to your present — and probably future — levels of confidence.

chapter **14** | # MANAGING BY COMPARISONS

"Why Can't You Be Like Your Brother?"

We live in a society that is highly competitive in both work and play. For example, sports represents one of our most valued areas of leisure, for spectator and participant, and sports is all about ranking, winning and losing. The statistics are infinite and almost always comparative. As we go through school, we receive specific marks or grades and our evaluation is often based on our position on the bell-shaped curve. That is, our final mark does not represent what we achieved with regard to score, but how we placed with regard to how everyone else placed. Concerning our careers, often the level of our success is largely dependent upon how well we are performing, or perceived to be performing, relative to others. Competition is an ever-present reality.

Witness some of the conversations that children have with each other when providing information about themselves or their families. The statement, "My father is taller than your father" has, as its hoped-for objective, to make you devalue your father's height, not simply value mine. When observing two adults discussing their achievements, one with the other, it frequently doesn't take long to recognize that rather than an information-sharing session, a verbal wrestling match is going on in which each person is either attempting to devalue the other or protect his own sense of value through a game of one-upmanship.

Perhaps because we see it happening so regularly, soon we don't need anyone else to play this destructive game of one-upmanship with us. We become very good at doing it ourselves. We frequently determine the value of our performance solely by using the performance of others as the ruler. Instead of using comparison with others constructively, we use it to debase our confidence level. We too often ask ourselves the question "Why can't I be like my brother?"

Let's first look at its constructive use. At times, it makes sense to compare our performance with others so that we know how the external world is likely to judge our performance. That is, it helps answer the question, How do other people think I'm doing? — a different question than, How am I doing?

Comparisons can be helpful in establishing an objective. Comparing ourselves to others can at times help us reach the conclusion that we could be doing better and determine by how much. Looking closely at someone else's performance vis-à-vis our own can also help us determine how we might reach more ambitious objectives. By the same token, it can also help us make the decision that we're not willing to pay the price needed to reach or exceed someone else's performance. We might even realistically be able to determine that, want to or not, we may not be able to get there.

However, comparing ourselves with the performance of others, if we're not careful, can be a costly de-activator. The process can go something like this. We have just reached a performance level, higher than ever before and are about to start internally celebrating what is clearly a positive achievement. Just as the celebration is about to begin we become aware that someone else has done it better. This someone else does not have to be competing with us, but the celebration rapidly becomes, instead, a self condemnation. What was good just a moment ago has somehow become bad because of a totally unrelated achievement by someone else.

For those of us who are really good at using comparison with others to attack our own self-confidence, we don't have to stumble on someone else's better performance in order to trigger this de-activator. The moment we achieve something or note a strength in ourselves, we begin casting around for the evidence that someone else has done it better or is better than we are. That someone else can almost always be found and as soon as our discovery is made, our sense of achievement disappears. It's as if, somehow, a piece of performance by someone else, completely independent and unrelated to our own, is able to radically alter our achievement. Our achievement remains the same and yet becomes something very different. Champions at this form of de-activation are consistently able to avoid building their self-confidence.

I remember once speaking to an acquaintance who related what I now realize to be an example of managing by comparison at its worst. He had been an amateur classical guitarist and experienced much joy from playing this difficult instrument. One night he went to see for the first time the celebrated guitarist, André Segovia, in concert. By the end of the evening, somehow his playing and Segovia's had become closely tied, with the result that he determined to never pick up his guitar again. He was as good as his word. Even though his previously accepted level of playing, one that he had enjoyed, had not changed at all, from that night on he was never to play again. In the equation Performance = Ability x Activation® he had used comparison to lower activation to zero. Some of us are clearly better at this form of self mismanagement than are others.

THE ACTIVATION HABIT: ELIMINATE DESTRUCTIVE COMPARING

The self-management challenge is to reduce the negative use of comparison to its absolute minimum. It is often meaningful to use someone else's performance as a way of determining where we want to go. It can be destructive to use it in determining where we are. For that, a very different kind of comparison should occur. The comparison should be with ourselves.

When assessing our immediate performance we should use ourselves as the frame of reference. *Does my performance represent an achievement for me?* is the self-management question to be asked. *Have I achieved what is, for me, a realistically high expectation?*

To determine the level of accomplishment represented by today's performance, a self manager must look at his own experience, effort, skills, aptitude, other demands and overall support, not someone else's.

I do not suggest that the question How am I doing? relative to someone else or for that matter, to everyone else, is an invalid one. It is, however, very different from another valid question, How am I doing relative to myself? The first question is appropriate for many situations, competitive situations for which positioning is important to the individual. The second, again, a different question, is valid for all situations, including the competitive ones. Amateur world-class athletics gives us a good illustration of both.

Anyone who has watched televised competitions in individual sports has likely seen interviews after the contest of extremely satisfied "losers," athletes who haven't won any medals but are, nevertheless, very happy with their performance. The explanation: they just surpassed their previous personal best. They recognize that much was accomplished. Would they have liked to have won a medal? Absolutely. Is that still their intention? Most likely, but a separate issue. Did I do well? is a different question than, Did I do best?

Many of us behave as if we are in a competition even when we're not. We don't ask the question, Did I do well? We simply ask, Did someone else do better? As self manager, ensure that you ask the first question. Whether or not you ask the second, as well, depends upon the specific situation and your own goals. There is nothing wrong with wanting to do better than others. There's nothing wrong with wanting to be best. *In assessing your own immediate performance, however, remember that the critical comparison to make is with yourself.*

chapter **15** | # MANAGING CHANGE

SELF-CONFIDENCE AND THE PROCESS OF CHANGING

As individuals, we are required to carry out two responsibilities with regard to change — we must respond to it and we must bring it about. Both responsibilities are growing and so how we manage the change process and ourselves within it is an extremely important self-management issue. This chapter deals with one crucial and largely ignored aspect of change management — managing confidence within the context of change. Without strong confidence management, effective response to, and creation of, change is at risk.

One thing we know about the demand to change — it frequently creates a resistance in us. Resistance to change is a common characteristic and one that is becoming more and more expensive as the demand for change accelerates. We don't necessarily like to experience change within and outside ourselves, and so there are times when we try to avoid the experience. The trouble is that successful avoidance can turn out to be very costly.

What is it that we resist? It's not usually the idea of change in the abstract. Most of us are willing to accept that change has become a constant, and that a high degree of adaptability is a necessary condition for success in today's

146

world. It's not that we're resistant to change — just the specific changes that we're being asked to make at this point in time. We don't mind the idea of change. It's changing that we have trouble with.

Why the resistance? One reason might be that the recommended changes really don't make a lot of sense and we refuse to fall into the trap of holding that the new is good simply because it is the new. However, another reason might be that we *desperately want to believe* that the changes being recommended don't make a lot of sense. In this instance, it is unconfidence rather than objective judgment driving the resistance.

There is an understandable reduction in confidence around an untried situation or skill set in that neither come with yesterday's proof of success. The only thing that we can have is faith in our ability to succeed. If self-confidence is low, however, there is not likely to be an abundance of faith. It isn't easy to embrace change when you see yourself probably falling flat on your face because of it.

The resultant sense of vulnerability is likely to push us in the direction of avoidance. Fear of failure becomes a strong motivator, especially when it is coupled with the belief that failure is likely. We look for all kinds of reasons to justify turning away from new opportunities or new ways of dealing with old ones, trying to convince ourselves and others to stand still. We want to believe what we are saying because the belief represents our escape from anticipated disaster. It is not that unconfidence necessarily undermines our integrity, but it can undermine our objectivity.

There are times that we can't avoid change in spite of ourselves. It is irresistible and, like it or not, demands to be confronted. The trouble is that when we find ourselves having to deal with situations while we are in a relatively unconfident state, we don't activate well. Even if we can, in fact, deal effectively with the situation, we might not. To make matters worse, a lack of confidence can easily breed even less confidence. When the expectation is one of failure, even the slightest setback can be interpreted as proof of impending disaster. De-activation habits, like the crusade of self criticism and catastrophizing, are more easily triggered and so confidence, and with it performance, spiral downward.

Flexibility and change are closely aligned. We know that we have to become more and more flexible with regard to the application of abilities we already possess as well as the acquisition of new skills we don't yet have. In business, for example, we must have a heightened flexibility if we are to effectively respond to the ever-changing needs of our specific customers and of the marketplace. A high level of confidence strongly supports this necessary adaptability. Unconfidence and its ensuing desperate hold on yesterday's successes make for an inflexibility that organizations and individuals alike can ill afford. While the unconfident may know the importance of adaptability, their chances of becoming sufficiently adaptable are seriously undermined.

The relationship between proactivity and confidence was discussed earlier. In part, proactivity refers to the responsibility that individuals have to create new worlds; to make changes happen. Initiating change takes confidence. Often the initiator has to overcome resistance in others, which was triggered by his initiative. The proactive have to respond to the new world that they have created and so all the indefiniteness, the lack of history associated with the new, the unknown, now have to be dealt with. The very act of identifying or creating a new, previously undiscovered opportunity takes a relatively high level of self-confidence. Keeping on this previously untried road may take even more.

Adaptability and proactivity are very much a part of change — the change we respond to and the change we create. Managing change is largely an issue of managing confidence.

THE ACTIVATION HABIT: FOCUS ON THE NEW

When faced with change, what is it that we are likely to focus on? Understandably, we tend to look at aspects of the external world we have not previously dealt with: knowledge and skills within ourselves that are as yet untested or unacquired. We focus on the perceived gaps in our abilities and experience that need filling if we are to face the new challenge, prepared. We don't spend a lot of time considering our strengths because they are already in place. We ask, "What do we need to succeed that we don't yet have?" rather than, "What success factors are now in place?" But what might focusing almost entirely on what we don't have do to our level of confidence?

When our immediate awareness is filled with a picture of our deficits, in a sense, that is what we become. Our sense of vulnerability increases significantly because we are attending almost exclusively to our perceived vulnerabilities. It's easy to lose confidence in oneself when *all* the focus is on what we might not have or what we might not know. While planning the doing requires that the spotlight be on the weaknesses, activating the doing requires that attention also be given to the strengths.

New demand situations, however, are seldom — more likely never — totally new. They do not consist only of elements never witnessed or never dealt with before. They do not demand only skills, knowledge and experience never demanded before. In fact, while the ratio of new to old is different for different challenges, in most instances we walk into new situations having, in both skills and experience, very much more than we are missing. Although we may never have faced the same challenge before, chances are that many, if not the majority of the abilities needed have already been acquired and many aspects already experienced. We walk into new situations with relevant strengths and while planning the doing requires that the spotlight be on the weaknesses, activating the doing requires that attention also be given to the strengths. Noting those strengths can realistically increase the awareness of the positive potential we bring to the new challenge.

There is little point in pretending that you have all the tools and experience when you haven't. However, it makes no sense to carry the distortion that you have much less than is, in fact, the case. *As a self manager, when faced with the demand to change, take an inventory of the strengths, the relevant abilities and experience you bring to bear on the new challenge. The weaknesses, the gaps, must be dealt with, but in order to have a realistic, optimistic picture of your potential, take note of your strengths.* This will help to constructively protect and build your immediate level of self-confidence.

FOCUSING ON PAST ADAPTABILITY

One particular strength that should be given attention on its own has to do with our ability to adapt to change, and so part of the self manager's inventory check should focus on past evidence of adaptability. The speed with which our world is turning suggests that in all likelihood we are handling situations and know how to do things to which we were strangers only a very short while ago. There is also a good chance that some of these new demands, while now we give them no thought, at first appeared as insurmountable challenges. Hindsight tells us that the high degree of insecurity we may have experienced was unwarranted. We are adaptable. We can change and a quick look at the evidence of our adaptability can, itself, increase it.

Noting our general ability to adapt, registering the knowledge, skills and experience we already have that are relevant to demands of change, can be as important in determining performance as is the identification of gaps and filling them.

Performance requires potential and the conversion of that potential. While taking an inventory of what's missing or is as yet untried helps ensure that the necessary potential will be installed, recognizing the strengths and relevant experience that already exist can support the critical conversion process.

chapter 16 | MANAGING COMPLACENCY

It's difficult to talk about building self-confidence without dealing with its dangerous variation — arrogance. People often resist the strengthening of confidence in themselves or others for fear that, ultimately, they might create too much of a good thing. Arrogance is dangerous for a number of reasons and so, deserves attention when looking at the issue of self-confidence. However, it's important to make a clear distinction between arrogance and self-confidence, no matter how high the level of that self-confidence might be.

If confidence is defined as a realistic, optimistic awareness of one's abilities and potential, it would seem impossible to have too much of that good thing. However, arrogance is not simply an overdose self-confidence; confidence is optimistically realistic, but arrogance is optimistically *unrealistic*. Self-confidence is deserved. It is reality based and all the activation habits recommended in this chapter are grounded in the reality of one's achievements and strengths. Arrogance is undeserved and either misinterprets, exaggerates or fabricates the positives. People often suggest that the arrogant are fundamentally insecure. There is likely some truth in that if only because basing one's internal reputation on, at best, the inflation of truth, must put one on shaky ground.

It is sometimes easy to mistake strong self-confidence for arrogance. We tend to frown on people, not because they think they're good, but because they all too readily broadcast their achievements. That represents a second kind of arrogance. Although the confidence may be deserved, the volume of the horn blowing may be too high. (Perhaps the truly confident have little need to be boastful and are not likely to get swelled heads. The arrogant, on the other hand . . .)

The highest cost of arrogance is not social ostracism, however. It comes in the form of a de-activator of a much higher order — complacency.

Complacency and Activation

Complacency promotes a kind of resting state, a condition that allows one to rest on one's laurels, real or imagined. There's a sense of self satisfaction that carries with it the bonus of not having to do any more work, exert any more energy, in the area of perceived excellence — "I'm so good that I don't have to work at succeeding. Success will simply come." In the past, resting could easily promote rusting. With today's rate of change, rather than becoming locked in a standing position, resting can quickly lead to rapid backward descent.

It is somewhat of a paradox that success, largely a result of activation, can, and frequently does, lead to complacency, a potentially serious de-activator. When we are successful, it is important that we recognize the success and our role in it; that we not ignore this valuable confidence-building material. At the same time, we must beware that the recognition doesn't create complacency. Success can beget success or it can beget its absence. Which it will be is largely a self-management issue.

Complacency can be a quiet kind of arrogance, an internal realization that application may have been required in the past or may be necessary for others but for the complacent, it isn't needed. Success will come without effort. We have all witnessed the destructive effects of complacency, if not in ourselves, then in others.

Relationships between people are often built through conscious, careful consideration. Frequently they unravel because the strength of the relationship is taken for granted and when that happens, the work stops. Complacency is reflected in the belief that the relationship is strong, not because of what I do, but because of what I am.

In business we see some people of apparent promise who experience a high degree of success and then, instead of their growth continuing, it ends. This occurs, at times, because they've gone about as far as they can go, sometimes further than they should. At other times, however, it's because they've convinced themselves that they no longer have to do anything to continue their upward climb. While they haven't used up their potential, complacency has slowed down their conversion of that potential into performance. The level of activation has dropped and so has their apparent promise.

In new learning situations you can almost hear the complacent saying to themselves, "Everyone else is probably going to have to pay attention to what's being taught right now but fortunately for me, handling this new situation will be a breeze. Whatever has to be done I'll be able to do and with ease." It's not until some time later when, for good reason, complacency has vanished, that they can be heard to say, "If only I had listened." There's nothing like a few good falls to reduce overconfidence.

That complacency is a highly dangerous enemy can be seen not only from the blocked performance of individuals. We have, in recent years, seen corporations, previously perceived as being virtually untouchable, especially by themselves, experience a rude awakening. These corporations had arrived. They believed the success formula to be so deeply entrenched that it seeped from the very walls of their offices. Their culture would, by itself, sustain the magic. Complacency, in some instances, brought about the vanishing of the magician. Others survived, humbled and dramatically altered, after having almost disappeared from the organizational horizon.

The trap of overconfidence can have many victims. We've seen not only individual corporations, but entire industries caught in its jaws. North America's automobile industry, needing to concern itself only with competition from within, gives us perhaps the most dramatic example. However, its highly inflated self evaluation may have been a reflection of the complacency disease, suffered by the entire industrial community to which it belonged. We've seen elected governments fall largely because they believed themselves invulnerable, and countries under serious threat because past victories convinced them that they were unassailable.

The Invisibility of Arrogance

The trouble with arrogance and its quieter but often more dangerous cousin, complacency, is that the sufferer is, by definition, unable to diagnose his condition. "Me, complacent?" laughs the victim. "Certainly not. I am simply intelligently and comfortably secure in the obvious promise of my future." The arrogant, accused of being so, may reply, "You confuse arrogance with greatness. But then, how could you be expected to understand?"

We self managers have a problem. We are responsible for activation and one of our tasks is to protect and strengthen self-confidence. However, though confidence and arrogance are not the same, though complacency is not a necessary result of strong self-confidence, if we are not careful, the line between the two can be crossed and the crossing can go unnoticed. Overconfidence is a de-activator and so the self-management function is to work toward its elimination. As self managers then, it is important that we guard against something we are unlikely to recognize — a tall order, especially considering that arrogance, undefined, can be very comfortable.

Because of its invisibility, fighting arrogance as an ongoing self-management activity becomes even more important. The aim is not to necessarily diminish the belief that with regard to a certain performance area you're the greatest. For that matter, you could be right. After all, someone deserves the title. Your job, as self manager, is to avoid the danger of complacency that can easily accompany the championship.

THE ACTIVATION HABIT: DETERMINE THE STRETCH FACTOR

It is important that you continuously compete with yourself, in all your critical achievement areas; that you attempt to surpass your personal best. Successful people can easily fall into the trap of no longer doing the very things that brought the success in the first place. By increasing your targets after reaching an objective, that trap will likely be avoided. *Review your important areas of achievement regularly and determine a new stretch factor for each. By doing this you will be building protection against the de-activation of complacency.*

Review "The Climb"

One other self-management practice, that, if done habitually, can help guard against overconfidence. When a successful result has been achieved, a large objective met, recognize the success, appreciate your accomplishment but at the same time, do a quick mind's-eye review of the climb — the time, energy, skills acquisition, persistence, attitude and self-management practices that were necessary to bring about that success. By carrying out this review, by revisiting the success determinants, you are much less likely to abandon the very things that brought the success about.

PART II

MANAGING SELF DIRECTION

Determining What Should Be Done

> *A person must have the ability, must be aware of that ability, must make the right immediate-activity decisions regarding the application of that ability and must translate those decisions into action, if the ability is to bring about anything close to optimal performance, if the ability is to be optimally activated.*

INTRODUCTION

I put myself through school as an undergraduate by spending my summers working at an oil refinery, mainly in its grease plant. The grease-plant foreman had the official title "Pusher," very simply because his job was to push me and everyone else at the grease plant. Our job was to move in whatever direction his push sent us. We were to make no activity decisions at all. When not pushed, we just stood still, waiting — all that incredible potential bursting to get out. (We seldom had to wait for long.) Together we — the pusher and his workers — managed to get the job done. The pusher managed. We did the job.

Self direction, the second activation area, is concerned with making immediate-activity decisions. Everyone must have a pusher and for yourself, you're it. As self manager, you stand with your performer all the time, barking orders: "Do this." "Stop doing this." "Do that." "Continue." Your performer, the person that looks just like you, represents a tremendous amount of potential, but that potential is triggered only by you. You, the self manager, decide what portion of potential to trigger and where it should be aimed. Your performer is like a highly capable robot who awaits your orders. Activating the robot is your responsibility and you carry it out, in part, through immediate-activity decisions. Those decisions determine the direction your performer should go. (That is not the end of the activation process, however. The push is still to come and will be dealt with in the chapters on self commitment.)

What should I be doing now? is a question that we are answering, virtually moment to moment. At any moment in time, in both our occupational and personal lives, we have numerous activities to choose from and as our world, and with it, our jobs, become more complex, the number of choices grows. We had better choose right. Any immediate-activity decision that is not the best we could have made at that moment, taking into account the situation, our objectives and our abilities, represents wasted potential. The lower the ranking, the greater the waste.

Making the right activity decisions is a responsibility, difficult to carry, not only because of the numerous choices available and the attached consequences, but because it is never ending. In a sense, it's a decision that is continually in the making. We may, once having decided upon an activity, carry it through to completion but even then, moment to moment, it is because we continued to choose that activity over the many possible others. Frequently, whether good or bad, we move from activity to activity, deciding on different ones as the day goes on. During our waking hours the requirement to decide on immediate activity is ever present. The self manager is the "pusher" extraordinaire. We all continuously make our own immediate-activity decisions even when it is to follow the instructions given by someone else. The question is not whether we are self managers. In that we have no choice. The question is how good we are at it.

The activation habits discussed in "Managing Self Direction" are designed to help continuously strengthen the quality of our immediate activities — to help us continually move closer to the top of the list of today's best possible decisions.

chapter **17** | # MANAGING SELF COMMUNICATION

"So I talk to myself. Nothing wrong with that. It's when you hear me start answering. That's when you'll know I'm in trouble."

A SOCIAL PROHIBITION

Old joke, but one that reflects a predominant societal belief — there is something very wrong about talking to oneself out loud. Some of the reasons for it are probably not difficult to identify. People in the midst of a hallucination can often be seen talking to themselves precisely because they've lost touch with external reality. They tend to be labeled as acutely psychotic, not a classification we especially like, and so most of us try to avoid talking to ourselves out loud, in public. But it goes further. The negative attitude taken with regard to this, what, on the surface, appears to be a rather harmless activity, is sufficiently strong that many of us resist talking to ourselves out loud even when there is no one within hearing distance. Sins done in private are sins, nevertheless.

There are other kinds of communication that can be practiced in public without censure. It's perfectly acceptable to say most anything to an infant, especially before the baby is at the stage of being able to understand one word you are saying. Feel free to carry on a conversation with your dog, your cat or even your canary, no matter who may be watching. Even your machinery, particularly your automobile, is an acceptable passive partner in a conversation, especially when it's been misbehaving and deserves a good talking to. But remember, the one thing you musn't do is talk to yourself. Understanding why the social prohibition exists doesn't make it less expensive, however.

As self managers, one of our primary areas of responsibility is determining the best activity decision for our every moment in time — a heavy job. A major tool we employ to carry out the job is that of self communication. We must analyze situations, understand problems, identify conflicting objectives, define action steps and do all of this through some form of self talk. However, most of us have a restriction on how that self communication is to be carried out. It has to happen largely in our mind's eye: "Mum's the word!"

The Drawbacks of Thinking Silently

Let's look at the process of silent self communication for a moment. First, we do it all the time. In fact, there's no way to avoid doing it nor should there be. The world would be an even noisier place if all our self communication were to be spoken out loud. Also, we don't self-communicate only in words. It may happen through images or through distinct memories. We think much more quickly than we speak, and so it is often significantly faster to self-communicate silently. There is certainly no language barrier between the "speaker" and "listener" and, of course, we escape being labeled as someone to be avoided, "someone not quite right, if you know what I mean."

However, there are also some real drawbacks to silent self communication that can, at times, get in the way. Our thoughts are often not ordered. We think very quickly and can easily move from one topic to another, back and forth through different time zones, all in a matter of moments. An internal trail of unfinished thoughts is a common experience. But there are times when what's needed is an orderly analysis of a situation and a solution in the form of specific, immediate action steps. This mix of incompleted thoughts crossing many topics, this free association that frequently typifies internal thinking, does not necessarily lend itself to some kinds of problem solving with the result that we can carry around both problem and solution for a very long time without clearly perceiving either.

THE ACTIVATION HABIT: EXTERNALIZE SELF COMMUNICATION

There are times when, for the sake of arriving at a solution, an understanding of a situation or a specific-activity decision, it is important to externalize our self dialogue. This forces us to put some temporal and rational sequencing to our ideas and perhaps most importantly, to stay on topic for more than a few moments so that we can see, with greater clarity, what it is we really think regarding a particular issue. We may discover a degree of understanding that we weren't aware we possessed or an action step previously hidden.

The Sounding Board

Even for those of us who believe that we never do, and never would, talk to ourselves out loud, chances are good that sometimes we come awfully close to it. We feel the need to "talk out" the solution to a problem and so we go looking for a "victim," someone who will serve as our sounding board. The unspoken function of this unsuspecting target is not to share his ideas with us; not even to render an opinion about our opinion, unless the two correspond. In fact, when opinions are offered we may get impatient, not necessarily saying but certainly wanting to say, "Would you please be quiet and just listen to me!" This sounding board's function is exactly what its title implies — to give us a surface from which to vocally bounce our thoughts; in other words, to allow us to talk to ourselves out loud. We realize, somehow intuitively, that we need the discipline that external communication gives us to work through the issue and so we go looking for our "excuse." Of course, there are times when people get caught at this subterfuge. The tell-tale expression signifying the identification is, "He's speaking just to hear himself talk," which is, of course, exactly the point of the exercise.

When available and willing, the sounding board can be an excellent way to externalize self communication. The problem is, the demand far outdistances the supply. We tend not to be the only people around who think they have something important to do or say.

The answer — be willing to break from tradition and make externalized communication between self manager and performer a regular practice. Talk to yourself out loud.

Thinking By Writing

There is, of course, another safer form of externalized self communication — writing. Paper and pencil can do much to help organize thoughts and keep us on topic. Much of the noise, the interference that occurs, when we are thinking, is eliminated through this process and as a bonus, socially, it is much safer. Although writing can be a very effective form of self communication, it carries with it a few drawbacks.

First, we talk faster than we write. There are times when we have a lot to say to ourselves and not enough time to say it on paper. Second, we think faster than we write. Our hand often can't keep up with our brain and we either return to having a silent internal conversation or we leave ourselves at the starting gate. Writing is a good externalizer, but not always the best choice.

Thinking Out Loud

Back to the social embarrassment — talking to yourself; this can be a powerful self-management tool. I, personally, have often inadvertently experienced its effectiveness when composing a letter or note, using a tape recorder. I start with the assumption that I know exactly what it is I'm going to say. However, dictating is simply talking to oneself in the presence of a machine, and so the benefits of this form of self communication kick in as soon as the exercise begins. Many's the time that I've been pleased to discover that I ended with very much more than I believed I had started with. There was much more inside than I had realized. It took talking to myself to discover it.

Self managers have the responsibility of coming up with the commands that direct their immediate activity. There are a lot of possible orders to choose from, the aim being to make the best available choice. To do this requires that we sort out our thoughts, comprehensively, quickly or both. One way of supporting this objective is to talk those thoughts out loud to ourselves. It's not something that can or should be done all the time. It is a tool to be taken seriously, however.

An interesting observation about this self-management practice. I've been recommending it for a long time and although people mention the impact that many of the self-management practices have had on them, this is the only one that sometimes gets these qualifications. "It made me very uncomfortable at first but after a short time it became a lot easier," and the more dramatic, "I've never gotten comfortable with the technique but I find it so useful that I practice it, regardless."

In seminar, I ask people to identify a problem for themselves, personal or work related, that they've been carrying around with them for a while and to take five minutes, standing, sitting or wandering around the seminar room to examine the situations by talking to themselves aloud. I've had as many as 30 people wrapped in conversation with themselves, some pacing back and forth, others, seated, chin in hand, staring up at the ceiling, mouth continually moving, and still others facing the wall, standing in one spot and going at it. To say that it looks like Bedlam is no exaggeration.

I then ask, "Did anyone get further with the subject under 'discussion' than you had, perhaps, expected?" Most often, at least one person will say something like, "Get further? I resolved the situation completely." Many report that they had made much more progress than expected and a common observation is that "I felt very uncomfortable at the beginning but soon I wasn't even aware of anyone else. I was too busy concentrating." I then point out that if the technique is effective in this group setting, how much more effective, when being done in private.

Of course, there are many work situations that do not allow for complete privacy. What then?

In spite of social opinion, talking to oneself aloud can be an extremely effective self-management tool. Tell people around you that you use it; that if they hear you mumbling to yourself it's because you find talking your thoughts to be a most effective method of problem solving. Even if some wisecracking occurs, it will disappear quickly and you will be free to use this activation tool, unhampered.

When to use this technique. Many self-direction practices are supported through externalized communication. For example, the daily planning meeting that you have with yourself, recommended in the next section, is often enhanced when carried on out loud. If you practice talking to yourself when you are alone, you are more likely to do it at other times when you think it might make a positive difference. The very act of practicing it makes it a nonissue, at which point it becomes a readily available self-management tool. You will soon get to know when it is useful. Chances are that, with time, its use will grow.

chapter **18** | # PLANNING FOR PROACTIVITY

You ask if daily planning is important for me? The answer is yes, absolutely. Why is it important? Well, I guess there are as many reasons as there are days. So much to get done. So little time to do it. And to make matters worse, I always have more to accomplish than is humanly possible so I've got to decide what gets done and what gets cast aside, temporarily or forever. Planning does that for me. It helps guarantee that my attention is focused where it is most needed. You know the old saying, "There are never enough hours in the day." Well, planning can't change that, of course, but it can help ensure that those precious hours aren't wasted. Is daily planning important? I should say it is.

What's that? Did I draw up a plan for today? Well, to tell the truth, no, I didn't. Just wasn't enough time.

Whenever I ask a group of people to tell me why daily action planning is important, I'm always impressed at the comprehensiveness of their answers, whether or not they have ever taken a course in time management. Living in a demanding world tends to give us all the insight we require into the need to plan our activity.

And now for another "whenever." Whenever I ask a group — the same group that just listed the reasons for planning one's activities daily — whether they seriously plan their every day, the answer from most group members is a resounding "No." I figure that planning is, perhaps, the most valued and at the same time, the most ignored activation practice that exists.

The reasons given for not doing this important activity are numerous. Perhaps you might recognize some of them.

"I've got so much on my plate that I don't have time to plan!"

"I meant to plan but I just got too busy."

"Don't worry. The work will come to me without my having to plan, whether I want it or not!"

"My appointment book is so full that there's no need!"

"I don't have to make a plan. I've got one already. It's in my head. I just know what has to be done."

"I'm in meetings all day, today. What's the point?"

"Why bother? I've got so many things being thrown at me that there's no point in having a plan. I'd never get it done anyway."

So many reasons to plan, reasons that are used as excuses to not.

THE FUNCTION OF DAILY PLANNING

Planning is, of course, a critical management practice. For the self manager, the most important is planning the day's activities. The primary responsibility of the self manager is managing immediate performance and to do this, effectively, requires high-level decisions with regard to his performer's immediate activities. Although all immediate directions pertaining to a day's activity cannot be plugged into the daily plan, it can nevertheless serve as a frame of reference, as a platform from which the self manager can command the day's activities.

In a sense, the well-executed daily action plan includes the very best self directions that can be generated, taking into consideration one's potential and one's objectives, both occupational and personal[1]. In part, it requires a crystal ball as it must attempt to anticipate the day's demands. Invariably the crystal ball will, to some degree, distort the immediate future. And so the self manager is likely to be forced to improvise at various points during the day. Having a well-thought-out daily activity plan, however, supports the quality of those improvised decisions. The cost of replacing one activity with another is better understood. The decisions to be protected, if at all possible, are identified. Some, if not all the apparently high-priority decisions, have a better chance of being carried out because they have been identified. Those that are not acted upon are less likely to be lost and can be carried over into tomorrow's daily action plan.

Supporting the Proactive

One of the critical changes occurring in the workplace, today, is that not only are we being asked to march to orders given and then expected to cover more ground, but the demand is that we initiate more of those marching orders for ourselves. This, in itself, is a tall order since few of us sit around with nothing to do unless we create the work. There are many things, and often many people, out there screaming for our attention, asking us to react to their need. If we were to draw up no plan at all, we would likely be busy every moment of our day. We don't need to initiate to be busy (not necessarily the same as being optimally productive) and, in fact, if we respond to immediate external demand, there is a very good chance that initiating travel in a new direction will simply not occur.

It is easy to fall into the trap of deciding to get to the proactive just as

---

[1] There is no attempt here to provide a time-management system. There are enough of those already in existence to choose from. Choose one that suits you best but most important, even if your choice is a pencil and blank piece of paper, choose one and use it.

soon as time allows. Without our active intervention, in all likelihood, time will not allow and we will continue to be almost completely reactive, perhaps effectively so, but reactive, nevertheless. The daily action plan provides the needed protection for the proactive. Unless we protect our initiatives by assigning them a time to be done, there is a good chance that the day will roll over us. The only way to ensure that, instead, we do some of the rolling, is by sitting down and asking this question seriously: "What should I best do today?" *making sure that those things that can only happen through our initiative are considered first.*

The Action Plan as a Stress-Management Tool

A few other benefits to daily activity planning are worth considering. The first is related to the heavy load of anxiety that busy people frequently carry on their back. This excess weight has to do with the reality that most of us have a lot that needs to be done at any point in time. Although we may have 200 different things that need attending to, we can only possibly get "seventeen" of them done today, not because we're lazy or slow, but because we're human and the day, finite. Without a plan, we are, in a sense, always carrying around the whole 200 things, all through the day. At day's end, rather than a sense of fulfillment from having accomplished the seventeen, we feel the frustration of not having dealt with the remaining 183. What's worse, in all likelihood, on our travels we picked up at least another seventeen things to do.

A daily plan, on the other hand, makes it clear at the day's beginning, that the only things in existence for the reality that is today are the seventeen things to be done, or perhaps some other activities that may take their place. Only seventeen things are being carried around and as the day progresses the load lightens. For today, the 183 don't exist. The anxiety that comes from carrying around an impossible expectation is diminished, if not removed, and the day ends with a realistic sense of fulfillment rather than its unrealistic opposite.

Often, during a busy day, it becomes difficult to pace oneself. There are many factors outside our control that work against a balancing of effort. However, by planning the day, as imperfect as the plan may turn out to be, we often can gain some control.

Strengthening the Self-Management Function

The daily activity plan is not only a direct method whereby the self manager can more effectively manage his performer, but it can also direct the self manager's ongoing development.

You will see throughout the "Activation Habits" portion of this book the suggestion that the specific activation exercises you are working on at any specific point in time be part of your daily action plan. In some instances, the writing itself is part of the exercise. For example, the exercise related to "Managing Self Criticism" begins with the instruction, "Look out for destructive self criticism," a simple way of promoting the awareness necessary to elicit the "Stop it!" command. Minimally, the daily activity plan should include the specific activation habits to be worked on.

THE ACTIVATION HABIT: ACTION PLAN EVERY DAY

The bottom line is this. The self manager has the responsibility of generating the decisions that are meant to choreograph the day's immediate activities. Many of the directions, because the day will invariably include the unexpected, have to be made on the spot, and the focus must be entirely on the present moment. The daily activity plan allows the day to be looked at, as a whole, just before it begins. It asks the question, "As performer and as self manager, how can I best use the day?" and then becomes the background upon which to make the continuing ongoing immediate-activity decisions, which are the responsibility of the manager of immediate performance — the self manager.

In contrast, a day without a plan is a day of improvisation for which the melodies are determined largely by the external world. Although the immediate-activity decisions will still be made by the self manager, the day will be shaped almost entirely by the outside world, a day to be reacted to rather than one to be controlled. It may be a productive day, but the responsibility of the self manager to make it as fulfilling as it can be will not have been honored.

chapter **19** | # MANAGING BY LEAST NUMBER OF DECISIONS

That's it. That's the ticket. It's about time I made that decision. I know. I should have made it months ago. OK, I should have made it years ago, but as they say, better late than never. I feel terrific. Funny, isn't it, how good you feel after you've made an important decision even though the results of that decision may not be experienced for months? Well, that's the way I feel right now. Like if I looked at myself in the mirror I'd already be pounds lighter. This has turned out to be a very important day. I must remember everything I can about this moment, the date, the time, the name of the restaurant. It'll be a kind of anniversary to be celebrated for years to come. The day I made the decision to stop eating desserts! My thin-day, the day I started on the road to svelte. I'll probably need a new wardrobe in not too long. Pretty expensive, but definitely worth it. Feel better, look better and be a lot healthier. Small price to pay. Why should a ban on desserts make such a difference? Because my sweet tooth has been my downfall, that's why. I'd hate to actually figure out the extra calories a month I have force-fed myself on desserts alone. Well, I don't really need to figure it out. I just have to remember my waist size. Thank goodness, those days are over.

What's that, waiter? Would I like dessert? No thanks. I don't do dessert. What was that special again? Dutch chocolate cake. Well, what's one more dessert, especially when you know it's your last. Might as well go out with a bang. Anyway, as I said a few minutes ago, I want to make this day a day to remember!

THE TWO CATEGORIES OF IMMEDIATE-ACTIVITY DECISIONS

One of the major responsibilities held by the self manager is to make the decisions that direct immediate behavior — a heavy and never-ending task. There are so many immediate-activity decisions that have to be made on the spot, that can't be anticipated even moments before the point of decision. These decisions make up one large category that requires the focus, energy and action of the self manager. They are the decisions that relate to the one-time events that form a large part of virtually every day of our existence — the category of unique-activity decisions.

There is second category of immediate-activity decisions that is at least as important, but is easily self-mismanaged — the category of recurring-activity decisions, (RADs). Whereas a unique-activity decision directs one immediate activity, a RAD, made once, may have the potential to direct hundreds of like activities. If it is a good decision, it can account, over time, for the effective conversion of a great amount of performance potential.

Recurring-Activity Decisions (RADs)

In our personal lives there are a number of RADs many of us have in common, decisions that we have made or considered. A lot of them relate to the area of health. We decide that we are going to exercise every day or a certain number of days every week, for example. Over ten years that decision, if honored, can be responsible for over 2,500 workout sessions — the making of fairly serious conditioning. We make decisions about what we will eat regularly. We make decisions about what we won't eat ever, whether it be the kind of food, amount or both. We make a decision that we will never smoke another cigarette again — ever. There is a form of financial decision making that, itself, includes other recurring-activity decisions that can serve to direct our personal spending and savings — the decision to operate within a well-defined budget. A very popular arena within which to make any number and kind of RADs is our list of New Year's resolutions. This list will often include a number of decisions that, if kept, would likely positively change the direction of our lives and in the relatively short period of twelve months. Considering the number of people that make New Year's resolutions and the likely size of their list, there must be a large number of fulfilled people every year by the time December rolls around.

In the occupational world, the category of recurring-activity decisions can also be very important. While many decisions are relevant to numerous occupational situations, others relate to specific kinds of work. Planning, the activation habit discussed in the previous chapter, is one example of a common RAD that relates to virtually every occupation (and for that matter, most aspects of one's personal life). For salespeople, the level of prospecting activity represents a critical RAD. For people managers, it might be a decision about the number of individual performance-appraisal meetings to have with each managee, annually, or it might be the frequency of staff meetings. For students, it could be the number of hours to be spent doing homework per night. Some RADs may deal with one project over a limited time period, while others may be applicable throughout one's entire work or personal life.

Many of our recurring-activity decisions have the potential of making a large performance difference. They can be extremely powerful activators precisely because they can activate our performance potential over and over again. They can serve as the activity foundation blocks of success in the significant areas of our lives in that they frequently deal with the fundamentals of positive performance.

Whenever it is appropriate to make a RAD, the self manager is well advised to do so. The great thing about them is, once the decision is made, that's it. Very little effort will be needed from then on with regard to making decisions relating to the relevant recurring activity. The decision has been made not only for one point in time, but for many decision points to come. The return on investment for one good decision can be great, and the time, the energy, the focus can now be concentrated on those unique-activity decisions that need the self manager's attention. Recurring-activity decisions allow a redistribution of self-management energy and protect good decisions already made.

Is the recommendation to self managers, then, to consider making more RADs? Although that may be good advice, it probably isn't necessary for most of us. The self-management problem is not that we don't make enough recurring-activity decisions, as much as it is that we make them and then behave as if the decisions never happened. So often we treat the recurring activity as if it were a unique event, a once-in-a-lifetime choice point in need of an immediate decision. In our illustration at the top of this section, our somewhat over-zealous self manager made the decision, no desserts, potentially applying to numerous decision points to come. The moment the first one appeared, the question, "Should I have dessert?" was asked as if a decision were needed. Regardless of what decision our gourmand would have made about that specific piece of Dutch chocolate cake, no decision making was required, and so no opportunity to give the wrong direction needed to be opened. He had made a decision on what should be done about desserts, but not any specific dessert. He may as well not have bothered.

Mismanaging RADs

In fact, he may have been better off had he not bothered. There is one thing worse than not making a RAD when appropriate — pretending to make one; that is, making a RAD and then treating every activity as if it were unique; making the one decision for all future similar activities and then asking the question again each time the activity becomes a possible part of the here and now. What makes it worse than not having made the decision in the first place is that we can lull ourselves into a false sense of security based on the illusion that one set of immediate-activity decisions has been taken care of and so the rewards of that decision will be forthcoming. Our dessert eater had better not order up any new clothes in anticipation of his soon-to-be-altered waistline.

THE ACTIVATION HABIT: MANAGE BY LEAST NUMBER OF DECISIONS

Self managers should make a practice of regularly determining those activities that fall under the category of recurring-activity decisions. Make the appropriate decisions and assign them a time frame. New challenges, new responsibilities and new projects may occur over time, resulting in new recurring activities that should be decided upon and then added to the category. There may be reason to change the decision related to some activities, perhaps because the conditions surrounding them may have altered. On a regular basis, self managers should review the list of activities that belong in their category of recurring-activity decisions and should review the appropriateness of the decisions and assigned time frames for each.

The more critical self-management practice is, when presented with an opportunity to carry out on RAD, to not treat it as if it were a unique activity decision. When the potential for a recurring activity arises, don't ask the question again, "What shall I do?" That question has already been asked and answered. *You are not at a decision point. You have already made the decision. Don't make it again. Simply apply it.*

Self managers have the responsibility of generating numerous immediate-activity decisions every day, and the higher the quality of their decisions, the greater the level of activation. As the manager of your immediate performance, self-manage by the principle of least number of decisions. Recognize that there are two categories of activity decisions — *unique-activity decisions* and *recurring-activity decisions* — and that they should be dealt with differently. For the unique decisions there is no short cut. They require your self-management energy whenever they appear. For the recurring decisions, on the other hand, your responsibility for self direction has already been carried out. Don't waste energy and risk mistakes by making the decision again. By not dealing with unnecessary decision points, you free yourself to focus on those areas that require your energy. By not asking the question again, you allow a number of important immediate-activity decisions to direct your performance effortlessly and glean the performance rewards.

chapter **20** | # MANAGING THE MANAGEABLE

THE VICTIM

Just great. I get up, ready to greet the day, look out the window and what do I see? Blue sky? Sunshine? 'Course not. Why would I even think such a thing? I should know better. Rain. Wet, dreary, depressing rain. Sixth rainy day this month. Perfect setup for what I'm sure is going to be an even more perfect day. After all, in the next few minutes I'll be fortunate enough to find myself in the middle of a jammed parking lot, pretending to be a road. I fully expect that one day I'll walk out my front door and see a sign at the end of my driveway, "Lot Full" and won't even be able to get to work. Mind you, that probably wouldn't make the slightest bit of difference to anyone, anyway. It's not as if they let me accomplish anything there.

Hasn't the place changed? I mean, you used to be able to get things done. 'Course, one of the reasons for that is you knew what needed doing. They'd tell you. Not anymore. Take the last few weeks. Over three weeks ago my boss said he'd get back to me about whether project plans had changed or not. Have I heard a thing? What do you think? Not a hint. For all I know,

I'm working on a project that doesn't even exist anymore. What's worse, they might be creating a huge mess down the road because they think I'm busy doing something else. I can see it all now. My boss calls me into his office in about six months and reads me the riot act because I haven't met my objectives. Won't he be surprised when I tell him that I didn't meet them because I didn't get them in the first place. Makes you feel pretty useless, I can tell you. And when it's promotion time, who won't be on the list again? Me, of course. And the reason? "Didn't meet your objectives."

Whether they believe it or not, I want to meet my objectives, but I don't have enough information! And that's not all. I'd like to be more productive but they haven't given me the necessary resources and for that matter, they should know that a course to update some of my technological skills is certainly in order. There have been a lot of changes recently, after all. I guess the bottom line is, I'd like to be more productive but they just won't let me! Well, enough of that. Read a bit of the morning paper and then I'll be off.

Now, would you look at that. How's a person supposed to stay positive when things like that are going on in the world? Politicians these days! And the weather forecast! Miserable for the next five days. I should have known. I mean, what can you expect? A little sunshine every now and again? Right. And what planet do you come from? I guess I'd better get going. I mean, why wouldn't I want to get soaked on my way to the car and then drive to work at two miles an hour so that I can begin my undefined job. And all for what? I'll tell you what. So that I can give away most of my earnings to those useless politicians that run the country. What a life!

FOCUSING ON THE UNMANAGEABLE

In the equation, Performance = Ability x Activation®, an ability value of zero represents no opportunity for self management other than wasting time and energy. In the absence of performance potential, the self manager has nothing to activate. There is another significant opportunity to waste time and energy — focusing on areas and objectives outside our control. From a performance perspective, concentrating on the unreachable is not a good thing to do, a conclusion so obvious that it might seem advisable, once stated, to simply move on quickly.

But is it, in practice, really that obvious? In fact, focusing on the unmanageable may be one of the greatest de-activators that confront self managers. Not only is it a trap, easy to fall into, but often, when we're caught, we don't even know it.

Some Common Traps

We cannot control today's weather. We can't even influence it. Oh, we can dress for it. We can escape it to some degree by going indoors or traveling to a different climate. But control? Influence? Sadly, no. And yet were an interplanetary visitor to spend only a short time on earth, he could be forgiven for coming to the conclusion that meteorology is one of the primary passions of the creatures inhabiting this small piece of the universe. We talk about it all the time and to whoever is near. It's true that sometimes it serves as an icebreaker or represents the only common ground we know we have with a complete stranger, but at other times many of us go far past the icebreaker stage. Especially when the weather has been unpleasant for any length of time, we want to talk about it or even just think about it to ourselves. Some of us, myself included, are extremely fortunate in that our cable network not only supplies numerous channels with newscasts, followed or preceded by the weather, but the luxury of two channels devoted entirely to that one topic. Not only can we get the current weather of virtually any spot on earth if we wait long enough, but we even receive detailed weather history, pictures and all! And that for an impactor we know to not even try to influence. What about impactors for which the picture isn't as clear?

Let's take a look at the character in the illustration at the top of this section. After wallowing in the weather for a while we saw him move to the traffic, another easy attention trap that is likely to lead nowhere. He then focused on his place of work, certainly an arena in which he can have an impact. However, let's take a closer look at the objects of his concentration. He didn't spend a lot of time thinking about what he can do. Instead, he looked at what might be stopping him from doing it. All his energy was spent considering the actions or the perceived inaction of others. He then moved to politics and taxes, topics perfectly suited to our action hero. He appears to see himself as a leaf, moving in whatever direction the wind happens to be blowing. His concentration is almost totally on what the world is doing to him, with little left over to spend on what he might be doing to the world — a self manager, spending all his energy on things and people outside his control, on managing the unmanageable.

Of course, people aren't generally as totally victimized in outlook as is our speaker in the opening monologue. In its "purity" it might be considered an exaggeration. However, the seriousness and the popularity of this de-activator are real. The workplace frequently provides examples of it in full operation.

A decision comes from on high in the corporation, one that most people consider to be less than brilliant. But the decision has been made and everyone realizes that there's nothing to be done. It is now part of today's reality. A significant portion of those affected (and probably some not touched) figuratively don sackcloth and ashes and meet in small groups, wailing and bemoaning the decision. Their energy is being wasted and their performance potential frozen as they focus on that for which they can do nothing. *(Invariably, however, there are some people invited to the wake who disagree as vehemently with the decision as do the mourners but who refuse the invitation. They don't do wakes. Too busy focusing on areas in which they can make a difference.)*

Another common example. All one has to do is listen in on workplace conversations to know that one of the most popular topics of discussion in the occupational world is the boss, the external manager. Special focus is given to his weaknesses and he is often identified as being a reason for failure or reduced success. As was demonstrated by our "victim," it is not uncommon to hear someone say what boils down to, "I would like to be doing a much more effective job but my manager won't let me!"

Whether or not that might be the case is not the issue here. There are good external managers, managers that aren't good and many in between. Should we, therefore, assume there is an extremely high correlation between manager and managee performance? Do great managers have great managees and poor managers have people who are dramatically unproductive? Sometimes the correlation between the two is high, but generally the quality of external management is only one influencing factor among a number of others, the most critical being the quality of self management. Many are the inadequate external managers that somehow manage to have some highly productive managees, in spite of themselves. By the same token, if effective external management were the primary determinant of managee success, every good manager would have no performance-problem people working for them. Reality suggests otherwise, however.

Another occupational example. There can be no doubt that the general state of the economy can have a significant effect upon sales. I've done some work with various salespeople in different industries and I've observed external factors at work that can have an effect on the performance of virtually every member of a particular salesforce. I have also observed something else. There are almost always some members of a salesforce in an organization or industry, that, while affected by negative external conditions, continue to do relatively well. Despite the economic situation or, for that matter, the quality of their sales manager, corporate advertising, presence or absence of incentives and so on, they continue to succeed. I have also observed that while their peers spend many hours discussing, over coffee, the sad state of the economy, this consistently effective minority are off activating the skills that bring about performance, regardless of external conditions.

We see many examples of focusing on the unmanageable in other arenas. Many students who come home with a less than sterling report card say with great conviction, a conviction perhaps honestly felt, that they had little to do with their lack of success. The blame lies with the poor quality of teaching they received.

Might they be right? They might. Quality of teaching is extremely important. A horrendous teacher can have a devastating effect on students. The likelihood of their being right is more to the point, however. The fact is that most students who blame their teachers, not as being a secondary but as being the primary reason for their lack of success, belong to a group of students, all taught by the same teacher, in which a small number may have done poorly, a large number, not badly and a small number, very well. Was the teacher not as bad as all that, then? Perhaps, but that's not the point. It is not the teacher who does the learning. It is the student. Both are important members of the formal learning process but the student is, by far, the most important. Many are the wonderful teachers who have some capable, but nevertheless, failing students.

We looked earlier at the weather as something we can do little about. Focusing on this highly independent element of nature can be extremely de-activating. I've often encountered people who are, at the time of meeting, relatively joyless, not because anything significantly negative has befallen them, but because they are bored to death. Why is that? They'll tell you without you even having to ask. "It's the weather," they say. "Who can go out in weather like this? Who, but an idiot, would want to?" Of course, if they bothered to check, they'd see all kinds of "idiots" in restaurants, movie houses and theaters, but they won't. It's too cold or too wet or too hot or . . .

The Cost of "Malfocusing"

There is no intent here to suggest that external, influencing factors are not at work and don't affect performance to some degree. It's the degree that's at issue and more to the point, the cost to the individual of imagining very much more outside determining power than, in fact, exists.

Overfocusing on externals wastes potential. If I can do little or nothing about a situation, there isn't much performance-related value in spending time and energy focusing on it, especially when the alternative is to focus on the doable. However, if, for example, I am convinced that it is not I, but my external manager or my teacher or the weather that determines my success, I will not be as likely to take control of my potential. Why bother? Not only am I attempting to manage the unmanageable, I'm avoiding managing the manageable. The result on both counts is serious de-activation.

THE ACTIVATION HABIT: MANAGE THE MANAGEABLE

The Reversal

Now to the most subtle and cumulatively, perhaps the most destructive variation on this theme of focusing on things that have impact on us, things that are outside ourselves.

When we want to attain a goal but something is in the way, a barrier between us and our objective, it is very easy to automatically overfocus on that barrier; to allow that barrier to fill the visual field in our mind's eye and within moments, to walk away from our objective. It's a kind of focusing on the negatives but in this case, the negatives are usually outside ourselves.

We will again use the weather as the illustration. Here's a simple and rapid thought process that you may have experienced at one time or another.

I want to take a walk, but it's raining.

Let's examine the statement a little more closely. If someone else were to make that statement to you, would your guess be that you've just listened to someone about to take a walk or someone who has just decided not to?

Although you can't know for sure, chances are you're not dealing with a soon-to-be walker.

The Exercise

Before continuing, please do the following exercise. It takes only a few minutes but can help bring home the significance of this section.

The above statement about walking and the rain is a wish statement, the wish being, "I want to take a walk . . ." followed by "but" and the statement of a barrier, something getting in the way of satisfying the wish — in this case, the fact that it's raining.

I want to _____ but _____.

The exercise is this. Take the next five minutes to generate and write down as many of your own "wish . . . but . . ." statements, personal or business, that you can — realistic wishes that have something standing in their way, statements of goals, real for you, but with something getting in the way to attainment.

Now, back to the text. Here is the statement we looked at a few minutes ago.

I want to take a walk, but it's raining.

It has two pieces of stated information: one about a desire and one about the weather. There is also a strong, but unstated, piece of suggested information that, in all likelihood, the wish will not be granted; that it will not even be pursued. What is the point of pursuit? There is something standing in the way.

Let's now look at a variation of the first statement.

It's raining, but I want to take a walk.

What is communicated by it? The chances that we are in the presence of a walker have increased considerably. Even though the stated information given in the two variations are exactly the same, the suggested information is very different. *One suggests that walking won't happen, the other, that it will.*

In the first, the objective is stated at the beginning, the barrier at the end. This is the order to be expected in that there's no reason to register the barrier to an objective that we don't have. In the second, the order is reversed. What's standing in the way comes first and "what I want" completes the statement.

In both instances, it is the end of the statement that gets the focus. In the first, the spotlight is on the barrier and so the barrier looms large. It tends to become the significant reality. We think very quickly and in an instant the issue feels closed and we walk away.

In the second, the statement finishes on the desire, on the objective and the fact that it is I who wants it. It no longer feels like "case closed." We are back where we belong, looking at ourselves and what we wish to achieve. The spotlight instantaneously falls back on us and the question automatically arises, *What can I do?*

The focus is back on our potential to make a difference. We may now find a way to achieve our objective, to approximate it or perhaps we may discover that, in fact, the objective is unattainable. The important thing is that if there are any activity decisions — any directing of our ability that would help us to accomplish our objective — we will now be considering them. When we don't ask the question, however, the potential, even if it does exist, will be wasted. By focusing on the barrier we can easily miss what it is *we can do* to overcome it. *Again, as self managers, we must concentrate our energies on the manageable, on what we can do, on how we can make a difference.*

Please return to the wish statements that you generated a few minutes ago and reverse them. By making yourself a more significant factor, you may discover potential previously missed.

This reversal, while very simple, can also be an extremely powerful self-management tool. However, as with all the tools in this book, it becomes useful only when it becomes automatic. Through practice, make the reversal of your "wish . . . but . . ." statements a habit.

Focus on the Manageable

The simple, but important summary statement is this.

As long as we're not focusing on what we can do, we are unlikely to generate the activity decisions that will activate our potential.

The only impacting factor that we manage and control is ourselves. We make a difference only through what we do. We get results only by what we do. We influence others only through what we do. With regard to activation, the sole justification for looking at impactors outside ourselves is to help us answer the question, "What can I do about this situation?" If this answer is, "Nothing," move to something for which you can make a difference.

We have incredible control over a powerful resource — ourselves. The more we focus on managing that resource, the more we accomplish. The moment that our primary focus moves elsewhere, our potential as both self manager and performer is de-activated.

chapter 21

MANAGING EXPECTATIONS

PATIENT: *Doctor, after my operation will I be able to play the piano?*

DOCTOR: *Of course you will.*

PATIENT: *Gee, that's great. I never used to be able to play the piano.*

An old joke but with a timeless message. One hopes our patient will not immediately purchase a concert grand and rent a recital hall, but the fact remains that unrealistic expectations can be very expensive.

THE COST OF UNREALISTIC EXPECTATIONS

We self managers have an awesome responsibility. It is up to us to convert our potential into performance as effectively as we can in carrying out our objectives. It gets heavier. We're also the ones that often have to determine what those objectives should be. The immediate objectives are almost always ours to set and frequently, especially within the context of our personal lives, so are the mid- and long-term goals. We determine our expectations and then we're the ones that have to activate our abilities within the context of those expectations, all of which suggests that as expectation setters, we'd better be good.

We have to be wary of setting expectations that are unrealistic, either unrealistically high or unrealistically low. If our expectations are too high, we are in danger of wasting potential through activating our abilities in pursuit of the unattainable. Not only might we accomplish nothing, but by following an unreasonable objective, we may miss pursuing a more reasonable one. By not recognizing what we can't achieve, we may achieve nothing.

When we become aware that our objective may be getting away from us, in spite of what we feel to be our best efforts, a sense of frustration may set in, we may begin spinning our wheels, taking short cuts, become scattered and in a desperate attempt to catch up, our performance may deteriorate rather than improve.

In addition, when we create unreasonable expectations, we set ourselves up to fail and there is nothing like failure to seriously lower self-confidence. By lowering self-confidence, de-activation may continue long after we have stopped pursuing the false hope.

Expectations that are too low can, for different reasons, have the same overall negative impact on our performance. If much potential remains locked, there is no apparent reason to stretch. Not only do we not achieve what we could, but we may not find out what we are capable of accomplishing. While confidence may not be lowered, the increased confidence that can come from greater achievement is denied us.

The self manager's responsibility, then, is to set expectations that are optimistically realistic; to create a constructive framework within which to manage immediate performance. The critical issue, however, is not whether to set meaningful, ambitious but attainable objectives — that would be rather like recommending clean air. It is how to go about doing so.

The "Feel Good" Myth

When I was a young boy I had an uncle, someone who mattered to me very much, who once presented me with what he considered to be a very valuable gift. It was a truth that he thought to be important enough to share. "Young man, I want you to know and remember," he said, "that there is no such word as can't. There is nothing you can't do if you want it badly enough." Looking back these many years later, I realize that either he was not altogether right or there are times that I'm just not able to muster up enough "want" for my own good.

I also have found that my uncle is not alone in holding this valuable truth. We are told the same thing through the words of some popular songs, through hopeful movies and writings aimed at helping people with their personal growth: as long as you believe that you can do something and have enough desire, you will get it done. The implication is that "performance = desire x faith" — that ability has little to do with it.

This is nonsense, of course, albeit a "feel good" kind of nonsense. While it is true that if you have the ability to do something, but don't have the motivation to do it or the belief that you can, or both, in all likelihood you won't. That does not mean, however, that without the ability but with the confidence and motivation, you're there. In the absence of the skills, resources, time and energy necessary to make something happen, that "something" will not happen. We really know that, of course, and yet when setting expectations it can be all too easy to fall into the "feel good" trap.

What helps us get caught is that all too frequently our setting of objectives begins and ends with the result that we want. It's not that the result is obviously out of the realm of possibility. If it were, we'd know and reject it out of hand. It's that while it may well be realistic, we don't check to see if, in fact, it is. The result does not obviously belong in the realm of the impossible. We want to achieve it and that's enough. The trouble is, however, self managers don't do results. We achieve them and while, at times, they're the results we want, nevertheless, results are not what we do. *We do activities.*

It is through the managing and doing of activities that results are achieved. Often, our activity is not the only factor determining the results we get, but it is the only determining factor over which we have control. As self managers, we determine, we manage our activity. To begin the setting of expectations with a desired result makes all kinds of sense. To stop there, however, is to ask ourselves to manage that which we cannot directly manage — to manage the unmanageable.

THE ACTIVATION HABIT: TRANSLATE EXPECTATIONS INTO REQUIRED ACTIVITIES

It is important to have as a general direction, one that is achievable. We must generate realistic expectations from which to springboard our immediate performance. However, the only way we can determine whether or not a result represents a realistic expectation is to first translate it into what we do. Then we can be in a position to answer the following two questions.

- What must I do tomorrow and each day after, to reach the objective within the desired time frame?
- Considering what other things I have on my plate, do I have the skills, knowledge, resources and time necessary to carry out the activities during the tomorrows making up the time frame?

Only when we have translated the expectation into the activities necessary within an immediate time frame, only when we are considering the immediate performance required for success, are we in a position to answer. If the answer is Yes, it is because we want to and know that we can, and not simply because we want to and would like to believe that we can.

Of course, we don't always have the luxury of determining our own objectives, especially in the workplace. There are times when the expectations are imposed on us and considered immutable. What then?

As self manager, the one responsible for making the immediate performance happen, it is still important to be able to assess, to the best of our ability, whether or not an assigned objective is a realistic one. By translating an apparently unreasonable objective into what we must do to reach it , it may appear reasonable. On the other hand, we might discover that, everything considered, the goal cannot be reached. Now we are in a position to explain that we see the inevitability of failure and why. We might also be able to suggest what might be done to positively alter the situation. If we are not listened to, at least we will have protected our confidence, recognizing the failure to be one of unrealistic objective setting and not of ineffective self management. We may still have to suffer the other imposed consequences of not being able to do what we perceive to be the impossible, but we will have realistically reduced the cost to our capacity to activate.

When we think of setting objectives we tend to think long term. Much of the above discussion was generated with longer-term expectations in mind. And yet most of our setting of objectives is relatively short term, relating to the day or week at hand. Some of it gets written down in a daily or weekly action plan. Much of our short-term setting of objectives is done on the run and in our heads, however. A situation arises, or a request for our time, energy and expertise is made and granted with the result that a new expectation is now in place.

Is it realistic? Can it be carried out? If so, at what cost? These are important questions, but it is all too easy to commit oneself without giving them due consideration, one of the reasons being that there generally isn't a lot of time to go through the decision-making process. However, we tend to think very quickly, and especially if we develop the habit of daily action planning, as self managers we should have a fairly comprehensive picture of what is on our plate right now. Since we are responsible for managing immediate activity, it is also our responsibility to not issue directions generated through a knee-jerk reaction.

A self manager can increase the probability that immediate objectives will represent realistic expectations by developing the following habit. Ask yourself these questions:

- What must I *do* today or this week to reach the objective?
- Do I have the necessary skills and resources to succeed?
- Can I afford the pursuit?

Some of the self-management decisions may not be the best ones, but there is little doubt that your "batting average" will increase. Your immediate directions will represent self-management decisions rather than self-management reactions, and your immediate objective setting will continue to grow in effectiveness.

chapter 22

THE COACHING
SELF MANAGER

Most jobs require a lot of training. Some of the training is general and is received through the formal education system. Some is highly particular, tied to a specific job and often provided by the employing organization or by a highly specialized and applied educational setting. However, there are few jobs, regardless of complexity and degree of specialization, that do not have, as a critical training component, the training that occurs on the job. We learn many of our skills, we acquire much of our knowledge, through doing. By the very activating of our potential we are able to increase that potential. Salaries often reflect, at least in part, the worth we assign to on-the-job learning. A belief that hands-on training is valued is implied by the automatic increase in compensation that often is tied to time spent doing the job.

In both individual and team sports, the role of coach is well established. Not only does the coach have a strategic planning function, but an "in-your-face" on-the-job training function as well. Continued *learning by doing* is not a responsibility assigned only to experience, but is shared by the coach who observes immediate performance and then derives and delivers lessons arising from that observation. The coach takes an active stance in the training of his athletes.

In the occupational world, as the demand for continued growth in performance potential increases, the coaching function is being seen more and more as an important part of people management. Managers are given courses in how to offer more effectively, not only before-the-job, but on-the-job coaching to their managees, in an attempt to accelerate their rate of development through the use of immediate performance as a learning tool.

There is a problem, however. Practice suggests that the external manager is viewed as the only person worthy of the title "coach" and yet he is seldom in a position to observe the immediate performance of his managees. On-the-job coaching is, by necessity, a rather rare happening.

That does not mean, of course, that in the absence of an external manager, experience cannot, by itself, function as a learning tool. It can and obviously does. Our learning by doing does not necessitate that there be someone else watching. The problem is that with the coach not on the scene, there may be no one taking an active teaching role. Much of the value of experience is in danger of being lost, because no one is watching.

THE PASSIVE ON-THE-JOB COACH

But someone *is* watching — the self manager. After all, we do learn from experience, from doing things poorly, better and extremely well. Even when we have not been receiving feedback from someone else about our immediate performance, we can still see ourselves advance, day by day, up the slope of the new learning curves. However, as self manager, the important question to ask is not Am I self-managing? In that, we have no choice. We are the managers of our immediate performance, by necessity. The critical question to ask is How effectively am I carrying out the function? or perhaps more critically, How much better could I be doing?

We all have an on-the-job trainer with us at all times. Most of us do not purposefully take advantage of that and likely pay a high cost for the oversight. We may read articles and take courses and although that kind of learning activity can be important in increasing our performance potential, it is not what is meant here by on-the-job training — the learning that comes from the actual *doing* of the job. We certainly tend to take note of at least some of the larger errors we make and try to take advantage of what we learned by not repeating the blunders. We register some of our more forceful positive-performance advances and attempt to retain them to support future success.

However, most of the lessons to be learned from a day's performance do not fit under the category of "momentous," positive or negative. Most of our experiential learning is cumulative and made up of small and subtle lessons, minor adjustments, the fine tuning of knowledge and skills that serve as the steps we use to climb the learning curves placed before us. Unless we are purposefully watching, the majority of those lessons are apt to go unnoticed.

One reason that many of us aren't great at self-coaching on the job is because we pay little active attention to the role in the first place. We don't do it well because we don't try to. Another reason is that doing two significant, highly involving things at the same time is difficult and so, often, we become too busy *doing*, to simultaneously focus on our teaching role, on consciously registering what we can learn from the doing. When we have a job to do, our focus lies primarily in reaching our objective, not on self improvement. The result of this inattention, while understandable, can also be expensive in that small mistakes, mis-applications of potential, may go unnoticed and therefore are more likely to be repeated. Useful variations of immediate performance, small improvements in the way we do something, doing something differently, doing something well for the first time — these examples of the positive activation of ability, if not registered, are less likely to be repeated. In these situations, we still learn from doing, of course, but we learn very much more slowly.

We've been referring mainly to climbing new learning curves, the transition between rookie and veteran. What about situations and responsibilities at which we have become accomplished? What are the implications of leaving our totally dedicated on-the-job coach in bed, figuratively speaking, in situations for which we have already attained veteran status?

It is not uncommon, once we have become proficient at our job or at a specific task, that our performance reaches a ceiling. We get to the point where it's as good as it's going to get. We've plateaued. It's not that there isn't room to grow or even that we're satisfied with the status quo. It's that we are now doing things sufficiently well that, while there are still opportunities to grow our performance, virtually all the mistakes we make are minor and the improvements in functioning, easily missed. We may become bored and walk into our all too familiar demand situations like robots, mechanically going through what have now become the almost automatic motions of performance. For the want of a self-managing coach, actively present, opportunities for further growth of performance potential are lost.

THE ACTIVATION HABIT: EXERCISE THE COACHING FUNCTION

The coach is available, always with us wherever we go and in a position to witness our every move. The challenge for all of us is to put that coach to work and keep him on the job, actively observing our immediate performance and applying the resultant learning so that we continuously strengthen our performance potential. However, at the same time, the carrying out of that function must not detract from the performance being observed. The coaching musn't get in the way of the play.

There are simple ways of effectively carrying out the self-management role of on-the-job coach, of utilizing immediate performance as an active learning tool without taking the focus away from *doing* the job; of capturing the data necessary to increase our performance potential without detracting from our here-and-now performance. Let's focus on the workplace for illustration.

The primary on-the-job-training question the self manager as coach is really asking is, What do I see in my own performance that could serve as data to increase my performance potential? However, while the external manager has only to coach, the self manager must both observe and manage the doing, simultaneously. That leaves little time to identify and then deliver the lessons of observation.

The good news is that the coaching self manager is always present. He couldn't miss observing all performance even if he wanted to. He's got the raw data. Even though he often can't use it on the spot, it can be considered soon after, preferably the day in which it occurred. The subtle lessons of a day, precisely because of their subtlety, are likely to disappear without a memory trace by the following day.

The self-management habit is an easy one to develop and to practice. At day's end, ask yourself the following questions and answer:

What did I do well today?

Regardless of how often a job is done well, if the specific performance is identified there is little chance that it will inadvertently be dropped from your performance repertoire. We generally have enough new potential to acquire and apply without placing the already effective potential at risk. Maintaining strengths already developed takes much less effort than does the acquisition of new ones.

What did I do poorly today?

This question represents the opportunity for the self manager to constructively criticize any negative performance that he has identified. Here an activity plan can be generated to help strengthen future performance potential and, if possible, reduce the impact of today's weaker showing.

Did I remember to bring my strengths to bear on today's challenges?

There are times when the issue is neither that we did well or poorly, but that in relation to our potential, we simply didn't do. We have the ability to handle certain situations much better, but somehow, the potential just wasn't activated. It's important to identify the waste of specific performance potential to ensure that our strengths don't atrophy.

What did I do differently today?

This is, perhaps the most important question of all. When we have performed an activity for the first time, handled a situation differently than any other we've encountered, dealt with a common challenge in a different way, it's important to take a close look. The new performance may not yet be a part of us. If we're looking at something positive we want to identify it, in a sense, preserve it, so that it becomes part of our performance repertoire; if a fresh negative is revealed, we want to eliminate it so that it doesn't.

How well did I carry out my self-management function?

This end-of-day meeting is a good time to review your performance as a self manager. You may find that many of the positives and the negatives of that day were the direct result of the quality of activation that you, as self manager, generated. Were there examples of highly effective self management? Were there opportunities to protect your confidence better, to come up with better activity decisions, to "run interference" and clear the way for decisions to be carried out that you missed? Identify both the positives and negatives of your self management so that this critical function can continue to grow.

This meeting, at the end of the day, is an important one. It is here that we can, usually very rapidly, critically analyze our performance of the day before its subtleties have disappeared. It is in this brief meeting that we can take advantage of the fact that we have been present and an observer of our immediate performance, in total, for that day and have, at our fingertips, the most important data for continuous improvement. By making this daily meeting a habit, rather than simply depending upon immediate experience to do its teaching job, we actively use experience to ensure that its lessons are learned. This short meeting, held perhaps while traveling home at the end of a day, ensures that we have an on-the-job coach constructively critiquing every move. The cumulative result of hundreds of these meetings over a year can be extremely significant in continuously increasing our performance potential. Serious on-the-job training.

chapter 23 | # THE SELF MANAGEMENT OF NEW LEARNING

THE CONSTANT REQUIREMENT

"You can't teach an old dog new tricks." Interesting saying and especially interesting considering the number of "new tricks" most of us dogs, young and old, are being asked to learn on what seems to be a daily basis.

"You're learning all the time." That's another one and when it was said even in the very recent past, there was a kind of quiet reassurance about it. It seemed to say, "Life never stands still and just by living it, bit by bit, we become wiser and wiser." Perhaps a slight variation of the statement would be more in keeping with today's reality. Perhaps it should read, "You'd better be learning all the time or else!"

So much to learn and at the same time so much to discard. Not long ago our life cycle might have been described as having three primary phases: the learning phase, the doing phase and the resting phase. We prepared ourselves to be contributors, we contributed and then we retired. If we decided to make Phase 3 an adventure rather than an extended rest in preparation for the final one, then learning, again, became a very much more prominent and active experience. Of course, learning continued through Phase 2 but only as a secondary characteristic.

Teaching versus Learning

Today, if we decide at the end of life's first phase, the learning phase, that the lion's share of active learning for us is done, there's a good chance that it is we who will be "done" and in very short order. As was said in Chapter 6, "Activation," the individual — the primary change agent — is the receiver, processor and the deliverer of change. Looking at the front end, the receiving end where the "bulk learning" often takes place, we tend to behave as if once the necessary learning has been defined, an effective method of teaching determined and the teaching presented, the job is done. The targeted increase in potential has been reached. Witness the fact that if there is any kind of evaluation of new training in organizations, it usually begins and ends with a questionnaire looking at the quality of the teaching experience. Whether learning then takes place is not even questioned. The responsibility appears to be seen to lie with the teacher, not the student. The assumption seems to be: Give us the necessary new knowledge, presented effectively and it will be learned.

But will it? We all have, in varying degrees, the potential to learn. However, just as we cannot assume that knowing how to perform a certain task means that the task will be performed, nor can we assume that because we can learn, we will. One of the reasons that flexibility is becoming a more necessary characteristic today, is its contribution to learning. Not only does new learning make us more flexible, but flexibility is important in bringing about new learning. Revisiting self-confidence for a moment — if I have a confidence deficit, I'm more likely threatened by the new. Within moments of being presented with the opportunity to acquire a new skill set, I may, as a kind of protection, become inflexible. I may rapidly generate numerous reasons that the material is simply not worthy. The mind closes and so does the opportunity to learn. Effective self management of confidence is important in activating the potential we have to learn.

In organizations, often what is labeled as "adult learning" is not learning as much as it is understanding. Attendees of a seminar, designed to provide a new or strengthened skill, leave the seminar appreciating the application of that new skill set and perhaps having a method with which to acquire it but without having, as yet, learned the skills. The skills are not yet a part of them, only the understanding of what those skills are and that they can be acquired. However, acquisition requires eliciting specific activities such as rereading the relevant material and systematically practicing application until the skill has been mastered or the new approach internalized. The self manager must effectively generate the immediate-activity decisions that over time will produce the desired learning. He must then ensure that those decisions are carried out. A tall order considering that the new learning not yet in place is usually competing with old learning already established and productive.

We self managers are responsible for activating our learning potential, and the mechanisms that free the potential are the same activating habits that convert all performance potential. There is no doubt that the better self manager we become, the better learners we are. However, there are some potential traps to new learning that suggest that it may deserve added attention.

The Cost of New Learning

First, new learning often tends to have a high cost. Just its newness suggests that acquisition and application will take a fair amount of energy. The newer the learning curve, the more mistakes we are likely to make and confident or not, making mistakes is not, for most of us, a terribly enjoyable pastime. Also, often the new learning is intended to replace information and skills already learned and practiced and discarding them can feel costly. The higher the cost we perceive something to be, the less easily we are willing to pay the price.

The Passive Critic

Second, because of the almost exclusive focus the world puts on the teaching, we can easily be lulled into believing that the learning is something done to people rather than something people do. For this reason we can easily become critics of the learning situation rather than learners. Our energies go to looking for evidence that the new material is not worth learning rather than making sure we are first opening ourselves to its possible usefulness. We look for things we disagree with and don't look for things we don't know but perhaps should. We focus on the weakness in the teaching methodology rather than attempting to apply the strength in our ability to learn. We look for what the world will do to support our continued learning after the seminar is over rather than focusing on what we, the learners, can do to establish and strengthen the new skills.

THE ACTIVATION HABIT: PUT NEW LEARNING TO WORK

What can a self manager do to support the acquisition of new skills, knowledge and approaches — other than the ongoing strengthening of the habits of activation?

For starters, we can remind ourselves who, primarily, determines the value in the new learning situation. Ourselves. We must keep, front of mind, that if there is something useful to be gained it is our responsibility to find it. We must be ready to listen, be willing to attempt to understand the material being presented, *before* making a decision as to whether or not it is worth learning. Of course, it may turn out that we decide there wasn't anything of value and so we walk away from the content of the new learning experience. In that instance, the important thing to ensure is that we really are looking at the new material, and not at our failure to activate our potential to effectively understand what it is. This first step consists of *turning what we are presented with into what we know about.*

Then the next crucial part begins. The teaching has been completed. We've determined that its content should become a part of us and so we must now decide what we have to do, specifically, with regard to our immediate activity, day by day, to learn the new material, and to make it part of us. *Turning what we know about into what we know* becomes our objective, likely supported by our daily action plan. If there is outside support to help us with the transformation, all the better, but regardless, the responsibility is ours.

The next step also belongs primarily to us. Rather than concentrating on activating our learning potential, the shift is to the potential we've learned. We now must take responsibility for *turning what we know into what we do.* At that point the new learning has been effectively self-managed.

The Self-Management Challenge

The questions to ask of ourselves and then demand answers to are:

- Is there anything new and of value being presented?
- Is there anything of value that I already know but am not applying?
- How can I convert the teaching experience into a learning experience?
- What must I do to ensure that the new learning is activated?

Putting new learning to work is the business of the self manager.

chapter **24** | # MANAGING DECISIVENESS

Self managers are in the business of making decisions. We often must choose between two directions, the objective being to choose right. To do otherwise is to waste potential. At times, the correct choice is clear. We know what should be done, what directions we should give ourselves. At other times we can't be sure and at still others, we can't really know. It's the last two categories, the "not sure" and the "can't know," that deserve some special attention.

Frequently, alternative directions have different positives and different negatives associated with them, and it becomes difficult to assess with certainty which will ultimately prove to be of greater benefit. There is some risk involved in choosing. Although there may be things that can be done to reduce the risk, what the best decision would be may never be completely revealed. There is often an unknown factor that, for the want of a working crystal ball, will remain unknown. One decision that can be made in an instant is the decision not to make one until the situation becomes clearer.

This indecision isn't all bad or certainly doesn't feel all bad. By postponing, the risk and its accompanying discomfort have, at least, been delayed. We know we haven't made any mistakes simply because we haven't done anything. While we may be paying a large opportunity cost, we're not in a position to see the future that would have been, and so we cannot see the price tag. What we don't know can't hurt us or at least we don't feel the pain. Instead, we may feel somewhat self-satisfied for having been wisely protective. And perhaps we should. Time may serve to make the right decision clearer to see.

There is an accompanying cost to not deciding, however, and that is the burden of unfinished business. We must now spend energy revisiting the undecided. If indecision comes too easily, we carry with us the excess baggage of many unresolved issues that continue to be revisited until dealt with or forgotten. As the habit of indecisiveness grows, so does the volume of the unresolved. Our desk becomes cluttered and we can't easily get to the decisions that need attention or have difficulty giving them the focus that they deserve. Most of us have more on our plates than we can handle. We can ill afford to add, unnecessarily, to the load.

THE ACTIVATION HABIT: MAKE NOT DECIDING AN *ACTIVE* SELF-MANAGEMENT DECISION

Certainly the activation habit to develop is not, "When in doubt, decide!" There is no intrinsic value in making a bad decision or one that is blatantly premature. At the same time, when there is little to gain from postponement and perhaps much to lose, not deciding becomes poor self management.

By developing the following activation habit, the self manager, when at a potential decision point, can rapidly determine whether deciding for postponement is in order. Start the day with the instruction: *Note when decision avoidance is about to occur.* Via this simple mechanism you will be sensitized to the challenge.

When you note that you are considering walking away from making a decision, ask yourself the following three questions:

- Will there be new information?
- Will it likely make a difference?
- Is there time to wait for it?

There may be times when you can't be certain of the answers to the above questions, when the only appropriate answer is "I can't know." If the stakes are high, postponement of decision making may be indicated. Here, the decision to not make a decision is a considered one.

When the answers to the three questions are Yes, postponement does not reflect indecisiveness but a quality self-management decision.

When the answer to *any* of the questions is No, make the best choice possible and act. Through this practice, carrying unnecessary decisions still to be made will be reduced and you will be able to focus better on those issues requiring your attention.

chapter **25**

MANAGING THE RELATIONSHIP BETWEEN SELF AND EXTERNAL MANAGERS

Some of us have external managers in our work lives, managers whose formal responsibilities include carrying out management functions with regard to our performance. Others of us, for example, the self employed, the owner, the most senior executive in a corporation, the homemaker or the retiree may not, in a formal sense, have an ongoing reporting relationship with an individual external manager. Regardless of whether we actually have someone with the title "manager" or not, we all have people in our work lives, often many people, who carry out the Phase 1, "Preparation," and Phase 3, "Evaluation," management responsibilities of our performance cycle.

Although we don't think of ourselves as having managers at all in our personal lives, the same, nevertheless, holds true. Many of our objectives are determined, at least in part, by others. Often our families are the source of some of the goals that we pursue. Can there be any doubt that the government sets certain tasks for us that we have to follow or suffer the consequences? Having friends means having some of our objectives determined by others, and keeping friends often requires the active pursuit of those objectives. In marriage, the moment that one spouse ceases to have any management responsibility for the other, and therefore ceases to be a source of short-, medium- and long-term objectives, is likely the moment that, for all intents and purposes, the marriage has ended.

We are all managed by ourselves and we are all managed by others. Like it or not, we are responsible for the managing of our own immediate performance, but the responsibilities of determining many of the objectives of that immediate performance and of evaluating its worth belong to others. How supportive the external managers in all areas of our lives are, is dependent, in large part, upon them. It is also very much dependent upon us, however — on the approach we take towards and on the use we make of those sources of external management. In addition, it depends upon the degree to which we recognize our self-management responsibility and appreciate that we are the owners and managers of our own potential.

We may be able to influence but we cannot control the perception and the performance of others. We have a much greater degree of control over ourselves. This book is about self management and so, with regard to relationship between the self and external manager, its focus is on the resources for which we can make the most difference — ourselves. But let's first look at the Traditional Management Model and the way it perceives the relationship between manager and managee.

Diagrammatically, it looks like this.

EXTERNAL MANAGER

PERFORMER

Pinocchio with Strings

Here, the managee plays the stringed puppet to his manager's Gepetto. It is the manager that pulls the strings, that determines all the moves. Of course, puppets differ in what the manager can have them do, depending on the number of strings, and how many joints, but within each puppet's limitations, what it does and how well, is determined entirely by the decisions and capacity of the puppeteer. The manager is master and determines every move, while the managee is totally reactive. It may be possible to create the illusion of self determination, but to tell the puppet to be proactive, to make him responsible for his own performance, can only be part of the show. While, perhaps sadly, the movable managee cannot really take credit for his positive output, he also is not in a position to take responsibility for mistakes and omissions. Both the applause and the hook belong to Gepetto.

"I Got No Strings"

The Shared-Management Model diagrams differently.

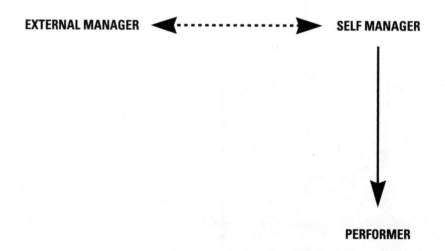

The strings are off. Although the manager may have a significant part in setting the stage, the performance is up to the managee. It is the managee's self manager that determines the moves; the degree to which the external manager influences those moves is ultimately decided by the managee. The puppet has no strings. Both applause and hook are rightfully his.

Of course, regardless of the management model, the management is, in fact, shared. The determiner of immediate performance is the individual doing the performing, regardless of what representation of reality a management model might put forward. While the managers are busy somewhere else, their managees are not crumpled in a pile, immobilized and waiting for the return of their external activators. Nor are they necessarily marching to the orders previously issued by management, assuming any orders have been given.

The problem is not the presence of strings, but the illusion of their being there. The assumption that managers are directly responsible for the immediate performance that happens in an organization has been a prevailing one for so long that, real or not, it can often color the way we look at others and, more importantly, the way we look at ourselves.

People who own something tend to deal with it very differently than do those who don't see themselves as having any ownership. It is easy for a self manager to deal with his immediate performance as if it belongs, not to himself, but to his manager. This illusion is often fed by the manager, holding the same mistaken belief and trying to behave accordingly. The result is that rather than focusing on what initiatives he can take to enhance his performance, the managee focuses on what his manager is doing or not doing that diminishes his performance. "Do you believe the foolishness that's going on here?" he says, arms folded and with a knowing look of frustration on his face. "But what can I do? It's not my responsibility. I just work here."

It's a kind of societal focus on the unmanageable, a general approach to performance management that can quietly close off the proactive conversion of potential into performance in one or more of three ways. The self manager does a poor job of carrying out his management responsibilities because he sees them as belonging to somebody else. The self manager easily becomes a diagnostician, expending his energy discovering what external interference from his manager is standing in his way toward greater productivity, rather than what internal resources he has that can be applied to further growth. Because his mode is reactive, he does not look for opportunities to utilize his external manager's strengths and resources to support his doing the job. He is more concerned with addressing the question, What isn't he doing for me? rather than What can he do for me?

THE ACTIVATION HABIT: LIVE THE SHARED-MANAGEMENT MODEL

There is no doubt that if an external manager recognizes that his managees determine their own immediate performance, he will be in a much better position to support their efforts and not get in the way. However, that is not the primary focus here. We all manage our own immediate performance. All of us are in charge of our own Phase 2, the Activation Phase of our performance cycle, regardless of what anybody else might think. Recognizing that our success is primarily up to us — that not only does the job get done by us, but that we manage the doing — supports in us a very different focus toward those with external management responsibility for us. The important question now does become, "What can he do for me?" In other words, as the owners of our performance, it only makes sense that we focus on the strengths, on the positive resources that our managers can bring to bear on our level of success and go after them.

For the self manager, because he is responsible for managing his immediate performance, it is he that is also responsible for determining the functional relationship between him and his external manager with regard to the doing of the job. Recognizing that success is primarily his to determine allows him to not trip over negative support coming from his manager, to neutralize it through realizing that it is not his manager but he, himself, that largely brings about success or failure. On the other hand, positive support from his manager should be identified and pursued; the better the manager, the greater the resource. External managers see their people as their resource. It is perhaps even closer to the truth to say that the external manager is his managee's resource and that it is the managee who has the responsibility of tapping it.

The self manager must ask this primary question. *What, in my occupational and personal life, can I influence my managers to do to increase the effectiveness of my immediate performance?*

chapter **26** | # SELF
STARTING

I am not a self starter. I freely admit it. In fact, I'm rather proud of it. Oh, I know that my position goes against mainstream thinking. I know that self starting is supposed to be a highly valued trait in today's occupational world. But that doesn't necessarily mean that it should be. After all, mainstream thinking isn't always right thinking, is it? Now, before you close your mind entirely, please consider my take on the issue.

You see, I'm an "other starter." I let other people "turn my crank," so to speak. You might think that it's because I'm lazy but I don't think so. I think it's because I'm smart, because I see things more clearly than most. You see, everybody wants a piece of me. By that, I mean that I've got more things to do in a day, let alone in a week or a month, than I can possibly get done. (I wouldn't be surprised but that you're in the same boat.) Since I can't do it all, I realized that I've got to accept the need for some kind of selection procedure, some way that helps me choose what things get done and what things don't. Oh, I know that accepted practice suggests a daily action plan in which the day's priorities are set, but like it or not, sometimes priorities change from hour to hour and besides, who's to know, in this complicated world of ours, what's important and what's not?

Well, I decided on a system that would help me make the right choices, the choices that reflect the needs of the world around me, the world that I serve. I decided to look at everybody, everybody in my work and in my private life, as if they were my customers and to let them determine where my efforts should go. I decided to work on the assumption that who knows better what's important to the customer than the customer himself. And so, before I make a move I wait until a need has been loudly and clearly expressed. I let others start my engine and the louder the demand, the likelier I am to move. Pretty clever, eh? Let me show you how it works.

At the beginning of the year, my boss sits me down and we discuss, meaning I listen to, what are to be my objectives for the next twelve months. I tell him that I fully understand what's expected of me, shake his hand, and then I wait. Oh, I keep busy, but I don't really get serious until he tells me that there's something specific that he wants me to do and right now! That's when I know that something important has been identified. I now have been given my impetus to action. I switch gears and off I go.

Now, before long, he's likely given me more to do than I can handle and so I move to Level 2 of my operating plan. Now, not only must he demand that I go in a certain direction, but that demand must be delivered with a sense of urgency. He has to ask twice or three times before I get going, or I wait for him to get angry and threaten some dire consequence. I then know that he's really serious and so I get really serious.

The point is that by taking this approach I don't waste my time with the less important things. I really get down to business, the significant business. I guess what it boils down to is this. By being an "other starter," I get the important things done — customer service at its best. Mind you, last I spoke with my boss he said that my job was at risk, but I'm sure that if he looks carefully, he'll see that I'm exactly the kind of employee he needs. After all, I'm doing all the things that he feels are important."

*　　　*　　　*

Foolish thinking? It certainly is, especially at a time when proactivity is at a premium and when things have become so complex that often we're the only ones that can provide the right immediate-activity decisions for ourselves; when we're the only ones in a position to know what needs doing, minute to minute, hour to hour. And besides, with everyone's plate getting fuller, there really is no one to start our engines and point us in the right direction but ourselves, most of the time. We cannot afford to wait until others tell us to do what's good for us. We must do both the telling as well as the listening. And so, unlike our speaker, there are few of us who would admit, even to ourselves, let alone to someone else, that we have made the conscious decision to be "other starters;" that we have carefully arrived at the decision that self starting is just not for us.

Trouble is, while it is not difficult to recognize the importance of self starting, it is easy to inadvertently fall into the trap of behaving like an "other starter," someone who is dependent upon others for their impetus to action. This is another example which, in spite of the fact that we know better, we don't necessarily do better. We don't necessarily translate what we know about self management into what we do as self managers.

FOSTERING DEPENDENCE

Being an "other starter" when self starting is what's needed can become the norm in spite of ourselves, if we're not careful. Here's what can happen.

We've got a responsibility that needs our attention. It may be one that we don't enjoy carrying out, that we don't feel confident about or it simply may have become lost among the many other things that need to be done. Whatever the reason, the responsibility is being neglected. However, this responsibility involves someone else, someone who is, in a sense, on the receiving end of that responsibility. It might be our external manager, a peer, a customer, or in our personal lives, a spouse, a child or a friend. If our neglect lasts long enough, there is a good chance that the someone else comes to our rescue. Because they require the results of our activity or perhaps out of concern regarding our nonperformance, they demand that we "smarten up" and get to work. We listen and soon we feel that we are now back on track.

The Cost of "Other Starting"

The job is getting done and as it should be, we're doing it. All's right with the world.

But is it? We didn't have only one job — the carrying out of the responsibility. We had another, at least as important — initiating the carrying out of that responsibility — and the latter job, the self-management job, was performed by someone else. We're back on track all right, but the question is, whose track? In a sense it has become someone else's, the someone else who took the self-direction responsibility that should have been ours. This doesn't have to occur very often until, inadvertently, the responsibility to initiate the activity is transferred from our self manager to the external source providing our impetus to action. We have become dependent upon someone else to get us moving. The more we allow the takeover, the more likely it will be to reoccur. We have unintentionally, and despite knowing better, become an "other starter."

The cost can be great. Our external starters are not around to jolt us into action most of the time and as a result, many of our responsibilities are attended to in an extremely untimely fashion, if at all. Without meaning to, and with the inadvertent and reluctant support of the people around us, we have fostered a dependence upon others as the source of our impetus to action. The chances are strong that our perceived value will spiral downward. We may not think like the speaker in our opening passage, like an "other starter," but we may behave that way and with potentially similar consequences.

There is another consequence of being a poor self starter, perhaps more costly than the disfavor we generate in the eyes of others. It has to do with those potential activities that begin as private, useful directions that only we can know about. This category includes the potential challenges, the potential opportunities that are ours to discover and act upon — or not. No one else can possibly provide our impetus to action because the action is only ours to know about. There is nobody else, for example, to push us into taking advantage of an opportunity that only we can identify. What they don't know about they can't insist upon. It's up to us.

However, the more dependent we become on others to provide our impetus to action, generally, the less likely we are to start ourselves in the directions that only we can know about — those requiring the greatest initiative, the highest order of proactivity. For those, if we don't provide the start, nobody else will because nobody else can. The potential opportunity will be lost.

The Invasiveness of Fostering Dependence

Whose responsibility is it to foster independence with regard to self starting, ours or the people around us? Occupationally, for example, does it belong to our external managers? Is it their responsibility to stay out of our way, to let us sink or swim, or is it ours to make sure that we keep afloat? Should we let our customers push us into action or should the push come from within? The answer is, of course, obvious. We are the managers of our own immediate performance and not because it's granted, but because it can only be so. Fostering independence is primarily up to us because providing the direction for our immediate activity, the independence itself, is primarily up to us. One of the difficulties is that the world can often appear to be hell-bent to wrest that responsibility from us or to not seem to want to give it to us in the first place.

We often learn "other starting" from our parents. Many parents, for example, have a tendency, while perhaps knowing the importance of independence training, to behave as if they're in the business of dependence training. This is a tendency easy to acquire, considering that we come into the world extremely dependent. Because our success is of great importance to our parents, when we're not initiating the activities necessary to succeed, understandably, they may well step in and try to do the initiating for us. Rather than allowing us to suffer the consequences of our inactivity, they intercede, provide our impetus to action and bring about the immediate success that comes from effective performance. Our present has been protected but what about our future, our future as self starters?

"Other starting" in the workplace is, at the same time, both frowned upon and virtually institutionalized. As was discussed in Chapter 2, the

Traditional Management Model leaves little room for self starting. The manager manages and the managee performs. The managee is the resource controlled by the manager. On-the-job management is ultimately seen as the responsibility of the external manager. When impetus to what is considered to be necessary action is not provided by the managee, it is seen as the manager's job to step in and see that the work gets done. For the welfare of the corporation, this is often a necessary intervention but can foster in the managee an unproductive dependence and a more defective self management. Of course, many managers, accepting the traditional mantle of owner of their people's performance, crack the whip, whether needed or not, thereby further fostering dependence.

The practice of fostering dependence is common and can be expensive to manager, managee and the organization. To the organization, because the positives that come from the proactive stance of a job owner as opposed to only a job doer, can be markedly reduced. To the manager, because it can lead to his increasing and ineffective takeover of the responsibilities of the people reporting to him. To the managee, because the critical activation responsibility of self starting is placed under attack.

One of the clearest examples of the insidiousness of fostering dependence was related to me while leading a self-management seminar a number of years ago, peopled by branch managers in retail banking. A participant shared this story. One of her employees had the clearly defined responsibility of submitting a particular report to head office at predetermined intervals. The bank manager slipped into the practice of reminding her staff member, just before deadline, that the task needed doing. One week, the manager's workload became too heavy to allow the inclusion of this, what was now, a traditional call to action. Not only was the report not submitted but, after the fact, the staff member stormed into her manager's office, angrily demanding the reason for her manager's having fallen down on the job! On the surface, the employee's outburst seems rather absurd, but a closer look at least raises the question of whose responsibility it had really become, not to perform the activity, but to initiate it.

Sales environments often provide a clear illustration of the tenacious nature of fostering dependence. Sales managers attempt to recruit for self starting and make it clear, from day one, that providing one's own impetus to action is essential if success is to be reached. Ask any sales manager, "Who must be responsible for motivating the sales staff?" and the answer will almost invariably be, "Each individual salesperson. It must come from within." At the same time, I doubt there is any management group that spends more time, on bended knee, trying to get their managees to breathe. The most concentrated management attention tends to be given in response to total inactivity, to an absence of self starting. The office door closes, the trumpets are sounded and while the tune being played may vary — anything from "Don't you care about your family?" to "Smarten up or suffer the consequences!" to "Is there anything I can do to help?" — an inordinate amount of management time and energy is spent attending to nonactivity. The meeting often results in a temporary burst of performance that rapidly dwindles until all is quiet, the silence signaling the need for yet another call to action.

The manager is spending the majority of time managing nothing, leaving little time for the people who could bring something to manage. The self starters tend to be ignored, precisely because they are doing the job. While the spoken message is "Self-start or else!" the behavioral message is "Self-start or I'll take over!" The large attrition rate seen in many sales-oriented industries may well be a result of the unintentional turning of budding self starters into highly consistent "other starters" and this, in spite of everyone knowing better.

The External Manager's Responsibility

This is a book about self management but because the area of self starting is so germane to critical issues like empowerment, job ownership and proactivity, and because, traditionally, performance management has often been aimed at creating effective "other starters," it is important to include a brief discussion about fostering independence and the external manager.

The tendency to focus on the negatives, discussed within the context of self-confidence, belongs to individuals not only when focusing on themselves. Often, for good, understandable reasons, the same tendency is reflected in the way we look at others, managers not being exempt. Because of its seriousness, employee nonperformance almost guarantees focus and is often the result, simply, of the managee not initiating the required performance — not self starting. Whether nonperformance should be attended to is not the issue. It obviously cannot be ignored. The issue is the kind of attention required.

When someone is assigned the responsibility of not only doing a job but being the initiator, the ownership of that initiating responsibility should be made clear, as should the consequences of not carrying it out. When initiation has not occurred, that is, when the individual's self manager has simply not done the job, care must be taken to deal with the situation; to ensure the job gets done while at the same time underlining rather than undermining the critical activation function of self starting.

The external manager must be careful not to fall into the trap of taking primary responsibility for managing people's immediate activity when they won't. He must recognize the deficit in self management, ensure the appropriate delivery of consequences and move on. He must stay out of the Phase 2, the Activation Phase, of the managee's Performance Cycle. Neither the self nor the external manager can afford the inappropriate intrusion. In the face of inactivity, energetic management support is inappropriate and potentially damaging. There is nothing to manage.

However, more intensive management attention should be given when self starting has occurred and a direction attempted. It is then that support for growth can be effectively offered and utilized. There is now something to manage. It is self starting and not its absence, performance and not nonperformance, that should be reinforced.

If you are a manager of others, help create self managers around you. It will not only foster their ongoing success but yours as well, by letting you focus your energy and expertise on the growth of your people.

THE ACTIVATION HABIT: PROTECT THE SELF-STARTING RESPONSIBILITY

While external management can have an important secondary role to play in fostering the independence of self starting, protecting and supporting the function is primarily the responsibility of the self manager, the manager of immediate performance.

The first critical step toward actively supporting self starting within ourselves is simply to recognize that the managing of immediate performance is primarily our responsibility; *that to effectively convert our potential into performance requires that we provide our own impetus to action*, regardless of whether others recognize the responsibility as being ours.

Whenever we find that someone else or some situation outside ourselves is calling us to action, that we are reactively responding to external pressure when we should have proactively self-directed, we must recognize that as a danger signal pointing to our not carrying out our self-management responsibility. Let this signal serve as a reminder that self starting is our responsibility, not as an excuse to give our "ignition key" away to someone or something else. "Other starter" is a label a self manager can ill afford.

It is important that self managers take seriously the self-starting function for those activities that only they can initiate, those areas of opportunity that only they can identify and act upon. Identify those areas and ensure that they get special attention. Include them first when generating your daily action plan, keeping in mind that for them, if *you* don't self start, you will not start at all. It's completely up to you.

PART III

MANAGING SELF COMMITMENT

Deciding What Will Be Done

> *A person must have the ability, must be aware of that ability, must make the right immediate-activity decisions regarding the application of that ability and **must translate those decisions into action**, if the ability is to bring about anything close to optimal performance, if the ability is to be optimally activated.*

INTRODUCTION

Motivation tends to be perceived as the primary factor determining performance, once things like the necessary skills and resources are in place. We know how important it is that a sports team be "up" for a big game. A good coach is seen largely as someone who knows how to motivate his players, individually and as a group. A strong leader in industry is perceived as being someone who can positively influence his people's commitment to corporate success. A good teacher is someone who knows not only what to communicate to his students, and can, but also can motivate them, can make them want to learn. We see our managers in society, from politicians to parents to teachers to supervisors, as having the critical function of serving as a source of motivation for those they manage. At the same time, we often appear to hold an opposing belief that no one can motivate an individual except the individual himself. In fact, however, our collective behavior tends to cover all the bases, to take no chances in this critical area. Regardless of our belief system, we hold anyone we can responsible for supplying this essential commodity — motivation. Once the potential exists, motivation is perceived as being a sufficient, perhaps the only sufficient, condition needed to bring about performance. Motivation is the key to success.

What is it that we mean when we talk about motivation? What does "to be motivated" signify? It means to want to — either to want to do something for its own sake or for what it brings. "I am really motivated to succeed" means "I want success in a big way." Assuming the potential is there, motivation is seen as being close to making success a certainty. After all, if a person has the opportunity to succeed, the skills to be successful and wants to, what could possibly get in the way?

However, all of us know people — often a lot of people — who are capable of success, truly want it and yet don't have it. There are even people, although fewer, who are capable of success, confident in their ability to get there, effectively self-directed and wanting it, who still don't get there. The truth is, few of us seek after failure *and there are a lot more capable people desirous of success than there are successful people.* Desire just isn't enough. Is it necessary? Absolutely. After all, if you have no desire to achieve something, why even pursue it? Still, it may not be sufficient.

Perhaps Samuel Johnson expressed it best when he said, "The road to hell is paved with good intentions." So often, we know exactly where we want to go (and it isn't hell), and we know exactly what we have to do to get there. Yet we end up doing something else, taking ourselves to where we didn't want to be and away from our desired destination. We give ourselves the right directions but still, we take another road. There are so many internal and external things that we allow to get in the way of translating our "shoulds" into "wills," even when we very much want the result that will come from the translation. What those things are and how to deal with them are discussed in the following chapters.

chapter **27** | # MANAGING EMOTIONAL MOTIVATION

At the beginning of a workweek, a manager asks one of his employees to make sure that a specific project gets completed, the file on his desk by Friday morning, at the very latest. The task falls well within the staff member's job description and ability and the manager makes it clear that the project must be given top priority, regardless of what else might be on the managee's plate. Thursday afternoon arrives and no file. The manager is tempted to say something but knowing that there is still time before the deadline, thinks better of it. Friday morning arrives and by eleven-thirty, still no file. Somewhat concerned, he goes to the employee's office, walks in and asks for the project report. The employee looks up from his desk and says, "It's not finished." The manager then asks, "Well, how far along are you?" The answer — "To tell you the truth, it's not even started." Now agitated, the manager asks, "Did I not make clear that it was essential that it be done by this morning?" "Yes, you did," answered the employee. "Then why didn't you do it?" asks the manager. "I didn't feel like it," is the reply.

*   *   *

When I ask people to give me some other words for the term "motivation," the list invariably includes entries like "drive," "urge," "desire," "energy," "enthusiasm" — words that suggest a "feeling-like-it" state. To be motivated to do something is to feel like doing it. To be highly motivated is to really feel like doing it, or to experience an almost irresistible urge. Is it any wonder that we see motivation as being important in supporting performance? It can provide a kind of push from within that let us pursue what we should, because we want to. We feel like doing what's good for us.

The trouble is, this state of "feeling like it," this emotional motivation, is somewhat difficult to sustain over time. For example, I really enjoy sirloin steak. It's one of my favorites. It would be fair to say that I'm pretty motivated when given the opportunity to partake. Still, if I've had steak for two nights running and get an invitation to a steak barbecue the next evening, I'd be motivated all right — motivated to find an excuse that would ensure my not having to face another New York strip. I can't sustain a high level of motivation for eating sirloin steak for three days in a row, and it's something I really enjoy. What chance, then, does my exercise program, or for that matter, my job have? In the abstract, sirloin remains something that I desire but for the immediate, it is not something I feel like having anything to do with.

There are few job-related activities that come close, for me, to being as motivating as a sirloin dinner. To wait until motivation hits might mean waiting for a long time and as far as consistency of performance is concerned — forget it. The fact of the matter is, if we had to depend on feeling like it, the kind of emotional state we attach to being motivated, to do the things we have to do to be successful, most of us would likely be in big trouble.

Imagine getting up, not now and again, but practically every morning and saying to yourself, with sincerity, "You know what I feel like doing today more than virtually anything else? I feel like doing all the things that are involved in getting my job done! Bring on the meetings, the paperwork, the complaints, more meetings, the conflicts, the reasonable demands, even the unreasonable demands. Let me at it!"

In truth, much of what most of us have to do to be successful places fairly low on our list of "feeling-like-it," and so being dependent on emotional motivation to make it happen can be dangerous. Is feeling-like-it motivation not a strong catalyst for performance? It certainly is. The critical question becomes performance of what?

THE DANGERS OF "FEELING-LIKE-IT" MOTIVATION

There are times when we generate optimal directions for ourselves, when we make a self commitment and elect, instead, to do something else. Much of the time, that something else is what we feel like doing, at least more than the commitment we abandoned and frequently, much more. Motivation strikes again. Motivation, as we generally think of it, feeling-like-it motivation, is, more often than not, not the support of success but its detractor. It gets in the way. Frequently, when we have "de-committed," it's in favor of something we're more motivated to do. Oh, we desire success, all right. However, the assumption that the desire to achieve something automatically becomes translated into the desire to do what has to be done to get there is somewhat suspect. Of course, we like doing what we feel like doing but in terms of the here and now, *what we feel like doing is often not consistent with what we intend to achieve in the longer term.* We may come up with the "right" direction but the motivation redirects. The salesperson intended to prospect but *felt like* having a cup of coffee with an associate who also had intended to prospect. The student intended to study but *felt like* watching the football game. The gourmand intended to diet but *felt like* having dessert. The manager intended to confront but *felt like* trying out that new computer program.

Perhaps the larger issue isn't "I feel like it" but "I don't feel like it." It isn't necessarily that we "de-commit" primarily because of the attractiveness of another direction, but because of the relative unattractiveness of the direction we were going to choose. We determine a direction and to ourselves we make a commitment to follow that direction. Its time comes and we simply walk away, telling ourselves, "I don't feel like it." We then cast around to find something we do feel more like doing. This process of de-committing need take only moments.

A Place for Emotional Motivation

Of course, for some things this motivation is appropriate. For example, there are times when we make decisions in the immediate present that are only about the immediate present. They don't relate to any larger time frame but have to do with determining how best to experience the "now." They are about feeling like it. Deciding early in the day to see a serious movie that evening and then, after an "I don't feel like it," choosing a comedy, is certainly appropriate. In fact, considering that the objective is having an enjoyable evening, to stick to your guns and sit through the drama would be the inappropriate decision.

There are other times, however, when "I don't feel like it" can become a serious barrier to self commitment, when the decision to de-commit is an inappropriate and costly one. The interesting thing is that at the moment of decision, we behave as if it is perfectly appropriate to walk away from the self commitment, a direction we've issued to ourselves, simply because *we don't feel like carrying it out.* The only cost we've considered is the cost to the moment and we've allowed that cost to determine our immediate performance. The direction is chosen, the ability in place, we're confident that we can carry it out but the feeling-like-it motivation is missing. The result — our performance potential remains unconverted. We don't activate.

"I Don't Get No Respect"

This chapter began with what I hope was seen to be a somewhat ludicrous illustration. A manager directs his managee to complete an important project. When it isn't done by deadline, the reason given by the managee is, "I didn't feel like it." Absence of performance, and especially the reason given for it, would be considered totally unacceptable. But let's look in the mirror for a moment.

We not only carry out our own immediate performance. We manage it. We have the responsibility of managing the performance moment of truth — that moment when the doing happens. As self managers it is our responsibility to decide what it is that should be done from moment to moment; to issue the directions intended to determine immediate activity. As performers, however, there is probably not one of us who has not pulled exactly what the managee did in the illustration that begins this chapter. We get an appropriate order from our self manager, we answer with "I don't feel like it" and then behave accordingly, as if how we feel about the order had some relevance.

The trouble is, it really seems as though it is relevant at the time. After all, there are many things that we do, only because we feel like it. We regularly make appropriate decisions based on our preference of the moment, and so it seems to be a perfectly sensible thing to do. In many situations, however, how we feel about doing an activity, whether or not we find it pleasurable, is no more relevant for us than it was for our managee in the opening illustration. We are the boss of our immediate performance and in certain areas of life, it is ridiculous for us to respond to our self manager's direction with "I don't feel like it and so I won't do it." It just doesn't feel ridiculous. We have a desired objective, we know the immediate activity needed to serve that objective, we intend to carry it out but at the moment for action we block the conversion of potential because we don't feel like it and the blocking can take an instant. Foiled by motivation — feeling-like-it motivation.

However, success motivation deserves a different definition. *Success motivation can be defined as the intellectual commitment to do what has to be done to bring about success, whether we feel like it or not.* There is no doubt that if we happen to feel like carrying out the direction, all the better. Nevertheless, we must not allow it to be a determining factor.

THE ACTIVATION HABIT: "WHO ASKED YOU!"

Primary versus Support Activities

Not all activity areas fit into the category, "Saturday Night At the Movies." That is, the activities are not fundamentally performed for their own intrinsic value. We arrive at a large number of activity decisions because of their anticipated effect on reaching other longer-term objectives. These support activities are not determined because of how they feel but because of what they do. It is when the objective that they serve matters to us, for whatever reason, that we must deal with them differently than we do with activities that are the objectives in themselves, that exist primarily for their own sake.

Manage Your Freedom

It is also important to appreciate that, when it is time to activate these support activities, even though there is usually no boss in sight, the presence of someone in authority is necessary. That someone is your self manager.

Although it's true that we have the freedom to choose whether or not we will listen to the directions of our internal boss, we can ill afford to abuse that freedom. It isn't difficult to fall into the trap of behaving as if there were no consequences to our deciding to de-commit simply because there is no one standing over our shoulder to prevent or immediately punish the decision. The illusion of freedom from responsibility is easier to conjure up when there is no external boss watching, but illusion it is and it must be recognized and dealt with accordingly.

For those immediate-activity directions, those should's that serve objectives that matter, it is important to make a contract with yourself that the word of your self manager is law. *Give your self manager the authority to manage your potential regardless of any momentary activity preferences that you might have.* However, because giving legitimacy to an illegitimate preference is such an easy barrier to trip over, it's not enough to only have this somewhat abstract conceptual agreement with yourself. It is also important to establish and continuously strengthen more specific activation practices.

First, define those life areas in which enjoyment should not be a primary factor in determining whether or not you follow through on immediate-activity directions you give yourself. You will likely find the list to be a fairly comprehensive one. For those areas, *assign authority to your self manager.*

Self-Manage Feeling-Like-It Motivation

Now for the day at hand. After you've determined the items of your daily action plan, review each direction to see which, if any, have an unwritten "If I feel like it" immediately following. (You may well find some. It makes us feel better to have the direction out there as part of the day's recipe, but deep down we intend to treat it as optional.) If so, ask yourself the question, Does momentary preference belong? If the answer is No, remind yourself that you're looking at a direction to be followed if appropriate, not if preferred, and be on the lookout for sabotage from within. If the answer is Yes, strike it from your list of commitments for the day. You may want to include it on your wish list, on those activities that you *might* do rather than those you've decided you *will* do. There is nothing wrong with having a wish list, but it's important that you not depend on its being carried out. When working specifically on building this activation habit, include one more direction in your daily action plan: Be on the lookout for the irrelevant "I don't feel like it." The instruction will aid recognition.

Now, to the immediate present, keeping in mind that many immediate-activity directions don't get written down. For those directions, appropriately issued as orders by your self manager, the instant that an "I don't feel like it" is noted, respond with an internal *"Who asked you!"* and order yourself back to work. Use those exact words. They will effectively serve as a reminder that how you feel about the activity under consideration is irrelevant and must be treated as such.

chapter 28 | MANAGING SELF TRUST

"MIRROR, MIRROR, ON THE WALL"

"Whom do you trust?" If you're looking in the mirror when you ask that question, the answer coming back may not be to your liking. That's not to suggest that people can't trust you — other people, that is. Chances are good that the statement, "My word is my bond" is one that applies strongly to the approach you have to the world. Most of us, after all, pride ourselves on our dependability. A promise given is, if at all possible, a promise kept. For many of us, however, there is often one glaring exception to this honorable stance. That exception — ourselves.

Of course, we don't intentionally treat ourselves shabbily. In fact, most of us aren't even aware of the discrepancy that can exist between the value of our word when given to others and its value when we are the recipient. I believe, however, that the discrepancy is not uncommon and this belief is supported by a survey I have often taken in seminars.

The participants are asked to approximate the number of promises to others that they have broken over the period of the past three weeks. Very few broken promises are reported. They are then asked to approximate the number of self promises that they did not keep over the same three-week period. *The number given is virtually always many times greater.* Some participants have suggested that the discrepancy may be the result of making many more promises to ourselves than we do to others and so there are more to break. That may be a factor contributing to the difference, but it is probably not the primary one in that participants report a high level of guilt associated with broken promises to others and little, if any, associated with promises given to themselves.

Possibilities Rather Than Promises

It would seem, then, that we look very differently at promises given to others than we do promises we make to ourselves. In fact, I'm not sure that we even consider the commitments we make to ourselves as belonging to that rarified category of promises. Promises are something we make to others. We give ourselves suggestions. Oh, we don't call them that but our approach to them implies that that is, in fact, what they are. The reason that the statement "My word is my bond" may not apply when directed at ourselves is that it isn't really our word that we give to ourselves. To us we deliver possibilities. To others we deliver promises.

A personal admission. Were I to promise a neighbor, one I hardly know, that I would help him with something next Sunday afternoon, even something unimportant, chances are very good that I'd be there, even if it meant refusing an unexpected offer of tickets to the ball game. I wouldn't necessarily be happy, but I'd be there. If, instead, I promised myself a few hours to work on an important project that same Sunday afternoon and got the same offer, chances are a lot better that hot dogs and crackerjacks would be the fare for the day and what's more, the choice would probably have been an easy one to make. (Easy and smart are not always synonymous.)

That we don't readily think of our self commitments as being promises has very serious ramifications with regard to our level of activation. In the first place, we are many times more dependent on our performance than we are on the performance of anyone else to bring about our own success, whatever the life area and however we define that success. Our fulfillment is primarily up to us. Conversely, no one (with the exception, perhaps, of young children) needs us nearly as much as we need ourselves. It doesn't matter how much we may want someone else to be successful or how much we may be willing to do to bring it about; unless they take the primary responsibility for making it happen, it simply won't. Just ask a parent.

For many of us, the person who is most dependent on us for their well-being is also the person toward whom we frequently manifest the smallest degree of dependability. If the answer to the question, "Mirror, mirror on the wall, who can you trust most of all?" is "Sure as heck not you!" the chances are awfully good that many of the objectives that you have are slipping, or perhaps plummeting, away.

Other Contributing Factors to Self Dishonor

Although the attitude we take toward self promises is probably the largest contributor to self dishonor, there are others that play a role. One of them has already been mentioned. We overcommit to ourselves. Of course, many of us overcommit to others as well, but because we need more from ourselves and because we are aware of those many needs and are with ourselves all the time, an overloading of self promises can easily occur. We don't keep our self commitments because we make too many of them. Related to that is the ease with which we can simply forget that we made them. In the rush of the immediate, they get lost.

Another factor has to do with the opportunity we have to play games with ourselves that we can't as easily play with others. We make a self promise, to be fulfilled sometime before the day is over. Time goes by and the window of opportunity is fast closing. Within moments, if we're not careful, we can bring about a remarkable conversion. "That wasn't an actual commitment, really," we say to ourselves. That was an, "I should try if I get a chance; if I have time on my hands." We instantly move the intention from commitment to wish.

THE ACTIVATION HABIT: TO THINE OWN SELF BE TRUE

The Plan

The daily action plan can serve to help support our level of self honor. First, it reduces the likelihood that we will overcommit, in that planning deals not only with what can be handled in a day but also with what cannot. That there are only so many hours in the day becomes obvious when those hours are being planned.

Second, for those self commitments that get written down, their very inclusion on our list of priority activities reduces their vulnerability. They cannot as easily be forgotten. Nor can we, as easily, believe the magic of turning promise to wish when we have evidence of the nature of the intention staring us in the face. We can't fool ourselves into believing that the intention really is not a priority when it has already been assigned high-priority status. Starting the day with a considered list of directions is a critical self-management practice.

Do Unto Self

Most important, how do we get closer to treating our self promises in the same way as we do our promises to others? How do we increase our dependability with regard to self commitments, our level of self honor?

Develop this habit. The moment that you find yourself about to walk away from a self commitment, from a direction that you have already determined to be a valuable one to take, ask yourself this simple question:

- Would I be walking away from this commitment had it been made to somebody else?

If the answer comes back a resounding No!, then think again.

We may still walk away, of course. However, both the question and answer can serve an important function. They can remind us of how dependent we are on our own level of self trust and that promises to self must be considered with at least the degree of seriousness we give to the promises we make to others.

chapter 29 | AIMING TO PLEASE

THE SOCIAL LESSON

We place a high value on altruism, on fulfilling the needs of others, not for our sake but for theirs. Its importance is very much a part of religious teaching that reflects and supports altruistic behavior. We see it reflected in our fictional heroes who are often largely defined by that characteristic. The well-known film, *It's a Wonderful Life*, for example, is about someone who spends his life almost entirely altruistically. In *Les Miserables*, Jean Valjean risks and loses his freedom, not in an attempt to feed himself, but to find bread for his younger sister. Adventure heroes are notable, not only because of the good that they do but because they risk life and limb to do it.

Some of our child-rearing practices also reflect the value we place on serving the needs of others. The sharing behavior by younger children is energetically celebrated, even when the sharing has been helped along through some serious parental pressure. A social lesson, received early and repeated often, is that serving others is important and valued. Understandably, throughout life, we continue to receive appreciation for our efforts on other peoples' behalf. The expression, "He'd give you the shirt off his back," meaning that person would do virtually anything for anybody, is seen as a positive statement about someone who takes his responsibility toward others seriously, so seriously, in fact, that he is willing to sacrifice dramatically, no matter the circumstances.

As can happen with other social lessons, some of us learn this one too well. We go in the direction of other people's needs, not as much because we decide to, but because we have been programmed to. We have an almost automatic response to a request — a well-developed knee-jerk reaction. Fortunately, the specific resultant behavior is often what we should do. That is, it not only fits society's values generally, but our own belief system specifically, so that the direction we follow is the right one both for us and for the person wanting our support. However, even though we may have taken the right direction, it may not be because we made a responsible self-management decision to do so. The decision was somebody else's. We were other rather than self directed — same result but a very different trigger.

RELINQUISHING MANAGEMENT RESPONSIBILITY

This *automatic* aiming to please can be a serious de-activator. We have a fundamental responsibility to others, no doubt. But we also have a fundamental responsibility to ourselves. At times, the existence of the two responsibilities does not create a problem; at other times, they conflict. This happens when we and someone else are in need of our services for the same period of time and we must choose. For the pleasers among us who "can't" (as opposed to "don't") say No, who say Yes virtually automatically, the choice is often made without thinking. We are propelled in the direction of the needs and wants of others, often trying to rationalize the appropriateness of the decision after it has been made, in the hope that we can comfortably justify it to ourselves. In making the decision, we have considered one responsibility while ignoring the other — the responsibility to ourselves. Again, I am not suggesting that we not attend to the needs of others — only that we also take our own needs into account.

This tendency can have a serious effect on the level of our self-management functioning — it can virtually eliminate the function entirely. We may have an objective, the ability to reach it, and know we can, and have decided on the activity needed to achieve our goal. The last necessary step is to convert the direction into activity, and were the world to leave us alone, that may be exactly what would happen. However, the world seldom leaves us alone. Just as we are about to follow our own direction, someone says "Me, please," and off we go, but in their direction.

We are not being self-managed. We are being managed by whoever happens to be nearest. No one else really knows what is on our plate and frequently, our plate is not what's on their mind. They are not in a position to determine what the best choice for us would be. Only we are. However, we've taken ourselves out of the action. We are allowing others to make our immediate-activity decisions for us, whether they are the right ones or the wrong ones for a particular moment in time. We may know exactly where we want to go, but instead find ourselves all over the map and often the map belongs to someone else.

The Cost of Reflexive Pleasing

The consequences of this barrier to activation can be clearly seen in many areas of life and in many occupations. I have seen managers become virtually dysfunctional because they not only practice an open-door policy, they, in effect, have no door. They are viewed by their managees as being the most supportive managers on the planet. The trouble is, they find little time and energy to pursue some of their own critical objectives and ultimately, they, the organization and their managees suffer. Inadvertently, rather than supporting growth they stifle it — in themselves and others.

Teams now form a larger part of the occupational landscape and within the team context, its members are expected to support each others' productivity. At the same time, it remains primarily the cumulative performance of each individual, functioning independently, that ultimately determines the effectiveness of the team. However, the team member whose response to the request, "Got a minute?" is an automatic, reflexive Yes, is, on the surface, seen as the teammate *par excellence*. Of course, the request really has little to do with time, the word "minute" being symbolic for anything from a real minute to hours. The problem, though, is that this team member, having little time to attend to his individual responsibilities, while perceived as being, perhaps, the strongest link in the chain, may really be its weakest. His primary job doesn't get done. Because a weak link can bring a chain down, there can be great cost to the team and to the organization, the reason being a severe deficit in self management on the part of this tremendously supportive team member.

The performance of the reflexively pleasing sales representative, whose sales arena is the client's world rather than his own, can be very much at risk, the dangers coming from various sources. Other colleagues, needing the ear of someone, know exactly where to go for that ear — the person who will leave whatever he is doing, simply upon request. Often, precisely because of the freedom or amount of self determination inherent in the job, the sales representative's friends and family, when needing some support during the workday, know exactly where to go for help. They can't seek out the people with a "real" job, people with a time clock, symbolic or actual, and so the available and willing favor giver gets the job, every time — but not his job. Theirs.

I remember one participant of a seminar, a sales representative, saying that her parents had moved to a warmer climate to live out their retirement, she and all of her siblings remaining in the home city. Although she had no doubt that her parents loved her and wanted her to be successful, it was always she and never her siblings who received the phone call that announced their impending visit. And they visited often, the expectation being that she would drop everything and support their stay for as long as it lasted. This was simply because, she later realized, that they didn't understand the demands of her job and she hadn't explained them. The problem was not, of course, the phone call but her automatic, accommodating response. Not surprisingly, however, until examining the issue, her cry had been "If only they would leave me alone," as if she had no part to play in creating this difficult situation.

The performance problems that the habit of reflexively pleasing can cause do not only apply to the area of work. Some of the stories shared by seminar participants over the years clearly demonstrate the destructiveness that this de-activator can have.

A number of years ago, at the end of a discussion of the issue, "Aiming to Please," a man nearing retirement, older than anyone else in the seminar, asked if he could address everyone from the front of the room. He proceeded to list a number of things — his job, various community services, his church and at the end of the list, his family. He then looked at us and said, "All my life, I have always said Yes to a request for my time, whether from work or . . . ." and he went down the list. "The result was that I was almost never home and the one item on this list that got virtually nothing from me was the item that was always the most important to me — my family. That was my self commitment and now it's too late. Take this discussion seriously." He had tears in his eyes. The room became very quiet.

At another seminar, during a coffee break, someone told me this story. He said that he loved carpentry and had recently decided that it was time to finish his basement. Because the year before had been very pressured, he made the difficult decision that it would be best for both him and for his family, if he hired someone else to do the basement, in spite of the expense. One week after contracting the renovator he got a call from a friend, completely inexperienced in working with his hands, requesting help on finishing his basement. The storyteller then sadly reported that he had spent his entire summer in the basement of his friend's home, hammer in hand, bank account depleted.

Please know that there is no attempt here to suggest that we should not support the objectives of others or that we should do it only when there is virtually no cost to ourselves. On the contrary, it is extremely important that we take our responsibility to others very seriously. Even were one to ignore the moral implications of the issue, none of us — our families, our organizations, our societies — could survive, were we to not take our responsibility to others seriously. In fact, many of our problems stem from not taking them seriously enough.

There is no doubt that when the two responsibilities, responsibility to self and responsibility to others, are in conflict, there are times when we should choose our commitment to others over our self commitment. However, when both responsibilities are vying for our potential, the choice must arise from a management decision by us as self managers, not from a knee-jerk reaction. There is a decision to be made about the immediate activation and de-activation of our performance potential, and we must take seriously the making of that decision. As self managers, that is our responsibility.

The Two Primary Responsibilities

The difficulty is that many of us have been, perhaps inadvertently, taught the lesson that we're not even supposed to ask the question. We are simply supposed to go in the direction of the other person's request. The issue is treated as being bipolar, and one can take one of two stances. One can be selfish and that's bad, or one can be selfless and that's good, the selfish person being only concerned with his own objectives and the selfless, only with the objectives of others.

In reality, both are bad. The universal condition suggests that we must, in fact, take both seriously. We have both responsibilities and both must be satisfied. When they're in conflict, we cannot afford to ignore either. Both must be considered and our potential then directed to the responsibility that needs us most. We must be continuously both self- and other-concerned. We must make a management decision.

THE ACTIVATION HABIT: MAINTAIN MANAGEMENT AUTHORITY

The habit to build is a simple one. When you have made a self commitment and someone else asks you instead to commit to them, ask the following two questions:

- What are the consequences to me if I go in the direction of the other person's request?
- What are the consequences to the other person if I go in the direction of my self commitment?

We think very quickly. By asking yourself these questions you will have rapidly analyzed the situation and be in a position to assess which responsibility requires your potential most. You will now be in a position to make a knowledgeable management decision, and you will have maintained your authority over managing that potential, an authority that only you can effectively exercise.

The choice will still not always be a clear one but most of the time there will be no contest. The "winner" will be obvious. Even when you know what the right choice should be, you still might not make it. However, the decision, good or bad, will have been a decision, not a knee-jerk reaction. It will have been your decision, its consequences understood.

A Word to the Timid

Some of us have great difficulty saying No even when we have determined that No is what should be said. This problem often has, as its underlying cause, a confidence deficit, and so working on building the skills of self-confidence will help. More particularly and perhaps as a quicker fix, practice saying No. Role-play different, direct, simple ways of refusing a request. "I have another commitment that must be attended to." "Sorry, I don't have a minute, right now." This will make it easier when your self-management decision goes in the direction of your self commitment.

It still may be difficult, especially at first, but after realizing that the sky hasn't fallen, it will soon become easier. If you have virtually always said Yes in the past, some people may become offended at your refusal, their expectation having been that a Yes from you had become their right. In the beginning, they may not like you as well, but chances are you will like yourself a lot better. After not too long, as your self respect grows, so will their respect for you.

| # MANAGING PROCRASTINATION

Procrastination is perhaps the most infamous of all barriers to self commitment. Virtually all of us put off doing things. We then recognize the costs associated with it, especially immediately after receiving the bill; still we procrastinate again. What makes this destructive practice so tenacious? Why do we continue to repeat it even though we know better?

We've already discussed one kind of procrastination, the inappropriate postponing of activity decisions. What we'll be looking at here is the inappropriate postponing of the activity after the decision has been made. Why do we do it and how can we diminish this destructive practice?

THE POWER OF PROCRASTINATION

Want to feel good? Want to get an instant rush and at virtually no immediate cost? If the answer is Yes (and why wouldn't it be, really?) here's what you do.

Put off something you have already decided to do today that you really don't enjoy doing. Don't postpone it for good. Simply decide that you are going to do it at some other time. Now, how do you feel?

One of the reasons that procrastination gets in the way of performance as often as it does and in spite of our knowing better, is that it frequently carries with it an immediate sense of relief. It's almost as if we regain positive time, simply by the act of postponing what we don't enjoy doing, and in a way, that's true. Usually we spend the newly repossessed moments more enjoyably than if we had honored our self commitment. If there is some tension attached to the activity targeted for procrastination, (and there usually is; otherwise, why procrastinate?), the moment we engage the "I'll do that some other time" lever, a sense of relief spills over us. Immediate reward and at no cost! We've done nothing and been rewarded for it, to boot, at least for the moment. Good deal. After all, how often do we get something for nothing? Is it any wonder that we keep coming back for more?

But there's still more to the power of procrastination. Even though we may not have carried out our commitment, our perception of ourselves as a responsible citizen remains intact. It's not as if we've walked away from our responsibility. We have simply moved its realization to some other time zone. Walk away from a commitment? Never! We've de-committed and still, our self image is untouched.

It can get even better. Often, at the moment of postponement, we see ourselves in the crystal ball of our mind's eye carrying out the deployed commitment more effectively than if we had actually kept it. We're not in an optimal frame of mind at this moment, the time just isn't right, but tomorrow will be different and then, why we'll be terrific! We smile, inwardly, just thinking about the high quality of our future performance. Postponement begins to feel like no ordinary self-management decision but one with Solomonic overtones. However, regardless of the reason for procrastinating, we do, momentarily, see the job being done during some tomorrow and almost always being done well. Why picture it being done poorly? Minimally, it would spoil our moment of immediate relief and imagined future success.

A personal illustration. One of the outdoor activities I enjoy least is raking leaves. In spite of my obvious disapproval, however, they continue to fall, covering the lawn, every autumn. As the weather gets colder my recognition that there is a problem in need of a solution grows, until finally I pick the date for raking — always a number of days away. The decision may be, for example, that raking will happen next Wednesday evening. The appointed hour arrives. I look out my study window at all the leaves covering the ground and make a self-management re-decision. Leaf raking is a weekend job, and by hook or by crook, this weekend those leaves get bagged!

Upon making this re-decision, two positive things happen instantaneously, both feelings. The first is the pleasant sensation that comes from knowing that tonight will be free of raking. The second is a feeling that comes from an image appearing as I gaze onto the lawn. I picture, in my mind's eye, the yard as it will look on Sunday afternoon, a yard entirely devoid of leaves. Not one fallen leaf to be seen anywhere. A perfect job. Not only by my procrastinating do I generate a sense of relief, but a rather remarkable sense of accomplishment, as well. During the act of procrastinating, alone, do I leaf rake at a world-class level.

Procrastination is such a tenacious barrier to self commitment because of the immediate, positive gains it brings with it. We de-commit, immediately feel better because of it (although there is often a quiet gnawing discomfort far in the background) and at the same time remain highly responsible and accomplished in our own view, at least if we don't look too closely.

THE ACTIVATION HABIT: BLOCK PROCRASTINATION

The self manager has to accomplish two things at this point. First, he has to check to see whether there are negative performance consequences associated with postponing the self direction, consequences that he may not really want to look at. Second, he must counteract the feeling of relief and the illusion of accomplishment that so often accompany procrastination.

Face the Consequences

The decision to procrastinate is usually made quickly. It's not an issue that is pondered at length, carefully evaluated and then resolved. The possibility is entertained and the self-management choice is made, often within moments. The question that we ask ourselves during those moments of decision is: "*Can* I do that tomorrow?" For some commitments the answer comes back quickly and clearly, No, but many, if not most of the things that we've committed to can be done tomorrow. Of course, eventually we run out of tomorrows but until that happens the answer we receive to the question is "Yes, you can do that tomorrow." The path to the decision, "I will do that, tomorrow," is now easily traveled.

The problem is, that was the wrong question. As self managers, if we are to support activation we must ask a different one. We must ask, not "Can I do that tomorrow?" but "*Should* I do that tomorrow?" This question may elicit a different answer. There are many commitments that can be postponed until some tomorrow but not without specific cost. Others may, in themselves, not suffer but *should* be honored today if for no other reason than that tomorrow's plate is likely to be full. It is the self manager's responsibility to find out. There is nothing negative about postponement of carrying out a commitment when it is without cost or with benefit. It becomes procrastination when there is a cost involved. The question, *Should* I do that tomorrow? allows us to make the distinction, and act appropriately.

Block the Delusion

Now comes the hard part. The relief we feel upon making the decision to procrastinate is real. While the "pain" may only be postponed, even a temporary reprieve often feels better than none at all. In addition, though the picture of tomorrow's accomplishment exists solely in our imagination, the sense of accomplishment generated is real and positive. The reward, deserved or not, gets delivered.

As self managers, to neutralize the illusion, it is important that we identify it. *Wipe the smile off your face.* The moment you note a decrease in tension or the welling up of a feeling of pride associated with the imagined job well done, ask yourself, "What are you smiling about? At best, you have done nothing and doing nothing is no great accomplishment."

By developing the habit of asking the "should" question and identifying the imagined accomplishment for what it is, you will have, within moments, both interfered with the dash toward tomorrow and increased the probability that decision rather than impulse will determine your immediate performance.

chapter **31** | # THE PRIVACY OF SELF COMMITMENT

THE POWER OF AUDIENCE

The presence of an audience can have a significant effect on our behavior. There are things that we do in private, things that are legal and allowed, that we would not even consider doing in public. We just wouldn't want anyone to know we do "that."

One of my favorite examples concerns a close friend, someone I admired, in part because of the even-tempered, supportive stance she took toward her children, regardless of circumstance. It wasn't that she didn't discipline them, but even the disciplining was done with a large measure of calm. One midweek afternoon I went to her door when she was not expecting me because I needed to pick up something. I was about to ring the doorbell when my hand froze in midair. I heard, coming from behind the closed door, an explosive and continuous scream of words, in which were included many that even my veteran ears were unused to. My finger then settled on the button, the chime instantly followed by silence and at the door appeared Mother Earth, enveloped by her cover of consistent calm. The power of audience.

Our self commitments are denied this power. The good news about breaking a self commitment, especially when its content has nothing to do with anyone else but ourselves, is that nobody knows that it happened. The de-commitment is our secret, and our public reputation remains intact. Of course, the bad news is also the same news. The fact that no one is there makes it easier so that many of the important self commitments that we make are vulnerable simply because they are self commitments.

I do not suggest that it is important to keep a self commitment simply because it was made. Also, the emphasis is not meant to fall on the concept of commitment. It is the "self" that is the concern. The honoring of some self commitments may not be important. However, there are many that are made because they are important to us; because their fulfillment becomes our fulfillment. They form part of what we are or what we want to be. When, because of something we do or omit to do, a commitment that serves our significant objectives fails, it is we who lose. This becomes clear the symbolic morning after, when the feeling of regret for what we did or did not do, dominates and we know it to be real.

THE ACTIVATION HABIT: MAKE SELF COMMITMENTS "PUBLIC"

One of the ways that various self-help groups — for example, groups on alcohol and tobacco use, gambling and overeating — support their members, is by having them share self commitments with the group. It's as if the members are saying, "I promise you that I will keep the promise I made to me." The private commitment has become a public one. Sales organizations often attempt to use the power of audience by posting everyone's sales results, the theory being that having witnesses to your level of productivity may increase it. Generally, setting annual objectives that traditionally happen between external manager and managee is not only a method of generating appropriate goals, but of turning them into promises made to someone else.

As self manager, you can support the activation of self commitments by moving them out of the private realm and into the public. One way of doing that is to put your reputation on the line. Rather than keeping the commitment to yourself, tell someone else that you've made it. Let someone else know about the promise, so that if you don't live up to it, you won't be the only one to know what your word is really worth. This might provide support in translating intention into action.

Of course, we can't, or wouldn't want to, do that with all of the commitments we make to ourselves. Some of them we may want no one else to know about. Others, no one else may want to know about. For example, my self commitment to eliminate all sugar from any coffee that I drink was probably as interesting to my friends when I made it as it was to you when you read it. Some commitments we make to ourselves, only we care about. Making them public could have some negative social consequences even if they were kept. More importantly, we make numerous self commitments, large and small, throughout a day and even if people were interested, we haven't the time to publicize, nor they to listen.

VIRTUAL PUBLICITY

We can, however, make our commitments "public" in our imagination. We all know, or have known, people whose respect we value, people whose opinion, especially of us, matters. We may not be able to physically convene this audience, but we can create them in our mind's eye whenever we feel their presence is required.

Determine the members of your valued "virtual" audience and when about to de-commit, ask the following:

- If my virtual audience were watching and knew I'd made the commitment, would I still be walking away?

Often, asking the question is enough to activate the commitment. Though the answer, "If they were witness, there's no way that I would be walking away," is no guarantee that the commitment will be converted into performance, it will give pause and the opportunity to reconsider. If a commitment is one that we would not want people we respect to see us abandoning, it may be one to take seriously.

chapter 32 | GENERATING ENERGY

In sports, it's not uncommon to hear a team or individual athlete described as having been "up" for the game. That's not to say, however, that when not "up" for a game, the team or player is "down." Being "up" doesn't simply imply being motivated, that is, wanting to win. It's really more than that. It means *really, really* wanting to win and as a result, experiencing the level of motivation, optimal for supporting performance. It means being optimally energized. It's that extra juice that provides a motivational edge. In a play-off, for example, both teams are likely to place very high on the motivational ladder. The team described as being really "psyched" is just that one notch higher on the "feeling-like-it" continuum, enough to bring victory, all other things being equal.

Earlier, success motivation was defined as being the intellectual commitment to do what has to be done to bring about success *whether we feel like it or not*. Sports has the advantage of also being supported by a relatively high "feeling-like-it" motivational level. You will hear veteran athletes say that they intend to stop playing the moment that it stops being fun and they mean fun, literally. Often, a manager in the occupational world will tell his people that it's important that their work be fun, but the pronouncement frequently has a somewhat hollow ring to it — a statement of the ideal rather than of the real. The truth of the matter is that for many of us, being up does not describe an emotional state associated with most of the activities that bring about success in our work lives. We'd better be intellectually committed precisely because much of the time, that's all there is.

Saying that feeling like it and the energy that it generates had better not be the kind of motivation that primarily determines success, is not to say that it isn't a useful, positive state to be in. There is little doubt that deciding something must be done, acting on the decision and feeling like it, beats acting on the decision but not feeling like it. Minimally, it makes the doing more enjoyable. There is also the possibility that when you are up for an activity, the likelihood of a higher activation level is increased. The increase in energy may result in your doing a better job. Saying that emotional motivation had best not be a necessity in bringing about the immediate performance needed for success is not to say it isn't a good thing to have.

However, a problem exists for some of us, precisely because we may like what we do professionally, but we do not often have our adrenaline pumping and experience a rush of excitement, "high-fiving" whoever is nearest, as we prepare to carry through with the next item on our daily action planner. Energy may not be commonly generated by our anticipation of work to be done.

Also, we tend to think of energy level as something outside our realm of immediate control. We're stuck. Our work may not generate it and we don't see ourselves as being able to, at least, directly. We know that it's valuable and it is certainly something we hope to have plenty of. We may pay attention to diet, physical exercise and the amount of sleep we're getting, in an attempt to increase our level of energy, but that is a far cry from being able to manipulate it at will. From the vantage point of the immediate present we see ourselves largely as victims rather than determiners of our energy level.

To some extent, of course, we are. State of health, age, time of day, biorythms, ventilation, lighting, all of these and more can affect our immediate level of energy. That is not to say, however, that we cannot exert some level of direct control, as well. We can, but most of us don't even attempt to do so.

THE ACTIVATION HABIT: ENERGIZE

The self manager's responsibility is not to light the motivational fire because of the task at hand, but in many instances, in spite of it. For one thing, most of us have to do some things, the anticipation of which simply does not and will not generate an energy increase. They are neutral, boring or downright unenjoyable, and no amount of rationalizing can up their intrinsic value. Rather than energizing, if anything, they can de-energize.

Many of us make little use of our ability to energize, to increase our perceived level of energy, not associated with any activity other than the energy raising itself. We often do it unintentionally. We're walking alone, for example, energy level relatively low and an acquaintance, unnoticed by us, walks by and offers a greeting. We look up, focus in and immediately, as we are about to engage in animated conversation, we not only appear to be more energized, but that is what we experience within ourselves. Did the behavior change bring about the change in energy, or did we automatically raise our energy level which, in turn, affected our behavior? Perhaps a bit of both. However, the how is not all that important. What is important is that simply by willing it we can change our energy level. Harnessing that ability to energize allows the self manager to take greater control of a kind of feeling-like-it motivation. Our level of emotional motivation then becomes somewhat dependent on us rather than the other way around. While we cannot afford to be dependent on emotional motivation as a necessary activator, that does not mean that it isn't nice to have and that it can't serve to increase our conversion rate. It is, and it can. Whether we enjoy the use of this activation bonus is up to us.

ENERGIZE UPON DEMAND

A Breathing Exercise

The act of inhaling can effectively be paired with the self instruction to energize. To accomplish this, simply take two or three fairly deep, slow breaths and while breathing in, give yourself the simple instruction, "*As you breathe in, feel your energy level increase."* Practice this a number of times a day until it becomes easy, and use it upon demand.

Be Your Own Cheering Section

We often give other people words of encouragement just before they are about to enter a demand situation, a version of "Go get 'em, Tiger." When spectators at a game, we often applaud our team or individual players, not only as a sign of appreciation, but as an attempt to raise their level of motivation. Sometimes in the press, players request that their fans add a source of motivation by getting into the game and making as much noise as they can.

There is no reason that we cannot act as our own cheering section, silently offering ourselves the kind of encouragement that we offer others. We may not always be as loud, but we are very much more available.

"Image" the Feeling

Every one of us knows what it feels like to be highly energized. One of the easiest and quickest ways to increase energy level is to simply image the feeling; to simply give yourself the instruction, *"Energize!"* and image it happening. Hone and apply your ability to self-energize as an inexpensive but effective activator.

chapter **33** | # MANAGING TEMPTATION

One of the most important functions we all have as our own self managers is that of advisor. While we seldom think of ourselves in that way, we are, in fact, our primary advisor. We seek our own advice numerous times during any and every day, starting with, "What should I do today?" to "What should I do right now?" to "What should I stop doing?" In reality, every time we choose or change an immediate-activity direction, we have given ourselves a piece of advice and since, ultimately, what we achieve is highly dependent upon what we do, the quality of that advice is critical.

When we de-commit, we are rejecting advice already given, readvising and then accepting the new words of wisdom. Often they are just that — words of wisdom. However, there are other times when our guidance may not fit the wisdom category, when we find it difficult to give good advice to the person most dependent upon it — ourselves. In fact, some of us have been known to deliver a quality of advice to ourselves that we wouldn't dare give to anyone else for fear of putting our lives seriously at risk.

Imagine, for example, telling someone with a weight problem that, in spite of what they had previously decided, they really should order that delicious ice cream sundae for dessert; telling a smoker, at the end of his second week of abstinence, that a few cigarettes, just to calm down, would probably be a good idea, considering the known ill effects of stress; telling a friend, recently committed to a daily exercise program, that considering the long day put in at the office, perhaps they should consider beginning their exercise program some other time and have a drink instead; telling a colleague that preparing for an important meeting first thing Tuesday morning is not nearly as critical as is watching Monday night football, especially considering the importance of the particular game. This is, generally, not the kind of advice we give other people. It is exactly the kind of advice that many of us give ourselves, however, on a regular basis.

Why is it that we tend to see the way to other peoples' solutions so much more clearly than we do our own; that the advice we give to others ranks as being almost Solomonic in contrast to some of the advice we foist upon ourselves?

Perhaps the main reason is that it is much more difficult to be objective when delivering advice to ourselves. When we advise someone else, although we may not benefit from it, we also aren't the ones that have to pay the price of carrying it out. They are. And what's more, the benefit will likely arrive at some future date, but the price has to be paid immediately. We all live in the moment and when we give advice concerning immediate activity to someone else, it's not our moment that's affected. It's theirs. The advice is good, in part, because our insight is not clouded by immediate cost.

When we are acting as both advisor and "advisee," the story is very different. The long-term benefit may be ours, but so is the immediate, the right-now cost. It is our moment that is at risk and so, just before the sacrifice, we automatically begin casting around for something that might save it. In trying to avoid the cost to our moment, we generate protective advice, attempting desperately not to consider what its price might ultimately be. We go on the "Buy Now — Pay Later Plan," trying desperately to ignore the cumulative interest that will be ours to deal with.

We Homo sapiens tend to see ourselves as thinking beings, living largely by our values, our vision and the beliefs we hold with regard to larger issues like freedom and culture. And we are that, certainly. But not only that. Perhaps, not even mainly that. So often we squander our larger objectives in favor of the now, without necessarily even recognizing the waste. Without exerting a high degree of control over our immediate behavior, we, too, as a part of the animal kingdom, tend to seek the comfort of the moment. Were self-discipline an easy thing to come by, we probably wouldn't spend so much time writing, talking and thinking about it. Unless the self manager exerts the necessary control, chances are good that the moment will win.

That is not to say that the moment shouldn't win. If victory is our goal, it should. The issue, here, is when it really isn't our goal; when we have determined to serve something else and still end up serving the moment; when our own fulfillment, our own well-being, as we define it, is negatively affected.

We live in the present and so to leave it unprotected is to leave living unprotected. It is perfectly understandable that we strive to protect the moment since, in a sense, that is all there is, the future being an abstract idea whose time has not yet arrived. We only experience the positives and negatives of the moment at hand with so little wonder that de-committing in support of that moment is so easily and so readily practiced. After all, if living is to make any sense, one of our primary objectives must be to enjoy the moment. Although we must protect the present moment, we must also offer some protection to our moments still to come or eventually our present, yet to be, may become intolerable. The problem is that often the immediate present and the future are in conflict. To serve one is to do a disservice to the other. It is the self manager's responsibility to achieve a balance, a tall order considering that the self manager, too, lives in the present — our present. It is the self manager's responsibility to live for the present, but not at undue cost.

Frequently, however, we don't see the cost. Is it that we can't; that for some reason, be it lack of understanding or lack of information, the cost is hidden from us? Sometimes. But more often we don't see the cost because we work very hard at not looking, especially when just the slightest glance would reveal the price tag. One way of protecting the moment is to ignore the cost of that protection so that we can just barrel ahead.

For me, Monday night football is a good personal illustration of this potentially expensive head-in-the-sand behavior. There are some autumn nights when I decide that football watching is exactly what I should be doing and for those Monday nights, that is exactly what I should be doing. There are other Monday nights when I make another decision. I decide that I should be doing something else and that's what I commit to, the corollary to that being I shouldn't be watching football. There have been some games that I've managed to see all the way through, however, because, just before the kickoff, I convince myself to change my previous self direction and commit to the football game instead. I convince myself that football watching is exactly what I should be doing. Interestingly, on those particular mornings after, I have yet to look in the mirror and see my reflection saying to me, "Way to go, Tiger. Another football game under your belt!" Instead, what I hear is, "Way to go, *Turkey*. Another football game under your belt." After the fact, and once the price has already been paid, I have no difficulty whatsoever reading the price tag. I could have peeked before the fact, but instead I made sure not to look.

A high level of self commitment is not about never revoking your commitment. It's about not doing so inappropriately. Frequently, we make a commitment to do something but when the time to honor that commitment arrives, something better, that is, something more enjoyable comes along. For the sake of the moment, we are tempted to choose the new alternative. *Inappropriate de-commitment is about giving in to the temptation when the price is too high.*

It can be easy to do, in that any one such self indulgence often looks quite harmless by itself. For example, one chocolate bar, chosen in spite of a commitment to the contrary, is not likely to bring about a significant weight increase. However, a series of such choices, influenced by bad advice and made one at a time, can carry significant weight.

THE ACTIVATION HABIT: ADVISE OBJECTIVELY

This chapter began by talking about the function of self manager as advisor. We looked at the difficulty we sometimes have in giving ourselves good, objective advice, one of the main reasons for the difficulty being that the advice often comes with an immediate cost to us. However, we not only give ourselves advice, we're handing it out all the time and so how well we do in life is highly dependent upon the quality of the advice we give ourselves. The cumulative cost of bad advice can be large. It is the self manager's responsibility not only to provide advice, but to make it good.

There is a simple way to raise the objectivity of the advice we give ourselves that relates to the oft-found discrepancy between quality of advice we deliver to ourselves and to others.

Pick someone whose well-being is important to you and when you find yourself about to walk away from a self commitment, very possibly in favor of a shorter-term gratification, ask this simple question:

- What would I advise that someone else, were he or she in exactly the situation that I'm in right now?

The nonsense you might have been feeding yourself tends to instantly fall away. The price tag is revealed. You now know the cost of the decommitment. You may still decide to pay it, but even that decision will be made with greater objectivity.

chapter **34** | # MANAGING INCENTIVES

Not long ago, I had a conversation with someone I had just met in the visitor's waiting room of a hospital. We both had time on our hands and we spent it talking. He was from a logging town on the west coast and had a partner in his own small business there. He told the following story.

One of the most important and challenging things I have to do is to get people to perform at a high level and stay there. We have a manufacturing process; the factory goes twenty-four hours a day and we know exactly how much product we have to ship daily just to break even. Over that amount means profit but for the business to work, productivity has to be consistent.

When we started we had figured out what maximum production per shift was reasonable and realized that there wasn't that much distance between level of performance needed to survive and the highest level we could expect, so, naturally, the optimal expectation became our target. Trouble was, we were just not reaching it but I knew that if we didn't come close, we were going to run into difficulty and it wasn't going to take long.

My partner is responsible for manufacturing and I take responsibility for sales. I'm usually on the road, away from the factory, but one day when I was there, my partner said that he just couldn't get the production up to what we needed and asked if I had any suggestions. This was early days and money was really scarce. All I had in my pocket was fifty dollars and that wasn't because I'd forgotten to go to the bank. I took the money out, pinned it to a wall and said, "The first shift to reach target gets to split the fifty bucks." That week we reached target for the first time. I then said that there's a case of beer for every shift that reaches target from now on, and any shift that breaks the record gets the new fifty bucks pinned to the wall.

It's now about five years later and in spite of a rise in manufacturing costs and no increase in price to customer, we have a very profitable business. We have no new technology and the same number of staff we had at the start, but the average production per shift is much higher than we imagined possible. We still give the case of beer when production surpasses a certain level and fifty dollars for establishing a new shift record. We've also instituted profit sharing, with the shares being given just before Christmas, at the company party. Everybody gets a good Christmas bonus, we've got almost no turnover and our profits are growing every year.

I thought that was a great story, one that had behind it a principle that comes as no surprise. Incentives tend to raise level of commitment. That is, a reward, tied to carrying out an objective, tends to increase level of commitment to that objective. The program worked out by this west-coast entrepreneur had built into it short-term, intermediate and long-term incentives. Interestingly, he suggested that the immediate incentives may have been the most significant in that it is when a shift is close to winning the case of beer or breaking the record that they come together and strategize ways of ensuring victory, ways that might include even abandoning sacred traditions like the coffee break, for that one shift.

We are aware of the important role that incentives can play in activating potential as demonstrated by the defined profit-sharing plans by many corporations, the graduated raises, depending upon levels of last year's performance, the rewards for suggestions adopted, the campaigns practiced by sales organizations and the glittering star pasted on the workbook page of a six-year-old for a job well done.

A MISSED OPPORTUNITY

Although we see the value of providing incentives for others and often appreciate others providing incentives for us, most self managers do not utilize this performance support consistently or systematically for their managees — themselves. For the self manager there is greater availability of incentives, a more responsive incentive-delivery system in place and the occasion to witness virtually every activity determined to be worthy of reward. A failure to utilize incentives represents serious opportunity cost because the self manager is the manager best positioned to utilize this effective performance-management tool. As a management tool, however, most of us use it little if at all.

Probably the biggest reason for this is that we understand that some of us have the responsibility of managing others, but we really don't perceive ourselves as having a self-management responsibility. The result of this selective blindness is that we tend not to apply what we consider to be good management practices to managing ourselves. We reserve those practices for "real" management.

Another reason. In "Managing Success," we looked at a common and well-developed tendency that many of us have, to not recognize our accomplishments, the small achievements that collectively bring about success. When considering others, we are often more open to seeing the cumulative nature of success. It is difficult to provide incentives for accomplishments not recognized.

Whatever the reason, however, the results are the same. We who are in the best position to witness and to reward positive immediate performance, to provide effective support for the quality and kind of immediate performance we, ourselves, desire, do not generally take advantage of that position. Managing by incentives is an area of self-management potential that tends, with any degree of consistency, to remain untapped.

THE ACTIVATION HABIT: PROVIDE SELF INCENTIVES

Oftentimes, reaching a major objective, the achievement of an important end result, is in itself an incentive, whether it be in the form of social recognition, a sense of self fulfillment or material reward. We are all on incentive programs but they are primarily long term.

It is not that long-term incentives are ineffective. Future reward, even distant, can act as an incentive that supports sustained activity. We see it all the time. We do it all the time. We may think about the future, but it is the present we live in and as was discussed in "Managing Temptation," often we sacrifice pieces of our future for the sake of our immediate present. Providing short-term incentives is a way of reducing the price that needs to be paid for future success. It is a way of bringing the needs of the present and those of the future together, of helping immediate behavior to serve both, simultaneously. The self manager is in the best position to accomplish this.

As the managers of our own immediate performance, we are in a position to create an active incentive program, one that supports the ongoing activity necessary for success. We are there when it happens, have an abundance of incentives to draw from and the delivery system that allows a timely honoring of promises.

The Campaign

Organizations, especially sales organizations, frequently use the campaign, usually a large reward-incentive program, as a way of attempting to boost productivity. The campaign asks for a high level of commitment to correspond to the large reward being offered. Much sacrifice, but with the hope that it will be perceived as being worth it.

Many of us are involved in high-demand projects of either a business or a personal nature for which we have to make significant sacrifice, but for which there is no incentive provided, other than the completion of the project itself. We experience the hardship of a campaign without its reward. Often the intensity of involvement is such that our lives are temporarily thrown out of balance. We don't have time for the kind of leisure or even work activities that we enjoy, the mini-vacations that help reduce stress.

We can, however, correct the balance, in some measure, by making the project a real campaign; that is, one for which there is an associated reward that we ourselves provide. We need not exclude the short-term incentives discussed below, but can also add something out of the ordinary — an incentive that will make the completion of the campaign something to look forward to.

The Cornucopia

We all allow ourselves small luxuries. Whether we have as many as we'd like, as often as we'd like, is another question but we have them, nevertheless. Some of them are expensive, financially or because of the time they involve, and some cost very little: a movie, a play, a restaurant meal, a glass of wine, a favorite TV show, a ball game, a book, time for reading, a compact disc, time for listening, a video, time for watching, a favorite food, a walk, a concert. Different strokes for different self managers, but for most of us, strokes aplenty.

We have them, but within the context of a possible self-imposed incentive program, we also waste them. That is, many of these luxuries could serve as highly effective incentives but we don't tie them to anything.

These are not necessarily extra luxuries but positives that we experience for no other reason than that we decide to do so. Why not tie them to a self direction, one we have already determined that we want to carry out? We still can experience the luxury but at the same time, increase the commitment to follow through with our own immediate-activity decisions. By bringing the reward for the activity into the present, we make the likelihood of it happening and often the enjoyment of the doing, greater. We also can increase the intrinsic value of the luxury itself in that it becomes not only something to be enjoyed but a deserved something.

A personal example. I believe that having sufficient exercise is important and its importance is related to state of health, long term. Although good health is a significant objective, it has some challenges as an incentive.

Intellectually, I know the importance of being healthy. However, I don't really exercise as much for the health of the moment as I do for my state of health in the future. When exercising, today's feeling of well-being is usually not at issue, precisely because I'm feeling healthy enough to exercise. My self direction to exercise is in service of the future and since I can't really classify exercising as being anything close to a favorite pastime, it is, to some degree, a disservice to the present.

I don't especially relish exercising, but music is a passion. Saying that my compact discs are my most valued material possessions does not exaggerate their personal importance. There are always discs that I want and seldom discs I want that I don't get. Although I consider them to be luxuries, they are not luxuries that I even consider being without.

I have joined exercise and music together. Compact discs have become part of my exercise-incentive program. A disc purchase requires four exercise sessions in seven days. Fewer than four sessions, and no visit to the music store or contact with the record club. I seldom miss a week, either of discs or of exercising.

Do I need the incentive program to lock in my exercising? Probably not, although I must admit that without it I tend to miss a few more days. I have found, however, that exercising is easier, less of a chore and that somehow the discs take on an even greater value when tied to something other than simply being.

Is it, perhaps, just a touch immature to be playing games with myself with something as important as maintaining my state of health? Maybe it is, although it probably wouldn't seem at all immature were someone else to be offering the incentive. Still, I'd have to admit that I exercise for discs more than I exercise for health. The nice thing is, I'm the winner both ways, in that the acquisition of music and health maintenance are both important objectives, not of someone else's but of mine.

As a general practice, provide ongoing incentives to carrying out your self-directed activities. Don't waste your luxuries. Tie them to honoring your commitments.

chapter **35** | # MANAGING OPTIMISM

Pessimism can be defined as the selective negative perception of reality. A pessimist is someone who not only sees but also focuses on what is wrong now and what could go wrong in future. The pessimist is constantly asking the question, "What's wrong with this picture?" and seeking an answer. Since few situations are perfect, an answer is usually forthcoming.

Pessimist Training

In "Managing Self Criticism," we looked at the ease with which we tend to recognize our own negatives, our mistakes, our omissions, our weaknesses and how that can have a significant and destructive effect on our level of self-confidence. The pessimism we're examining now has to do with the same kind of selective perception but aimed at the situations and people around us rather than at ourselves. It, too, can have an impact upon confidence, our confidence in the world, external to us and it, too, seems to come easily.

Whatever the reasons, it is not difficult to focus on external negatives. Many of us tend to notice the faults of people around us more readily than we do their strengths. Bad economic times get a lot more attention than good. We recognize and react to poor service more quickly than we do to acceptable or better. We are also exposed to the negatives around us by others, not only people we interact with but by the media. Judging from the content of newscasts, positive news must not sell very well and it isn't the "good" newspaper that we have delivered to our homes every day. This media focus on the negative is likely both cause and effect of what appears to be a well-developed tendency toward pessimism. Regardless of the causes, however, it seems very easy for us to gather the evidence that more strongly supports the view that things won't work out, than that things will.

The Difficulty of Self Diagnosis

One of the reasons that we may not even attempt to do anything about a residing pessimism in ourselves is that it's difficult to recognize. First, virtually everyone knows the benefits of realistic optimism, and it is easy to fall into the trap of believing that, if we know something, then we do it. After all, why would someone adopt a pessimistic stance who knows better? (Of course, if the distance between knowing and doing were really that small, we would all likely be consistently excellent activators.) Second, when we automatically and unknowingly overfocus on the negatives around us, the perception created is seen as real. The pessimist often believes that he is, in fact, an optimist, but one who has the misfortune of living in a bleak world. He is much like the person wearing sunglasses who goes inside forgetting about the glasses on his face, convinced that it is the room that's poorly lit. A pessimist's perception is affected by a pair of internal sunglasses that color the way he sees the world, but for him, it isn't his perception. It's the world that is dark.

Pessimism as a De-activator

Pessimism can have a strong negative effect on the activity directions we generate for ourselves. Why even consider an activity that is most unlikely to bear fruit? A daily action plan, generated within the context of a pessimistic stance, is likely to look very different than one supported by optimism.

Pessimism can strongly influence proactivity in that the dark-colored glasses of pessimism make identifying possible opportunities much more difficult. Risk is largely avoided in that low risk is seen as being high and higher risk is seen as being irresponsible. It can add to change resistance because a pessimistic stance makes it so much easier to "see" why the new won't work. The formulation of both short- and long-term objectives can also be dramatically affected.

Seeing only the half-empty glass can have a destructive effect upon self commitment. Even if an intention has been determined, the level of commitment supporting that intention can be lessened because, come the time for performance, the apparent reasons to de-commit are more likely to rule.

Overfocusing on the negatives in the people and situations around us can effect not only immediate performance, but can have significant impact upon our quality of life. Not only do we go through our days with less hope but with less joy as well, much of the positive potential of our moments going unnoticed.

Optimism as Activator

The optimist does not see the half-full glass as being filled to the brim but simply reads the reality positively. An optimistic stance toward the world supports the conversion of our potential. By being able to see the positive potential around us, we are better able to activate our own. The management of immediate activity becomes more positive. The daily action plan holds more promise in that more choices appear open to us. Our objectives, short- and long-term, are more ambitious because we have reason to make them so. Greater risks are taken because degree of risk is not exaggerated. Opportunities, invisible to the pessimist, are clearly seen by the optimist. Positives that exist in situations of change are more readily perceived and so resistance to change is lower. Level of commitment is strengthened because it is so much easier to go after the perceived attainable than it is the apparently unattainable. Quality of life is enhanced simply because life is experienced as having more quality.

THE ACTIVATION HABIT: PROMOTE OPTIMISM

It is the self manager's responsibility to promote optimism. The better we are at being able to see the positive possibilities in situations and the strengths in people, the more opportunities become available for the activation of our own potential. There is no suggestion here that we shut down our recognition of negatives. We need to take them into account. However, realistic optimism requires that we become keen observers of the positives and not allow the presence of negatives to cloud the comprehensiveness of our vision. It is important to be able to take the positives into account in deciding where we can go from here and whether we should.

The conversion from knowing the importance of optimism to being more optimistic is not a difficult one. It requires that a few simple questions be asked consistently and answered.

Build the habit of looking for the strengths in the people around you simply by asking the appropriate question that will get you there and making sure that you answer.

- What positive potential do I see in that person?

Build the habit of looking for the strengths in the situations you find yourself in by asking the following similar question and again, insisting upon an answer.

- What are the strengths of the situation being considered?

A more general question to ask when looking at the world and determining your immediate role in it:

- What is it that could, realistically, go right?

By promoting the habit of asking ourselves these simple questions, we can continuously build an optimistic platform from which to manage our potential.

chapter 36

MANAGING BY PERSONAL MISSION

In the "Introduction" to "Managing Self Commitment" we looked at desire — wanting success — as being a necessary, though not necessarily a sufficient condition to bring about activation. If I neither want to do something nor have any interest in achieving the results that stem from it, my doing it is most unlikely. After all, why would I pursue an activity that I see as having neither any intrinsic nor extrinsic value? So, we have to want to do something if it is to get done. The mistake we make is in thinking that the wanting will be enough. It does get us to the starting gate, however, and so, has an important function as an activator of potential. This want, this desire, does not have to be fire-in-the-belly motivation. It may also be an intellectual rather than an emotional commitment to achievement.

THE PERSONAL MISSION

All of us have a personal mission. That is, whether formally worked out and written down or simply carried somewhere within us, we all have objectives and achieving them is important to us. They may relate to the kind of people we want to be, how we would like to be perceived by others, the areas of life with which we want to be intensively involved — for example, the occupational or leisure areas — or the attainment of certain material goals. Whatever they may be, however, we all have critical, long-term objectives.

It is logical to expect that the objectives that make up our personal mission would serve as our primary source of motivation. They should provide the frame of reference from which our immediate directions and their translation are generated. If that were not the case we might find ourselves not even attempting to behave in a way that would bring fulfillment as we, ourselves, define it.

Understandably, in occupational literature, much energy has been spent recommending to people how they can effectively arrive at the formulation of their personal mission statement, the generation of which is intended to help people clarify the larger directions that they wish to pursue. There are, it would seem, two underlying assumptions that recommend this exercise.

The first is that in the absence of a systematic process, we are in danger of not really knowing what is important to us. We may expend energy, time and ability in the pursuit of objectives that aren't of primary significance to us, and more critically, we may not be pursuing objectives that are.

Fourteen years ago, in the earliest published version of my "Self-Management System," I posed three simple questions that can serve as a springboard from which to generate a personal mission statement, and I have been recommending them ever since. The three questions are:

- Who do you want to be?
- What do you want to do?
- What do you want to have?

People tackle them very differently. Some take many hours to generate their answers and arrive at a relatively detailed picture; some do it quickly, answering with a few sweeping inclusive responses, while others fall somewhere in between. Also, the questions are sufficiently similar that they tend to run into each other. Still, once answered, they provide a relevant and comprehensive frame of reference from which to choreograph one's immediate performance.

I believe the process, or one like it, is useful, but I am not convinced that people do not already know what it is that is important to them.

They may not directly ask the questions, but that is not to say that they don't have the answers. Five minutes spent with the three questions above, for example, is enough to give most people the substance of their personal mission.

The second assumption behind the recommendation that we generate a personal mission statement is that establishing the mission statement, itself, is enough to put it to work for us. Build it and it will activate. I am even less convinced that that is, in fact, the case.

Of course, if one doesn't have a personal mission statement, it isn't going to be able to play a performance-supportive function. Though it may not be fine tuned, we carry around within us a fundamental list of what we consider to be important. Ask yourself or someone else, "What, that matters to you, have you not yet achieved?" and see how quickly a personal mission statement is generated.

Is Having a Personal Mission Statement Enough?

Having a personal mission is not living it. Putting one's personal mission into an organized, explicit statement is not living it. *It is only when our personal mission becomes part of our immediate awareness that we can rely on it to generate the desire necessary if its objectives are to be reached.*

We see numerous instances of people knowing what's important to them in the abstract, but then forgetting about it in the immediate here and now. The rush of life can often take us away, even from our own most critical intentions. A few illustrations.

There are many highly responsible, productive people in the occupational world who have children at home. Commitments are made to their children, commitments to do certain things in the evening or on the weekend but habitually, many of the promises are not kept because something comes up at work. For these people, when there is a conflict between the needs of work and of family, work almost always wins, the choice being made virtually automatically. Were you to ask them to communicate their personal mission statement, in all likelihood, providing strong, supportive parenting would be revealed as one of their primary objectives. Their behavior, however, may suggest otherwise.

Many managers in the work world have as a primary objective the supportive, constructive managing of their people, and believe that to do so requires a high degree of time, energy and thought. In fact, however, they expend little effort carrying out their people-management responsibilities.

Many people have as a primary objective living as long and as healthy a life as they possibly can. They understand the importance that exercise can play in helping them reach their goal. Still, they may not give exercising a thought for weeks at a time.

Why the disconnect? The dishonored objectives might be a significant part of their personal mission statement, but it may have not been a significant part of their day, that period of time within which the activities that serve the larger objectives must occur.

The parents in the illustration gave thought to their children as demonstrated by the activities promised. They may not, however, have given much active immediate thought to their overriding objective as parents of those children, at least enough to turn intention into behavior. The managers and health seekers may not have given enough thought to their larger objectives to even generate any related commitments, let alone honor them.

In all instances, the desire may have been part of them but not a sufficiently significant part of their day to bring about the necessary directions and commitment to serve the objectives they themselves strongly value. In terms of the immediate, it is not only important to have a personal mission, it must be active, a part of one's immediate awareness. It's something that has to be carried into one's Phase 2. The people in the illustrations knew the importance of their children, their managees and their health. However, they ignored that knowledge in their immediate present.

THE ACTIVATION HABIT

Very simply, for "want" to play its role in activation, we must be actively aware of what it is we want. Unless we're aware of our personal mission, we are very much less likely to issue the directions that serve its objectives or generate the level of commitment necessary to ensure that the directions are carried out.

It is important to develop a personal mission statement, not primarily because we don't know what it is we want, but because the personal mission statement is a way of making that knowledge accessible.

Generate a personal mission statement either by asking the three questions mentioned above, or through some other process that you may prefer. *Then, at the beginning of every day, review the statement until it becomes an active part of you. Do this before you generate your daily action plan.*

The resulting awareness of personal mission will help you generate the directions that serve that which is important to you. When the time comes to carry out your self directions, the recognized importance of the commitments will increase the likelihood of their being carried out. Review your personal mission with a view to assessing its current relevance, at least twice a year. We change.

CONCLUSION

The self-management function represents a real and a very significant set of management responsibilities. The level at which those responsibilities are carried out in an organization plays a major role in determining the success of an organization. As individuals, with regard to all areas of our lives, how close we are to reaching our objectives is, again, determined, in large measure, by how well we self-manage.

The self-management function is not an abstraction. It is very real and very important. People are hired and paid not for what they are capable of doing, but for what they do — their output. That output is determined by their potential and their managing of that potential. It is the self manager whodoes the managing. Largely, we are employed and paid for the job of carrying out that function.

We tend not to look at the self-management function other than to acknowledge its importance with an all-knowing nod of the head. We don't even define it. After all, everybody knows what *it* is. Sometimes we express its importance more specifically. We say things like, "It's important to have self-discipline." "If you don't believe in yourself, then who will?" "You can lead a horse to water but you can't make him drink. That's up to the horse." Recently we have been saying things like, "It's important to be proactive." "Without flexibility, in today's world, it's difficult to function." "We must take ownership of our own performance." . . . and so on.

Oh, yes. We are very much aware of the importance of the activation function. We are so aware of it that we tend not to treat it at all seriously. After all, is not knowing a truth synonymous with living it?

In fact, all that we have to do is look at the amount of time and energy we put into thinking about or doing something about our self management functioning to see how little attention it is really given. And looking at the occupational world, how often do we see the self-management function recognized within the context of a performance-management system? How often do we see the specific responsibilities attached to the function, spelled out? How often do we see those functions monitored, evaluated, rewarded?

Yet, we are, in all earnestness, stating that we must see people taking greater ownership of their jobs if they, as individuals, and we, as an occupational community, are to survive and flourish. We ask individuals in our corporations to take more risks, more responsibility, to look for opportunities and then do what needs be done to take advantage of those opportunities, but after we've said how important this active, self-directed stance is, how often do we even look to see if it is being taken? And do we provide the core competency, the specific tools and processes designed to strengthen the kinds of behaviors that we continue to parade as being critical to our survival and success as we march into the next century, as the kaleidoscope continues to turn faster and faster?

INDEX